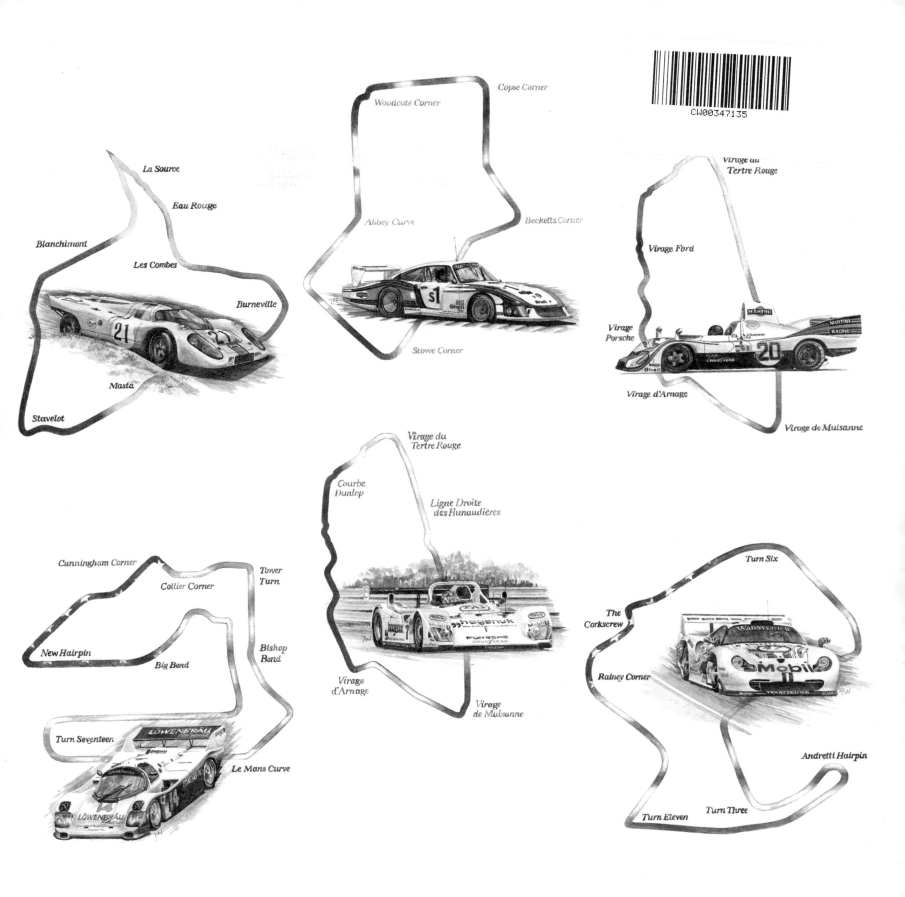

PORSCHE
IN MOTORSPORT

PORSCHE
IN MOTORSPORT

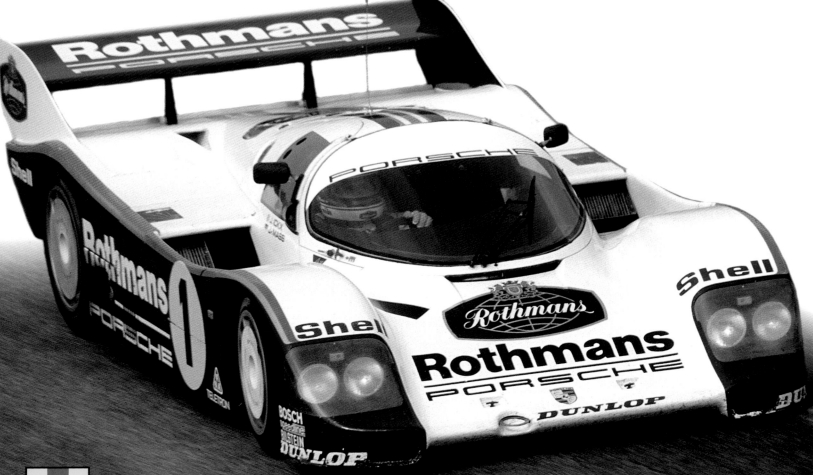

THE FIRST FIFTY YEARS
By **Peter Morgan** Foreword by **Derek Bell**, MBE

Haynes
THE
BOOK

First published in 2000

A catalogue record for this book is
available from the British Library

ISBN 1 85960 659 8

Library of Congress catalog card no. 99-80195

Published by Haynes Publishing, Sparkford,
Nr Yeovil, Somerset BA22 7JJ, England.

Tel. 01963 442030 Fax 01963 440001
Int. tel. +44 1963 442030 Fax +44 1963 440001
E-mail: sales@haynes-manuals.co.uk
Web site: www.haynes.co.uk

Haynes North America, Inc.,
861 Lawrence Drive, Newbury Park,
California 91320, USA

Designed by G&M,
Raunds, Northamptonshire
Printed and bound in England by
J. H. Haynes & Co. Ltd, Sparkford

CONTENTS

FOREWORD

by Derek Bell, MBE

MANY GREAT DRIVERS HAVE RACED for Porsche and others have dreamt of being included in the factory team, but those who have driven for the marque feel privileged to have been part of this unique history.

I remember with the 917 in the 1970s how many grand prix drivers of the time wanted to experience that magnificent machine. It was some time afterwards that I realised what an outstanding car it was – the most impressive of my career.

Over the years I have had the good fortune to drive almost every Porsche built, from the 356 to the GT1 and from the 917 to the 962. Each car was constructed with that basic Porsche logic of design and engineering that gave so many so much success. Factory drivers knew that when they raced a Porsche they had the car to win. One was confident going into races that the car would not fail, and never considered that something would break. However, one needed that confidence at Le Mans when about to drive down the Mulsanne Straight at over 240mph.

Sometimes I had to be reminded why Porsche went racing. On the rare occasions I became frustrated over a new feature on a car, Professor Bott (head of Weissach) would say, 'Derek, every race must be a development of something'. As a racer it was hard to accept his philosophy, but he was such an amazing man. Drivers all had the greatest respect for him and the Porsche development team.

It should not be forgotten that without Porsche's contribution to sports car racing over the years by supplying cars to privateers, this type of racing would never have been as strong and may not have survived. Without Porsche's commitment to racing, many drivers would not have had such glorious careers.

ACKNOWLEDGEMENTS

I N RESEARCHING FOR THIS BOOK, I became aware of the great characters from different eras who have played their part in building the Porsche motorsport name to what it is today. Of course, the automobiles and the challenge have changed almost beyond recognition over the 50 years, but I believe the individuals involved, although separated by generations, would find they have much in common. Then and now, their pursuit of excellence is both addictive and obsessional.

Fifty years of competition has established Porsche as one of the most instantly recognisable brand names in the world today. Racing has been the glue that has held the company together for half a century, despite the fact that this Stuttgart-Zuffenhausen based organisation has always been a production sports car builder first and racing car builder second. That the company has remained independent, when all around have surrendered to the corporate juggernauts of the industry, is down to a pragmatism that has become a hallmark of the product. In this time, the ride may have sometimes been rough, but history will record that Porsche – both the road and racing cars – has gone from strength to strength. Looking back of course, often indicates the trend for the future.

This book refers frequently to the event that has remained like a beacon of progress for the automobile in the second half of the 20th century – the Le Mans 24 Hours. Le Mans has been the anvil of development for so many manufacturers and perhaps none more so than Porsche. That the organisers remain open to lateral thinkers and innovators has guaranteed their survival and offers inspiration for the way forward. In the 1960s, turbine cars attempted to go beyond the accepted envelope and in the late 1990s, Don Panoz entered a petrol-electric car. Le Mans is ever the greatest test of automobile invention. Racing in the 21st century must surely move away from total dependency on fossil fuels and we can be sure it will happen at Le Mans first.

I have chosen just 12 cars to illustrate the evolution of the Porsche racing car, and in each of the stories I have profiled a different course to illustrate how the motor racing challenge itself has changed. You may take issue with the cars or the circuits I have chosen, but I believe these are particularly special to Porsche. That they are my personal choices is all part of the fun of writing such a text!

In my research I have spent many hours reading through records, magazines and books that have recorded the cars, events and personalities of earlier years. I am deeply indebted to Porsche AG, who have allowed me access to much valuable information. In particular, my thanks are due to Klaus Parr and Jens Torner in the Archive, Jürgen Pippig and Eberhard Scholl in the Motorsport Presse Department, and Professor Helmut Flegl and Norbert Singer in Weissach. In helping me tell this story I thank Paul Frère, Stirling Moss, Hans Mezger, Peter Falk, Manfred Jantke, Derek Bell, Reinhold Joest, Ralf Jüttner and Allan McNish – and the many others whom I have sought out to answer detail queries.

Special consideration must be made to the Le Mans organisers, the Automobile Club de L'Ouest, and to *Autosport* magazine for providing invaluable sources of accurate historical data.

Many of the illustrations are reproduced here for the first time and I greatly appreciate the permission to use photographs from the Porsche archives, the GP Library and LAT Photographic. I would like to thank Stephen Mummery for the Donington views of the WSC-95, while I have also used photographs from my own collection.

My concluding thanks go to Tracey Whant, whose absorbing water-colours you will find in each chapter. Tracey was somewhat apprehensive when she received this commission, but I hope you will agree that her delicate renderings bring a new dimension to the words and photographs.

Peter Morgan

INTRODUCTION

A NEW MOTOR RACING ERA began in Europe in 1950. It was the year when Giuseppe Farina drove an Alfa Romeo to victory in the first ever world championship Formula One event. The birth of Formula One was the spark that international motor racing needed, giving it the sense of purpose that would fire up the sport after a decade of war and austerity.

After several seasons of hesitant beginnings in the late 1940s, the dust-covered forms of Bugattis, ERAs and Alfas emerged from almost-forgotten garages to compete against a new generation of marques and drivers. By 1950 it was all coming together and across the bleak, war-torn landscape of Europe, competition events blossomed like the flowers in spring. It was a time when sporting drivers everywhere seemed finally to shrug off the past and go driving.

In sports car racing the trend was no less pronounced. The bulky pre-war Goliaths which had conquered the rigours of Le Mans were consigned to history as engineers used wartime advances in materials technology and engine design to produce lighter and faster machines. The first 24 Hours after the war – in 1949 – underlined the step forward that unconsciously had been taken. Prophetically defeating the 1938 victors, Delahaye, the race was won by one of the new Ferrari sports cars.

The following years would witness more new constructors coming to the Sarthe, and among those to race in 1951 was a single diminutive coupé carrying the name of Porsche. It was a name already well known in motor racing circles, since Professor Porsche himself had been renowned before the war as chief engineer of the famous Auto Union racers and the Mercedes-Benz record car. But the little Porsche at Le Mans in 1951 had none of the thunder of the earlier Silver Arrows. Under the guidance of the professor's son, 'Ferry', the new car marked the realisation of a dream that had already come a long way in a very short time.

It was just three years since the first prototype 356 had been developed from chassis and engine parts tooled for the professor's Volkswagen design. Despite the total disruption of war, the Porsche engineering consultancy business – established in the early 1930s – had maintained a momentum after escaping the allied bombing of Stuttgart in 1944. In 1946, and supporting a sizeable staff of 222, Ferry had resolved to start a manufacturing business alongside the consultancy. Initially, the output was agricultural equipment, but then, in 1947, the small band of dedicated engineers – the same engineers responsible for those famous pre-war racers – put down a marker for their future.

Out of nothing, Ferry Porsche and his small team produced a breathtakingly advanced grand prix car – the Cisitalia. The car was a commission from a wealthy Italian industrialist, and although it would never race, the Cisitalia was proof that the calibre – and the magic – of the Porsche design team was intact and was still the equal of any other group in the contemporary European automobile industry.

By the time the business moved back to its first home in Stuttgart-Zuffenhausen, the Porsche fortune was extensive. Royalty fees on every single Beetle made, combined with the accumulated rent paid by the occupying US forces on its Zuffenhausen buildings, ensured the capital was there to meet the growing demand for the first car to carry the Porsche name – the 356.

The 356 may have only developed 44bhp from its air-cooled 1,100cc flat-four engine, but it was packaged in a lightweight body and blessed with limpet-like handling. The dumpy little cars found themselves a ready market at home initially and, as the word spread, abroad too. There were more than sufficient enthusiast drivers who remembered the calibre of the Porsche name and who wanted one of the new sports cars. While demand outstripped resources in Zuffenhausen, it was left to those enthusiasts to test the little cars in the heat of competition.

One of those would make that first entry at Le Mans in 1951 – and so begin a tradition in international motorsport for Porsche that has continued to this day.

SOMETHING TO PROVE – 550

EUROPEAN RACING IN THE EARLY 1950s was a matter of dedication and enthusiasm. It was a time when cork-helmeted drivers in woolly jumpers or polo shirts rode 'on' rather than 'in' their cars. It was a cheerful time when a paddock would echo to the sound of unsilenced, slow-revving engines and loud laughter while the air would be scented with the addictive smell of castor oil. The mood everywhere was one of catching up on lost time and living life for the moment.

In Germany, a population that only a few years previously had felt cheated, now dusted itself down, becoming driven by a burning motivation to pull success from the ashes of catastrophe. This motivation was nowhere more evident than in the small world of motorsport, where the participants could experience the thrill of competition – and risk – that this generation seemed so ardently to crave.

Look at any photographs of German club race meetings in 1951 or 1952 and the sports car classes are filled with fleets of 356s, their drivers spiritedly hanging on while their machines adopt every angle except straight ahead. In Britain, they were in souped-up MGs, in France it was Renaults and in Italy they were racing almost anything that had wheels. The speeds were pedestrian by today's standards, but they were racing and that was all that mattered.

Almost from the beginning of customer production in Gmünd, the 356 had begun to feature in the sports results. While the fledgling Porsche factory concentrated on building up production car output – now moved back to the pre-war location in Stuttgart-Zuffenhausen – it was largely left to the customers to raise the company flag in competition. Names like Fürstenberg, Berckheim and Mathé appeared time and again in the results sheets as the little 1,100cc cars were campaigned in rallies and hillclimbs. These racing enthusiasts quickly found the 356 to be an effective weapon but it was not long before,

550 Spyder
Avus, Germany
1955

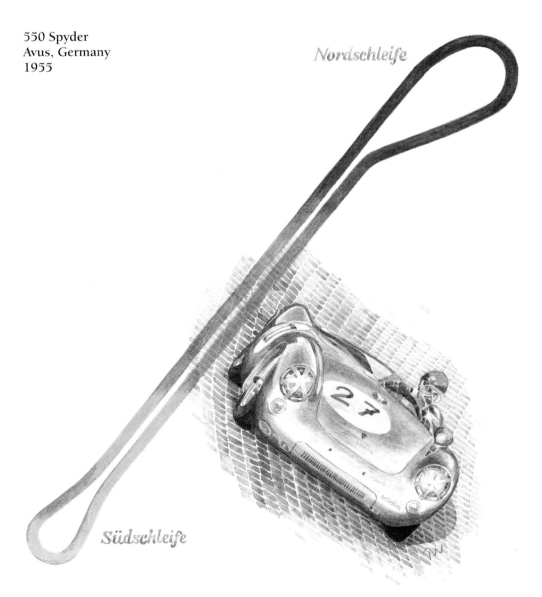

Nordschleife

Südschleife

Refuelling for the class-winning 550 coupé of Richard von Frankenberg and Paul Frère, Le Mans 1953. The hardtop was conceived to give the cars improved speed on the long straights. (Porsche Archiv/Günther Molter)

inevitably, some began to look for more. One of the company's pioneer distributors, Walter Glöckler of Frankfurt, was the first to probe what could be done with Porsche components in a pure-bred racing car chassis.

The Glöckler-Porsche was ready for the inspirational 1950 season (the first year of the new Formula One World Championship), the car being the product of hard toil over a cold German winter. The open two-seater was drawn by Glöckler's experienced workshop manager, Hermann Ramelow. He took the suspension, engine and other chassis parts from one of the first Gmünd-built 356s, fitted them to a light tubular chassis and clothed it in a boxy open body, formed by the Frankfurt coach-builder, Weidenhausen. Pretty it wasn't, but as a competition machine the car was highly effective. The 1100cc VW-based pushrod engine developed a well-tweaked 58bhp on methanol fuel and the whole car tipped the scales at just 455kg. Glöckler won a German national championship with the car in 1950 and this seminal machine would take two more championships in the following years.

It was in 1951 that the 'works' entered their first international sporting event – nothing less than the Le Mans 24 Hours – with a pair of alloy-bodied Gmünd 356s. Despite nervousness at being the first German team to compete at the Sarthe (a well-known centre of the French Resistance during the war), a single 44bhp car not only finished the race but won the 1,100cc class.

With increasing interest in his efforts from Ferry Porsche's engineers, Walter Glöckler had built a new sports racer in 1951 and this time powered it with a VW-based 1,500cc flat four engine. This second car moved closer to the 356 style of rounded body curves and cropped windscreen that would later be associated with the Speedster. Glöckler added another German championship with this new car.

While the factory's 'customer' 356 coupés in race trim now had 70bhp from their own 1,500cc engine, Glöckler's sports racer enjoyed a very highly tuned (and still methanol-fuelled) unit developing 98bhp. The performance advantage of the sports racer over the coupé was demonstrated at a record attempt at Montlhéry in September of that year, just ahead of the Paris Salon (motor show). A small team ran the cars in pursuit of distance records from 500km up to 72 hours. The Glöckler car did not prove to have the endurance of the coupé, but it did have greater speed, topping nearly 130mph (209kph) and being upwards of 20mph (32kph) faster than the coupés.

So while 356s became a regular sight on the European competition scene during 1952, highlighted by a repeat class win at Le Mans and a resounding overall victory in the Liège-Rome-Liège road rally, Ferry Porsche could not ignore the fact that sports car racing was moving on.

Using the Glöckler cars as the benchmark and their own 1,500cc pushrod four, a lightweight, mid-engined two-seater took shape on the drawing boards in Zuffenhausen during the autumn of 1952. The first pure-bred Porsche racing car was ready for the opening meeting of the 1953 season on the Nürburgring – the Eifelrennen, at the end of May.

Race record

By 1953, Ferrari, Jaguar and Mercedes-Benz had picked up the torch of motor racing progress and were locked in absorbing competition for the big-capacity sports car classes. The first year of the World Sports Car Championship witnessed engineers such as Mercedes' Rudi Uhlenhaut, Ferrari's Aurelio Lampredi and Jaguar's Malcolm Sayer producing inspirational designs for the racing sports car. These individuals and many other dedicated engineers were taking professional motor racing on from its post-war beginnings of racing for racing's sake, to exploring the limits of automobile technology. Against this quickening background, the emergent Porsche company began to take the first steps as a racing car constructor in the voiturette (up to 1,500cc) classes.

The appearance of the new Porsche sports racer at the 1953 Eifelrennen may not have caught the attention of motoring correspondents of the time in a way that say the

José Herrarte stands behind the Carrera Panamericana class-winning 550 coupé. Earlier in the year this car had been one of the pair that had run at Le Mans.

Porsche returned to the Carrera Panamericana in November 1954, this time using the new four-camshaft engine. Herrmann shocked the motorsport world by finishing third overall, easily winning the up to 1,500cc class.

silver 300SL, the red 375MM or the green C-Type had, but the class victory by Helm Glöckler (Walter's cousin), in pouring rain, suggested the little car was one to watch. The potential was further shown at Le Mans, when two new cars – this time with enclosed cockpits to give a top speed of around 124mph (200kph) on the famed Hunaudières Straight – captured first and second in the 1,500cc class. This impressive top speed was achieved with the trusted pushrod engine, running on regular petrol. The Le Mans victory, up a class on the wins of the previous two years, underlined the contribution of the four team drivers involved who, each in their own way, were pivotal to the early development of the Porsche racing car. Two journalists – Richard von Frankenberg and Paul Frère – drove the winning car, while teamed with Helm Glöckler was a young Stuttgart driver who had come to Ferry Porsche's attention after some stirring performances in a 356 – Hans Herrmann.

The slightly built and genial Frère, who epitomises the élan of that whole generation of sportsman racing drivers, recalled 40 years later the sometimes unnerving experience of driving the new Porsche coupé to victory. 'We still had the pushrod Volkswagen-based engine with about 83 horsepower. It was very little more than the standard engine. We had a big handling problem. In fact the car handled quite as badly as the rear-engined 356 of that period. This was because the rear suspension was 356 and came from the VW Beetle. It had a big tube with the trans-

verse torsion bars in it, plus two control arms and the swing axles. When you compressed the suspension, you got some toe-in (it was like steering). On the normal 356, the arms were just long enough to clear the gearbox in front of the engine. On the racing car we used at Le Mans, they used the same trailing arm set-up, but the arms were too short to clear the engine. So they just turned the whole thing round and when you cornered and the outside suspension compressed, you got toe-out. It was certainly as bad as the standard 356. Before my first time in the car, I did a few laps in the normal Porsche on the Wednesday morning. But when I took over the racing car I very, very nearly shunted it in the Esses. To cap it all, they didn't let me drive in daylight. They wanted people who knew the car to set it up properly and they were trying all sorts of things. So when it was 10 o'clock in the evening, they said OK, you drive. I was absolutely lost! All the cars were overtaking me and I had no idea how fast the headlights behind were catching me up.

Having to learn the circuit in those circumstances was just impossible. But after a while I learnt to drive it just like a normal 356 coupé and it was all right. We were quite fast on the straight – over 200kph – and the only real competition came from the Oscas, which were lapping about as fast as we were. We were going quite well, when around midnight the last Osca retired. Porsche only wanted the class victory, they were not interested in the Index (of performance). They slowed us down so much it became a terrible bore! I was furious because cars we had overtaken earlier were passing us. In the end we finished 15th and 16th I think. But we could have finished 11th or 12th. Any taxi driver in Le Mans could have driven faster!'

At the German Grand Prix meeting in August, Herrmann tried a few tentative laps with a slightly revised car, now coded 550 and fitted with what sounded like a heavily modified engine. The new car was not raced that weekend and its engine was shrouded in mystery. It was the first public run of a new four-camshaft, four-cylinder racing engine. The new machine did compete the following weekend at the Schauinsland (Freiburg) hill-climb. Driven by no less than pre-war Auto Union ace Hans Stuck, the car was a handful, especially as the power from the frenetic-sounding engine came all in a rush above 5,000rpm. Stuck was beaten into third place by new boy Herrmann – running an alcohol-fuelled 98bhp pushrod engine in one of the original prototypes – and a rapid Borgward. The two pushrod cars (the same two that had been entered at Le Mans) were then rebuilt and entered for the gruelling five-day Carrera Panamericana road race in Central America. Quite remarkably, and with very little support, Guatemalen driver José Harrarte succeeded in winning the 1,500cc class with one of these cars.

A new 550 was exhibited at the Paris Salon that autumn to gauge the level of interest in Europe to build a small series, while the US importer, Max Hoffmann, was leading the clamour for a production series of the two-seater. Hoffman knew that he would have no difficulty in selling the new car to the enthusiastic American racing community.

Over the winter of 1953–54 Stuck again raced the 550, fitted with the pushrod engine, in two races in Brazil. He achieved a class win and a fifth overall against strong opposition, while another Guatemalen, Jaroslav Juhan, won his class in the Buenos Aires 1,000km. By the spring of 1954, the new four-camshaft engine was ready to race in international events.

The highlight of the year was Hans Herrmann's resounding third overall in that year's Carrera Panamericana in a 550 fitted with the new four-camshaft engine. His average speed was over 100mph (160kph), easily leading home Juhan in his pushrod-engined 550. It was the success in this event that inspired Porsche's subsequent adoption of the 'Carrera' name.

That May, and with mechanic Herbert Linge next to him, Herrmann took on all-comers at the Mille Miglia – a time-warp 1,000-mile (1,600km) race on public roads around Italy. After an incident-packed drive (during which the pair went under a level crossing barrier with the train looming), they beat off a challenge from the Italian Oscas, won the 1,500cc class and finished sixth overall.

Le Mans was both a disaster and a triumph. Three 1,500cc 550s were entered and two went out with holed pistons – the von Frankenberg/Glöckler car in the first hour. When the third car suffered a similar fate with five hours to go, it was 14 laps behind the two leading Oscas. But far from giving up, the Porsche mechanics disabled the useless pot of the 550 and let the car chug on with three cylinders. With just two hours to go, there was a

This 550 was the car that was shown at the Paris Salon in October 1953. The photograph was taken some time later and reflects many detail changes. It would be nearly a year after Paris before the 550 was sold to customers.

In winning their class at the 1954 Mille Miglia, Hans Herrmann and Herbert Linge drew valuable publicity for Porsche. Here, driver Herrmann receives a welcoming bouquet of flowers on the pair's return to the factory in Zuffenhausen.

The class-winning 550 of Johnny Claes and Peter Stasse makes for the pits during the 1954 Le Mans 24 Hours. (Porsche Archiv/Günther Molter)

sudden rain squall and the two Oscas, each wanting to win, both slid off the road and left the crippled Porsche the only car in the 1,500cc class to finish – and win! Another 550 with a 1,100cc pushrod engine won the small capacity class. Porsche had maintained its 100 per cent winning record in the 24 Hours. This race saw the silver Zuffenhausen 550s identified with blue, green and red (while another had yellow) flashes on the tops of the high rear wings. Red stripes would later become fashionable on customer 550s as this was the colour used by star driver Hans Herrmann.

The problem at Le Mans was put down to inadequate cooling of the rear cylinders and incorrect ignition settings. This did not slow the confident roll two weeks later at the Reims 12 Hours, when Frankenberg/Polensky won their class. A month later at the German Grand Prix meeting, 550s swept to first, second, third and fourth in the sports car race.

However, it is correct to observe that where the works 550s could be expected to face their strongest European opposition – the UK – they rarely appeared. When they did, the German cars often went home empty-handed. For instance, at the Silverstone GP meeting in 1954, Herrmann was beaten into third place by a pair of MG-powered Lotus cars. The winner, in the stunningly compact Lotus 8, was the British car's designer, Colin Chapman.

Nonetheless, 1955 was a year when the 550 – now known as the Spyder – would become a major force in 1,500cc racing. Any post-war prejudice that might have been present was fast disappearing as it was realised how effective the little German machines had become. Max Hoffman's hunch had been correct and the cars found particular popularity in the USA and inevitably once further souped-up, certain cars began to feature regularly in race results. Among many, perhaps those entered by Californian John von Neumann for John Miles in West Coast Sports Car Club of America events, were the most successful.

At Le Mans – the year when Pierre Levegh's Mercedes cartwheeled into the startline tribunes, killing himself and 82 spectators – Porsche entered four open-topped and two closed (1,100cc) spyders. Five finished. There was no joy in the almost inevitable class win for Frankenberg/Polensky, but perhaps satisfaction at the first victory in the Index of Performance. Porsche 550s finished in fourth, fifth and sixth places overall.

At the autumn Nürburgring 500km, Herrmann and von Frankenberg found themselves outclassed by new cars from EMW (the East German rump of pre-war BMW) and Maserati. Edgar Barth won the event in his EMW and this led to frantic efforts to redress the balance before the annual thrash up and down the autobahn at Berlin's Avus Motodrom.

Avus was the antithesis of the sanitised, high comfort factor racetrack expectations of today. Located in the south-west suburbs of Berlin, the main road is easily recognisable as the E51, a dead straight section of autobahn through the Grunewald Forest between the Kaiserdamm in Charlottenburg and Nikolassee. The course was best described as a squashed speedway oval with the near 10km main straights separated by just 8 metres. The two turns at each end were initially banked only slightly, but in 1937 the brick-faced North Turn paving was pitched to no less than 43 degrees, permitting the highest average lap speeds anywhere in Europe. Avus was blindingly fast. The first race was held in 1921 and by 1937 Bernd Rosemeyer in his Auto Union set the all-time outright lap record around the 11.98-mile (19.29km) course at 171.74mph (276.32kph). After the war, Avus was still used for German national racing, but sadly the great banking has not survived today (although annual races are still held on a chicaned and shortened course).

It was at Avus that von Frankenberg would demonstrate his skills in the 550. As a result of the beating the team received at the hands of EMW at the Nürburgring, the spyder received some detail engine improvements that raised the four-cam's power from 114bhp to 125bhp, a new five-speed gearbox and a stiffer chassis. It was driving one of these improved cars that von Frankenberg staged a thrilling race with Herrmann (himself in a specially stream-lined 550) and Edgar Barth's EMW. Recorded at speeds up to 140mph (224kph), the racing journalist was reported as taking the North Turn banking at no less than 125mph (201kph). It does not sound much in absolute terms today but barely two years earlier, this had been the maximum speed of the 550 coupés on Le Mans's Hunaudières Straight. With such a furious pace, it was perhaps inevitable that the over-worked engines would suffer. Barth retired first and Frankenberg nudged ahead of an overheating Herrmann and claimed victory, to become 1955 German Sports Car Champion.

The winter allowed yet more improvements. For the 1956 season the 550A (also called the RS – for Rennsport) would give Porsche the extra performance they needed. But the debut of the new car at the Nürburgring 1,000km was almost upstaged by the Swiss May brothers. These enterprising engineers brought an old pushrod 550, to which they had fitted a large inverted aerofoil over the rear of the cockpit. The car was surprisingly competitive and threatened to eclipse the factory cars because of its increased cornering ability. Unfortunately, it is said a word was passed

The mechanics work on the Claes/Stasse 550 at the 1954 Le Mans 24 Hours. The Gustav Olivier/Zora Arkus-Duntov 550 is in front. Note the simple, but rugged mounting for the rear shock absorber.

By 1955, 550s were appearing in sports car events all over the world. This car is being refuelled prior to the supporting race for the 1955 Monaco Grand Prix. (LAT)

The start of the 1955 sports car race at Avus, on the outskirts of Berlin. Richard von Frankenberg in number 15 is surrounded by the four streamlined EMWs. Behind them is the fearsome banked Nordschleife.

to the scrutineers and reasons were found to exclude the car. The be-winged 550 was not raced again. Meanwhile, the factory was exploring other ways of increasing performance and an experimental car was built to explore the effects of reducing frontal area.

This 550 became known as *Mickey Mouse* and was a real handful to drive because of its narrow track and 200mm shorter wheelbase. The car was tried at various events during 1956. It made its final appearance in Frankenberg's

hands at Avus. He describes the handling of the car as 'not 100 per cent satisfactory', but his description of his exit from the race is so typical of the modest understatement that was so fashionable in those times. 'Finally, it appeared in the last German event on the Avus, where it shot over the top of the north loop in a most spectacular manner due to faulty material and burnt out completely.' In fact, Frankenberg was lucky to escape with his life, being thrown out of the car into a bush just as the car careered at high

Von Frankenberg in the specially streamlined 550 Spyder at Avus in 1955. He won a thrilling race with Herrmann and Edgar Barth in an EMW and was said to have achieved speeds up to 140mph (225kph).

speed over the top of the banking. The car itself plunged to destruction in a car park below. He says, 'the *Mickey Mouse* was not subsequently recalled to life'.

The emergent British constructors such as Lotus and Cooper had continued their increasingly inventive development in the small-capacity classes, and against this background the 550 was beginning to trail. While customers flew the flag internationally, the factory's attention turned to extracting more performance from the new 550A model. The importance of the 550 was that it was the first thoroughbred Porsche racing car. It was the car that put Porsche on the motor racing map and set the standard by which all later efforts would be measured. Being first in the line is not always a story of winning, but it is about being there and getting noticed. This the spyders did beyond measure.

Engineering

The 550 was designed as an uncompromising prototype two-seat racing sports car under the leadership of Ing. Wilhelm Hild. It would be Hild's seasoned blend of pre-war racing design and experience that would guide the 550 from strength to strength. The first 550's ladder-frame chassis was influenced heavily by Glöckler's cars. Since the still-secret four-cam engine was far from ready, the new mid-engined car was powered by the well-proven air-cooled, four-cylinder, 1,448cc pushrod engine, developed from the 1952 Le Mans-winning units. This reliable unit featured the fabricated Hirth crankshaft similar to the type which had been used on the Cisitalia Grand Prix project. Twin Solex down-draught carburettors resulted in a reliable 77–78bhp on pump fuel or 98bhp on methanol. The four-speed ring synchromesh gearbox (taken from the production 356) was outrigged behind the rear axle line with a hydraulically actuated single-plate clutch.

The front (laminated leaf) torsion bar suspension was lifted from the alloy-bodied racing 356s while the rear (cylindrical) torsion bars were enclosed inside a cross tube ahead of the engine. As with the Glöckler cars, the aluminium body was formed by Weidenhausen in Frankfurt, but was much lower than the earlier cars, with pronounced wings over each of the wheels. The dashboard formed an integral part of the body and chassis and so increased stiffness. A front-mounted oil cooler was given a narrow opening at the front of the car, along with openings to pass cooling air to the front brakes.

The first cars weighed just 550kg. A removable coupé top was built for the two works cars entered at Le Mans in 1953, which helped one of them achieve a top speed

In 1955 spyders were beginning to appear in events all over the world. This is the Wolfgang Seidel/Walter Glöckler factory car on the Mille Miglia.

Various modifications were seen on customer 550s. This car has a simple aero windscreen and small fairing behind the driver's head.

in France of 124.8mph (a whisker over the magic 200kph), but made the cockpit a very unpleasant working environment.

The cars taken to the 1954 Le Mans were significantly improved in detail over the earlier prototypes. The ladder frames were stiffened and efforts were made to reduce weight with many components drilled for lightness.

The cornering and high-speed stability took measurable steps forward during 1954, as a result of the work performed by a dedicated ex-school teacher who had turned his hand to engineering. With the help of Zora Arkus-Duntov, a Chrysler development engineer who had driven a 550 at Le Mans, Helmut Bott painstakingly analysed the dynamics of the suspension and it was as a

result of his work that the rear suspension changed from leading to trailing arms. At the same time, the parts of the suspension were stiffened and the result was much improved rear-end stability.

The small series of 85 1500RS models produced at the end of that year were to the same specification as the improved factory prototypes which had been run at Le Mans, but benefited from a complete review of the design detail to make the cars more suitable to less skilled mechanics. The man who wanted the 550s for sale most urgently, US importer Max Hoffman, also suggested the name Spyder. The more-catchy title recalled the exotic naming given to American two-seater bodied sports roadsters from the likes of Stutz, Cord and Duesenberg in the 1920s. It is Richard von Frankenberg however, who completes our understanding of the term 'spyder'. He notes that as used by Porsche, the term spyder with a 'y' is 'entirely incorrect, for the word is really derived from the insect spider'. Spider was the description given in the mid-1800s for a light, four-wheeled horse-drawn carriage called a Tilbury-Phaeton. With its large rear and smaller front wheels, combined with a lightweight folding top, it looked like a spider. It seems that even in the 19th century, coach-builders described their creations as spiders. When the horseless carriage came along, the term stuck as a means of describing a lightweight sports two-seater.

Over the course of the 1954 season, there had been much development work with several variations of body shape being tried. The final version of the 550 series produced at the end of that year – a full year after the car was shown at the Paris Salon – was the result of intensive testing in the wind tunnel and the fine art of long-time Porsche designer Erwin Komenda. The body, now formed by Wendler of Reutlingen, evolved from the bluff 356-derived profile and was identified by its more rounded front and rear wings which rose almost like fins at the rear. Almost inevitably the weight of these later customer cars crept up, although at 600kg it was still a very lightweight machine.

A new brake lining had been tried at Le Mans in 1954, but otherwise, these early 550s used the same braking parts as the production 356. In an effort to reduce unsprung weight, the steel wheels were given aluminium rims.

The 1955 Le Mans cars were fitted with larger drums (from 9in to 11in diameter, with the fronts increased in width from 40mm to 60mm). These larger front brakes were cooled by a small opening in the nose of the body. These improvements found their way on to the customer cars later that year.

Efforts were made to improve the famously flexible ladder frame in 1955 (if the car was jacked up, the doors could not be opened). A second truss tube over each longitudinal stiffened the basic ladder, with linking cross-tie tubes. This improved the bending stiffness, if not contributing to the torsional stiffness. Later in the year, a new five-speed gearbox was tried, which had first gear accessed through a locking catch and this Type 718 transmission became the standard equipment (with a limited slip differential) for the 550A.

In the four-camshaft racing engine, the young Ernst Fuhrmann gave Porsche its first racing powerplant, which, when viewed from nearly 50 years later, stands among the

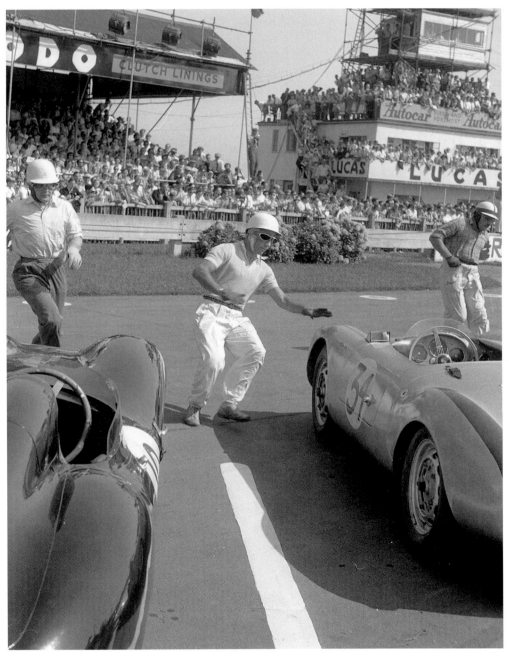

best in motor racing. In every sense the engine sparkled with ingenuity, deduction from experience and the influence of contemporary grand prix technology.

The type 547 four-cylinder engine was air-cooled, but enjoyed twin spark ignition from twin dynamos and twin distributors driven from the rear of each inlet camshaft. Lubrication was dry sump and the aluminium bottom end castings, barrels (the bores were chromium-plated) and

Stirling Moss runs for his 550 Spyder at the start of the 1955 Goodwood 9 Hours. That the spyders were being driven by increasingly important drivers was a reflection of the growing stature of the Porsche name.

Pit stop for the privately entered Ed Hugus/Carel de Beaufort 550A during the 1957 Le Mans 24 Hours. The pair would finish eighth. (LAT)

Hans Herrmann in the new 550A Spyder roars past a 356 in the Nürburgring 1,000km in 1956. He and von Frankenberg would win their class on this, the new car's debut. (LAT)

cylinder heads had some 40 per cent more cooling fins than the regular 356 pushrod engine.

The ten-piece fabricated Hirth crankshaft ran in four roller bearings and allowed one-piece connecting rods. The drive for the four camshafts was taken from the flywheel end of the crank, being a complex shaft and bevel gear arrangement. The engine was very over-square (having a short stroke and a large piston area) for its time, designed as it was for high power from high revolutions.

The cooling fan reflected the depth of consideration evident everywhere in the design. The dual inlet (from both front and back) fan was invented by Franz Reimspiess and was of such efficient design that for virtually the same power consumption it moved 70 per cent more air than the pushrod 1,500 fan.

It perhaps comes as no surprise that the 547 was a remarkably complex engine to build and maintain. It is said a factory-trained craftsman would take at least 120 hours to assemble one. But perhaps with racing in mind, this was acceptable.

The first engine ran in March 1953 and by the summer was good for 110bhp at 7,800rpm.

The first upgrade to the 547 was seen at the May 1953 Mille Miglia, when among detail changes Weber 40 DCM carburettors were fitted in place of the earlier Solex types to improve throttle response (although subsequent customer cars maintained the Solexes). The third series appeared for Le Mans a month later with increased crankcase and cylinder head finning, when the reliable output was said to be 114bhp at 6,800rpm. The 1500RS series in late 1954 were fitted with the fourth series of the engine, with detail changes to improve reliability (particularly stainless steel seats for the inlet valves). These later engines, rated to 125bhp at the flywheel, can be identified by a bulge in the housing over the driven bevel gear of each inlet camshaft.

SPECIFICATION
1954 550-1500RS Spyder

Engine: Type 547/1 air-cooled four-cylinder with two valves per cylinder. Dry sump lubrication (with 8-litre oil tank) with aluminium crankcase and cylinder heads with alloy barrels and chromium-plated bores. Fabricated Hirth-type crankshaft supported in four main roller bearings. Single-piece connecting rods. Two camshafts per side operated from the crankshaft by intermediate shaft and two vertical and two horizontal shafts (and using 14 bevel gears). 12-volt electrical system for dual coil ignition with twin ignition distributors driven from the ends of the top (inlet) camshaft each side and two spark plugs per cylinder. Two 40mm Solex PJJ down-draught carburettors. Vertical cooling fan with twin intakes driven by V-belt from the crankshaft.

Capacity: 1,498cc

Bore/Stroke: 85mm/66mm

Maximum power: 125bhp at 6,500rpm

Maximum torque: 130Nm at 5,000rpm

Compression ratio: 9.5:1

Fuel: Pump petrol

Transmission: Hydraulically actuated single-plate Fichtel & Sachs clutch. Type 718 five-speed rear-mounted gearbox. Second to fifth ring synchronised with the unsynchronised first gear accessible through a locking catch. ZF limited slip differential.

Chassis/body: Welded steel construction ladder-frame chassis. Front-mounted 68-litre alloy fuel tank. Sheet aluminium two-seater body with opening doors and removable front compartment and rear body section with plastic formed aero screen windscreen for driver. Lightweight, detachable all-weather convertible roof. Two leather trimmed bucket seats with front/back only adjustment. Very lightweight interior trim.

Suspension and steering: Front: Independent with twin trailing arms and transverse laminated spring steel torsion bars and telescopic shock absorbers. Adjustable anti-roll bar. Rear: Independent swing-axle with two universal (Hookes type) joints, located by trailing control arms with transverse round torsion bars and telescopic shock absorbers. VW worm and peg type steering with 2.4 turns lock to lock.

Brakes: Four 280mm (11in) diameter 40mm width drum brakes with hydraulic operation all round. At front, twin leading shoe design. At rear, one leading, one trailing shoe.

Wheels and tyres: 3.5 x 16in steel wheels with five fixings (nuts on to studs). Tyres : 5.00-16in front, 5.25-16in rear Continental racing tyres.

Weight: 600kg (48 per cent front, 52 per cent rear)

Length: 3,600mm

Wheelbase: 2,100mm

Track (f/r): 1,290mm/1,250mm

Performance: Acceleration: 0 to 60mph (96.5kph): 8.2 seconds (Source: *Road & Track*/Ludvigsen)

Maximum speed: Around 122mph (196kph).

PERSISTENCE PAYS –
718 RS SPYDERS

2

**718 RSK Spyder
Reims, France
Jean Behra
1958**

Virage de Muizon

*Virage
de la Garenne*

*Virage de
la Hovette*

Thillois

IN HIS 1973 BOOK, *The Design of Racing Sports Cars*, Colin Campbell notes, 'it would have been very enjoyable if we could have continued to use the same sports car for going to the movies, collecting the groceries and blasting round a race circuit at weekends'. In this snapshot of the way sports car racing was maturing through the 1950s, we capture the flavour of what was happening.

By 1955, it was all becoming very serious indeed. Mercedes-Benz had pushed back the understanding of materials technology in motor racing and their W196 and 300SLR racers were the embodiment of the most advanced thinking. Pitched against the German machines were Jaguar, Aston Martin, Ferrari and Maserati – all competing head to head in a struggle for supremacy. These were no longer practicable road cars, but thoroughbred racers – very highly tuned, peaky, noisy and with chassis and suspensions built for the demands of the race track.

In response to Mercedes, both Jaguar and Ferrari had produced cars that would underpin the stature of motor racing at a time when racing itself was under threat. The awful accident at Le Mans that year had resulted in a public frenzy of criticism and had actually led to the banning of motorsport in Switzerland. In many other European countries, racing continued but only as a result of intense diplomacy on the part of the racing community.

Racing responded to Le Mans 1955 in the only way it could – the show had to go on – and this it did with renewed obsession. The carefree atmosphere of the immediate post-war years somehow disappeared and at the top level a new kind of professionalism began to emerge.

Despite the death of so many spectators, Le Mans had run to the full duration in 1955. After the Mercedes team withdrew, Jaguar took a rather sober victory with the D-Type after Aston Martin failed to finish. In the 1,500cc class the 550s won, but Porsche could not have failed to take account of determined performances from their class competition, particularly the emergent and resourceful British

A superbly atmospheric view of the Le Mans pits during the 1957 event. Hans Herrmann climbs in while the mechanics complete the refuelling.

constructors such as Cooper and Lotus. The Lotus-Climax in particular had administered a thrashing to Herrmann on one encounter the previous year and had given the factory serious concern even at the race it considered its own – the Eifelrennen at the Nürburgring. At Le Mans in 1955, Lotus principal Colin Chapman ran one of his remarkable Lotus Mk 9s. After showing a clean pair of heels to the other 1,500cc contenders, the car was only eliminated when the designer himself was disqualified for reversing back on to the track at Arnage following a spin.

Porsche responded later in the year with the much-improved 550A. This car adopted a space-frame chassis in place of the previous ladder construction (although it did look like an evolved ladder frame rather than a full Chapman-esque space frame). This lightened and stiffened the car considerably. Most importantly, the rear suspension was revised to overcome the problem that increasing cornering speeds were accentuating swing-axle 'tuck'. The Porsche swing-axle design tended to drag the outside wheel under the car as the spring compressed. Cooper had already addressed this problem with their unequal length wishbone arrangement while Chapman had adopted a rigid De Dion tube layout for his Lotus 9. The swing-axle, so popular with Porsche since the days of the Auto Unions, suddenly seemed far too limiting. The solution on the 550A was to use a geometry proven by Porsche's Stuttgart

neighbours, Mercedes-Benz. Both the W196 and 300SLR had shown wheel camber could be controlled by lowering the roll centre and pivoting transverse radius arms from under the transmission. This was the arrangement used for the 550A.

The 550A brought Porsche back on the pace of the rapidly developing competition for 1956 and proved capable of scoring many high profile successes. That year brought the first of many overall victories in Sicily's gruelling Targa Florio – still a non-championship, but nonetheless highly respected, event. Italian ace and renowned road racer Umberto Maglioli was persuaded to drive the Porsche at very short notice. He beat off challenges from the large capacity entries of Maserati and Ferrari to complete the eleven laps of the tortuous 44-mile *Piccolo circuito delle Madonie* course in record time. The 550A overcame a strong challenge of the works Lotus team at the Reims 12 Hours and there was the now almost routine class win at that year's late-July Le Mans. With some 30 cars built, the 550A, like the original Spyder before it, became very popular with the company's racing customers.

But the opposition was not standing still. Durable though the 550A was – even with the outstanding 547 engine – more cornering performance was needed if Porsche was to go head to head with the best opposition in short events. The pressure to develop a new car grew further as the 1956 season progressed, particularly when Jean Behra won the late summer Nürburgring 500km in the new Maserati 150S. Away from the bustle of the race track and starting with a clean sheet of drawing paper, Wilhelm Hild and his small team of engineers began work.

However, Porsche was still a very small company and the development of an entirely new car would take time and considerable effort. The 550A continued to form the mainstay of the factory effort through 1957 and into the first months of 1958. Fortunately (and as the old English saying goes) there was life in the old dog yet. In the 1957 Mille Miglia, Maglioli achieved a remarkable class win, despite missing a scheduled refuelling stop in Bologna, running out of fuel and having to fill up at a local petrol station!

In the first big event of 1958, the Buenos Aires 1,000km, the value of having a top driver pairing was demonstrated in a near-giant killing result. When grand prix drivers Stirling Moss and Jean Behra crashed their own 3-litre Maserati, the opportunistic Porsche team manager Huschke von Hanstein offered them a 550A. Apprehensive about the speed of the little 1,587cc car on the 5.89-mile (9.5km) power circuit, the two drivers nonetheless agreed to try the car in the remaining practice. On his fourth lap Moss

The works cars did not fare well at Le Mans in 1957. Here, Richard von Frankenberg in a 550A leads Edgar Barth in the new RSK out of Arnage.

recorded a time that put him in among the big 3-litre cars, while Behra was only a second slower. After a dazzling display of driving, the two Formula One aces finished third, just seven seconds behind the 300bhp V12 Testa Rossa of Hawthorn/Gendebien. The red car had only managed to pass them just five laps from the end. In his history of Ferrari, Hans Tanner notes drily that there was 'quite a bit of difficulty from the Moss/Behra Porsche'. Moss, who would drive for Zuffenhausen again, found the car a joy to drive. 'The car was just bursting to have a go and it thrived on being driven hard.' He remembered many years later, 'In that race in Argentina in '58, we were third overall. My diary shows that my fastest lap was only two seconds off Phil Hill's pole time in the Testa Rossa!'

Race record

Porsche first took the wraps off the car planned to replace the 550A just minutes before the start of practice for the 1957 Nürburgring 1,000km. It was too new to race and the team fell back on the old 550As. This event is also memorable for another first. One of the factory cars was driven by former top EMW star, Edgar Barth, making his first appearance in a Porsche. Partnered by Umberto Maglioli, Barth could make little impression on the winning Aston Martin and the two trailing Ferraris, but the fourth place netted the almost inevitable class win. The popular Barth would become interwoven with the future fortunes of

the Porsche Spyders. However, the win was to lead to considerable upheaval for the Barth family, who at that time lived in the East German town of Chemnitz.

His son Jürgen, who would later achieve his own place in the history of Porsche, was only ten years old and remembers the time well. 'The EMW team had decided not to continue with their effort. So my father talked with Huschke von Hanstein and Huschke asked him to drive for Porsche. The idea was that my father was going to stay in East Germany and drive for Porsche, which he did for that first race. But the problem was he won the class and when he stood on the podium, they played the German national anthem and the East German guys didn't like it. He wasn't able to go back. So my mother and myself, we had to sneak out from our home near Chemnitz. When we left, we had to leave all the lights on in our house and we escaped through a forest and some friends of ours picked us up. We changed cars two or three times and we came to East Berlin on the first of November. It was Memorial Sunday and we went over with the Underground into West Berlin. They hadn't built the wall then and there were less controls at that time, but it was quite dangerous, and we left a lot behind.'

Edgar Barth would pick up his racing career with added momentum the following season. At Le Mans – and teamed again with Umberto Maglioli – the new Porsche, now named the 718 RSK revealed that it was in need of

Driving the old 550A Spyder, Stirling Moss and Jean Behra gave Ferrari 'quite a bit of difficulty' at the Buenos Aires 1,000km in early 1958.

Edgar Barth swings the 718 RSK through the banked Karussell Hairpin during the 1958 Nürburgring 1,000km practice. The tail fins brought mixed comments from the drivers.

significant development. Top speed was unimpressive and the handling was unpredictable. However, the run was ended prematurely after a collision with Tony Brooks's overturned Aston Martin.

The RSK only appeared subsequently in several mountain-climb events towards the end of 1957 and was not raced again until the 1958 Targa Florio. But after a winter's comprehensive development, and with Buenos Aires and a strong third at Sebring boosting their spirits, Porsche came to the Targa confident of a good showing against the dominant Ferraris. They were not to be disappointed. In the words of *Motor Sport*'s Denis Jenkinson, 'the little Porsche made them look silly'. Three drivers – Barth, Behra and Scarlatti – finished second ahead of the Testa Rossas of both Hawthorn/von Trips and Phil Hill/Peter Collins.

Four RSKs were taken to Le Mans and Behra/Herrmann led a 3–4–5 for Porsche after many of the leading larger capacity entries had retired in very wet conditions. At this race Edgar Barth was teamed with the journalist-driver Paul Frère.

'We were driving the 1500 Spyder while Behra and Herrmann had the 1600,' recalled Frère. 'I remember it was a horrible race because it was so cold and it rained for so long. At around 2 o'clock in the morning I was on the verge of stopping and handing over because I couldn't stand the

cold anymore. But I didn't do it. The next morning, around 11 or 12, the Behra/Herrmann car was running third and we were fourth, about two laps behind. But then they had brake trouble and they went into the pits to change the whole front suspension and brakes – everything. It took them about 20, 25 minutes. Then Barth and I were asked by Huschke to try and stage a dead heat. We had tried it already in '53 and well (he grins mischievously), we ended up winning by about a metre! It wasn't easy because they calculate where you are from the average of your lap times and you had to cross the finish line at the same distance apart as you started. Well, it was impossible, but stupidly, Barth and I agreed to do it. I did the last stint and I had to slow right down to let the other car catch up. And so at the end I tried to make a dead heat with them. But when it was all over I found out I was one lap behind. I never discussed it with Huschke, but I'm sure he did it on purpose, because he wanted Behra the team leader to win. We were robbed of third place that year.' It would be the last time Frère drove for Porsche as a professional racing driver, although their relationship would prosper strongly in other directions during the coming years.

Two cars were entered in the Goodwood Tourist Trophy, the final round of that year's Sports Car World Championship. The Behra/Barth RSK outpaced the rapid Lotus and Cooper entries once more to take the class win (behind three Aston Martin DBR1s). The placing ensured a resounding equal second (with Aston Martin) in the World Sports Car Championship behind Ferrari.

While the RSK's utilitarian lines may have lacked immediate artistic appeal, there was no doubting that the little cars from Zuffenhausen were now being taken very seriously indeed by all those from Newport Pagnell to Maranello.

Stirling Moss gives an impartial view of the Porsche at this time: 'The one thing they had from the start was reliability. They were under-powered compared to the bigger cars, but not because of their size. They were always potential class winners. Their handling was so good, you could look at them for the difficult circuits like the Nürburgring or the Targa Florio and think about getting up towards an overall win. They were very agile and extremely nice to drive because of their reliability.'

Perhaps the most surprising course where the RSK demonstrated its ability to upstage larger capacity opposition was the flat-out blind that was Reims. The July Speed Week became one of the most fashionable dates on the international motor racing calendar in the 1950s and early 1960s. The week began with first practice on Wednesday afternoon, leading up to a Formula Two race on the Saturday afternoon, followed by the 12 Hour sports car race (which began at 11pm or midnight) and then the Formula One Grand Prix on the Sunday afternoon. Organised with sometimes controversial efficiency by the Automobile Club de Champagne, it was no less than a motor racing fiesta. Significant partying and searing heat were the immediate challenges to racing at Reims, but the drivers would also tell – often with wide, haunted eyes – of the very high speed slipstreaming battles and car-breaking demands of the 5.158-mile course.

Sadly, business complications and growing safety concerns stopped the racing there in the late 1960s. Some 30 years later, the Reims-Gueux course can still be traced today. The Route Nationale 31 to Soissons just out of Reims itself was once one of the fastest places in motor racing. Take the local road to the village of Gueux at Thillois and you will come upon one of the most impressive sights from motor racing's history. While always under threat from demolition, the derelict grandstands and pits complex remain as stoic monuments to a forgotten age. Like a coliseum to brave endeavour long forgotten, their decaying majesty is a testimonial to the way things were – good and bad.

In the early 1950s, a new high speed curve skirted the village of Gueux itself (by-passing the narrow streets through which the Silver Arrows once charged) and swept

Relaxing after a hard day's work. Hans Herrmann (right) and Jean Behra unwind after placing third overall at the 1958 Le Mans 24 Hours in their 718 RSK.

Paul Frère brings the works RSK he shared with Harry Schell through the Karussell during the 1958 Nürburgring 1,000km.

After Jean Behra won the Formula Two race at Reims in 1958, certain customers wanted their 1959 production RSKs to be convertible to the central seat location for the formula. Dutch driver Carel de Beaufort campaigned his spyder in both the Dutch and French Grands Prix that year.

out over the rolling fields to link again with the N31 at a hairpin bend called Muizon. The whole course was a maximum speed experience and a drive around Reims will leave you wondering how the little spyders could have overcome much more powerful opposition. Only when you trace mile after mile of the course's flat out scream, do you realise the importance of that remarkable 547 engine's reliability.

It was not only on these long road courses that the RSK came into its own. Rising German driver, Wolfgang von Trips, benefited from the RSK's agility and rugged performance to win the European Hillclimb Championship in 1958.

The 1959 season continued much as 1958, with the first of some 37 RSKs being delivered to customers just before March's Sebring 12 Hours. Swedish driver Jo Bonnier

joined the factory team and partnered von Trips in a still-further developed car to third overall at the Florida airfield circuit behind the Ferraris. Behind them came two more RSKs – the privately-entered car of Sessler/Bob Holbert and ex-Mercedes driver John Fitch driving with Barth.

For the Targa Florio, now integrated into the World Sports Car Manufacturers Championship, Porsche sent four cars. To support them were two private entries from Paul-Ernst Strahle. It proved to be a tough race and all the works Ferraris retired as did two of the factory Porsches. Von Trips had the rear suspension collapse while poor Hans Herrmann was forced to wait by his car for 13 hours out in the countryside after his engine broke, to prevent the car being stripped by souvenir hunters. But by weight of numbers, Porsche took their first overall victory at an event which counted towards the championship. The

Barth/Seidel RSK was victorious, followed by a 550A driven by privateers Mahle/Strahle/Linge and two 356 Carreras of Pucci/von Hanstein and Strahle/Mahle/Linge (yes, they shared two cars!). Anthony Pritchard notes in passing in his book, *Porsche,* that after this event the cars 'were driven back to Zuffenhausen by way of Italy and the Brenner Pass'.

However, the elation did not last long. Le Mans was a disaster. Six cars were entered and six retired, the three factory cars succumbing after a pre-race gamble to find more power triggered three engine failures. August's Avus race brought more depression. Rain had made the North Curve bricks very slippery and Dutch privateer Carel de Beaufort had a very lucky escape when his RSK went over the top of the North Curve banking. Jean Behra was not so fortunate. When his RSK went out of control on the slick bricks, he hit a concrete foundation from a Second World

War gun. Beltless, he was flung from the car, hit a flagpole and was killed.

As the previous year, the final round of the sports car championship was at England's Goodwood circuit for the Tourist Trophy. In the Six Hours, Aston Martin continued their momentous year with victory and the championship, and it was said the von Trips/Bonnier RSK ran rings around the 3-litre Ferraris. The Porsches suffered from not having the knock-on wheels of the big cars, but with their smaller engines had to stop less frequently. Von Trips and Bonnier led overall at one stage and finished a headline-catching second after Stirling Moss in the winning DBR1 engaged in some tactical blocking of the third-placed Testa Rossa (which finally finished just a few seconds behind the Porsche). Moss's intervention ensured Aston Martin won the championship with 24 points since Ferrari could only

During 1958 the factory worked the bugs out of the RSK and the following year customers benefited from around 150bhp and a fine handling chassis. This is the old south loop of the Nürburgring. (Porsche Archiv/Günther Molter)

accumulate 22, with Porsche snapping at their heels with 21. As the previous year, it was *that* close for the spyders, who were showing that 140bhp could often overcome 300bhp or more.

Porsche's sports car momentum was not to be continued the following year however, as much of the attention of the small racing team in Zuffenhausen turned to Formula Two, albeit with a car derived from the RSK.

The 1960 season began with another resounding third in Buenos Aires with British driver Graham Hill partnering Olivier Gendebien, while at Sebring there came a momentous win for Hans Herrmann and Gendebien. To meet new sports car regulations, the RSK was updated to a new model called the RS60 and it was this revised model that overcame the new Ferrari Dino and the 'birdcage' Maserati to another great win in the Targa Florio. By the season's end, Porsche had accumulated equal points to Ferrari in the championship and only lost overall because the Italian cars had come third more times.

The RS60 became the RS61 the following year, with little change of chassis specification (and still typed 718 internally). The result at Sebring in 1961 is notable because a borrowed RS61 came home fifth. Its drivers were Bob Holbert and one Roger Penske. Holbert, partnered by Masten Gregory, would also win the 2,000cc class at Le Mans that year, finishing fifth overall.

Although by now committed heavily to Formula racing, Porsche continued to develop the RS61 prototype during 1961. Two types – the closed RS61 coupé and the much-liked W-RS Spyder – became the mainstay of the sports car effort over the next three seasons. One of the coupés finished seventh overall at Le Mans in 1961. The coupé design and the same W-RS re-appeared in 1962 with the 210bhp 2-litre eight-cylinder engine. The W-RS, driven by

Bonnier and American Dan Gurney, crashed on the 1962 Targa Florio. A single coupé driven by Palermo lawyer and Targa ace Nino Vaccarella (with Bonnier) came home third, despite the new disc brakes fading badly. The W-RS was rebuilt and continued 1962 with appearances in the European Hillclimb Championship and in a series of autumnal sports car races organised by the Sports Car Club of America.

Above: Jo Bonnier and Wolfgang von Trips drove this RSK to be placed second overall in the Goodwood 9 Hours in 1959. (LAT)

Opposite: Porsche claimed a dominant victory over Ferrari in the 1959 Targa Florio, although the winner was not this spyder of Umberto Maglioli and Hans Herrmann. The car would retire with a broken engine, stranding Herrmann out in the countryside for several hours. (LAT)

Far left: Porsche System team at the Nürburgring 1,000km in 1960, from the left: Ing. Hild (with his back to the camera), Maurice Trintignant, Hans Herrmann, Graham Hill and Jo Bonnier.

Left: Mechanic Eberhard Stortz vainly tries to rebuild the four-cam engine from the Bonnier/Graham Hill RS60 at Le Mans 1960. The car was retired when Stortz discovered a broken piston.

All that most drivers saw of Jo Bonnier and his co-driver Carlo Abate was the rear of their RS61 coupé. The 1963 cars featured wishbone front suspension and six-speed transmissions. (LAT)

Jo Bonnier's marathon effort on the 1963 Targa Florio (his co-driver Carlo Abate driving only three of the total ten laps) stands as one of the Swedish driver's and Porsche's finest wins. After nearly seven hours driving over twisting mountain roads, slick village streets and in extreme conditions of torrid sun that changed to heavy rain, the 718 coupé won by just 12 seconds from the very nimble factory 206 Dino driven by Lorenzo Bandini/Ludovico Scarfiotti and no fewer than six 250GTOs. Now nicknamed 'grandmother', the W-RS had limped home in Sicily for seventh place (Maglioli/Giancarlo Baghetti) despite having only first gear. In 1964, it was entered once again, but this time stranded Bonnier in the mountains with a broken driveshaft.

That same year, the 46-year-old Edgar Barth also confirmed his own and the W-RS's dogged competitiveness by winning the European Hillclimb Championship (for Barth his third). By the following May however, Barth was taken by cancer. It was perhaps a fitting point also for the spyders – in which Barth had achieved so much – to rest on their laurels.

Engineering

In the design of the RSK Ing. Hild sought to lighten and stiffen the chassis of the 550A, from which it evolved. The car was given a new internal type number – 718 – and this designation was continued from the first RSK through to the eight-cylinder RS61 Spyder of 1963.

The aerodynamic lessons learnt with the 550 and the

Mickey Mouse experiment resulted in the RSK having a lower, cleaner body profile. The nose in particular was sharper and an exquisitely manufactured surface oil cooler integrated into the underside of the front bonnet ensured there were no unnecessary openings to increase drag. Even the headlamps were faired in behind smooth, clear plastic covers and the car was fitted with a small, full-width windscreen. The mandatory spare wheel was housed in the nose ahead of an 80-litre fuel tank. A raised, but removable rear deck covered the engine (although the whole rear body was removable). Two openings at the rear of the tail section drew in air both for engine cooling and to the carburettors. The rear of the car was more rounded than the 550A, recalling the *Mickey Mouse* or the closed cars used at Le Mans in 1956. As with the 550A, a large louvred grille on each rear flank ducted air to the rear drum brakes.

The low pivot rear suspension was carried over from the 550A, while the front suspension was completely redesigned, not only to improve the handling but also to reduce the frontal area. The front suspension moved away from the Volkswagen Beetle-derived arrangement using spherical ball joints instead of bearing-type bushes, to a geometry that increased negative camber as the suspension compressed. The upper arms were raised and although they were lengthened, the traditional torsion bars were retained. These bars sloped downwards from the inner suspension mountings to the centre-line of the car, where their supporting tubes joined. The shape of these joined support tubes appeared as a letter 'K' on its side and led to the designation RSK. Various other frame improvements were made ahead of the dash bulkhead to stiffen the front section and reduce flexing resulting from the cockpit opening. It was planned that the RSK could be adapted to the new 1,500cc Formula Two that came into effect in 1957 and to this end the worm and peg steering box was mounted centrally and linked to the steering wheel by two universal joints.

The brakes were now operated by a double hydraulic system, the four 280mm drums being the twin leading shoe type and fitted with curving, radial finned drums called 'Turbofins' to help keep them cool.

As practised at the May 1957 Nürburgring 1,000km, the first car was fitted with the same 135bhp 1,500cc 547 four-camshaft engine as used in the contemporary 550A, with two 40DCM Weber downdraught carburettors. The new car weighed approximately 20kg less than the earlier model.

For Le Mans that year the plastic windscreen wrapped around the sides of the cockpit opening, together with two vertical fins on the tail. The value of these fins would prove to be the subject of some uncertainty, together with misgivings about the effectiveness of the new front suspension. The next race appearance for the RSK was the 1958 Targa Florio and, after a winter's development, the front suspension was completely revised to eliminate the camber-changing geometry, but still using torsion bars. At the rear the swing axles were reduced to complex lower transverse arms and to prevent toe changes with wheel movement. A Watt linkage and paired radius rods located each hub.

Externally, the 1958 factory cars can be identified by the additional oil cooler mounted under the left-hand door which was fed cooling air by a small sill-mounted scoop and was exhausted by an oval outlet in front of the left wheelarch. The extra oil cooler was necessary to cope with an improved output from an engine now fitted with huge 46IDM Webers and high-lift camshafts developed over the previous two seasons. At the start of the season, the remarkable four-cam 1,498cc engine was good for a reliable 142bhp. By interesting coincidence this is the very same output quoted for the 1,475cc Coventry Climax FPF twin camshaft in-line four used by Colin Chapman in the Lotus 15 – this being one of the cars the spyders had to beat on the international scene during 1958. The Lotus came out at around 30kg lighter than the RSK and in the hands of drivers such as Roy Salvadori, Alan Stacey and Graham Hill, it achieved much success across Europe. The front-engined Lotus chassis boasted sophisticated Chapman-designed coil spring suspension, rack and pinion steering, all-round disc brakes and a long 2,235mm wheelbase. This specification was in stark contrast to the much more conservative Porsche design, which used proven torsion bar springing, worm and peg steering, drum brakes and a hill-climb-influenced wheelbase, which, at 2,100mm, probably contributed much to the car's accepted nervousness. However,

The W-RS Spyder of Edgar Barth and Herbert Linge in the Nürburgring pits before the start of the 1963 1,000km.

With the principal racing effort being placed on Formula One, three RS61s were entered at Le Mans in 1961, including two of the new coupés. The Barth/Herrmann car was placed seventh overall.

the Porsche was in another category when it came to robustness and it was this feature that was the foundation of its enthusiastic following and string of endurance racing successes. It was in sprint events where the more fragile Lotus excelled and the English car ably demonstrated what could be done with a strong engine and a sophisticated lightweight chassis. In the words of the inimitable Graham Hill it was 'bloody fast' and often victorious.

The spyder wasn't slow either. After the frightening shunt with the *Mickey Mouse* car at Avus in 1956, it is perhaps a measure of Richard von Frankenberg that he continued to race there at every opportunity. Before the season closed in 1958, he achieved a speed of no less than 160mph (257kph) with an aerodynamically cleaned-up RSK with a 160bhp, 1,600cc engine.

In response to the technical pace being forced by Lotus and the other British constructors (including Cooper and the new Lola concern), the 1959 RSK featured a Porsche-inspired version of the double wishbone rear suspension that had become *de rigueur* in grand prix racing. The new design gave the factory drivers a significant edge over the customers during 1959, since the rear was more stable during cornering. It was a major reason why that year, the factory Spyder driven by rising stars von Trips and Bonnier finished third overall after 12 hours of Sebring's tar strips. The new rear suspension allowed much faster changing of

the transaxle ratios and simplification of the chassis frame tubes at the rear. Around this time, the gearbox casing broke new ground in being made from lightweight magnesium alloy. The 1959 RSK Spyder can be most easily identified by the fairing behind the driver's head.

Porsche's 1959 Le Mans fortunes were squashed by the decision to use the more powerful 148bhp engines. It was an attempt to stay on terms with the ever-improving class competition, but all six of the RSKs entered retired. It was a very uncharacteristically poor showing and the root cause – an earlier design change to the fabricated Hirth crankshafts – was rectified immediately afterwards.

For 1960, the RSK was named the RS60. The new model differed only in detail and the measures taken to bring the car in line with the FIA's proposed new regulations for GT racing to be introduced in 1961. This took the form of a full-width safety glass windscreen which was a minimum of 250mm high, a wider, 1,100mm cockpit with larger doors and a larger mandatory luggage bay that could take a suitcase measuring 650mm by 400mm by 200mm. A steering damper was included and the wheel size reduced from 16in to 15in. The tyre widths, minuscule by today's standards, were 5.50in at the front and 6.00in at the rear. Perhaps predictably, the wheelbase was increased by 100mm to 2200mm, bringing them nearly in line with the contemporary Lotus and improving handling predictability.

Graham Hill drove the RS60 regularly and was uniquely placed to compare it with the British competition. In his regular column in Britain's *Sports Car* magazine, he praised the engine for its smoothness and reliability, but felt the road-holding was not as good.

The factory offered the RS60 to their best customers early in 1960 with either 1,498cc or the 1,587cc four-cam engines, these highly developed units producing healthy outputs of 150bhp and 160bhp. To overcome the higher drag of the RS60's full-width windscreen, the works cars appeared at Le Mans with a high, full-width fairing behind the cockpit, with curved plastic side-screens over the doors.

The RS61 was virtually unchanged from the RS60, but it was the need for speed which drove the new body styles of 1961. An RS61 with an 'open' coupé body was first seen at the April Le Mans test weekend and later raced on the Targa Florio by Gurney and Bonnier. This car, still referred to as type 718 and later called the W-RS Spyder, deleted the extended rear hump that characterised the RS60, improving cooling and carburettor breathing and adopted a wide chord fairing behind the cockpit. The windscreen of this revised RS61 was deeper and more raked and featured more deeply recessed headlamps covered by clear plastic

Giancarlo Baghetti enjoying the W-RS Spyder on the way to seventh place with Umberto Maglioli on the 1963 Targa Florio. This eight-cylinder car was using experimental glass fibre bonnet, engine cover and doors. (LAT)

Edgar Barth jumps into the W-RS at the start of the 1964 Sebring 12 Hours. By this time the car had acquired a roll-over bar – a useful hand-hold for Le Mans-style starts – and a tail spoiler.

covers. The 1961 Targa Florio marked the debut of the enlarged 165bhp 2-litre four-cam four-cylinder engine, type 587, which gained its capacity by both extra bore and stroke and notably adopted plain bearings for the crank and connecting rods bearings (and finally dispensing with the complex Hirth crankshafts). This engine, destined for the road-going Carrera 2, was used in Sicily mainly because of its improved torque.

The W-RS Spyder also enjoyed an extra 100mm on its wheelbase to allow the 2-litre, 771 eight-cylinder engine to be shoe-horned into the car. The 2,300mm wheelbase dimension would become a 'comfort zone' for later generations of Porsche racing cars.

For the 1961 Le Mans race weekend, a new full coupé was entered for Herrmann and Barth. This was planned to replace the very successful Abarth-Carrera GT and continued the thinking of the Targa RS61, being styled by F. A. Porsche with a full roof and doors that curved over into the roof line.

The 1962 sports car development improved the W-RS and the closed coupé only in detail. The main attention went into improving the output and reliability of the 771 engine. Excepting capacity, these engines had the same

SPECIFICATION
1959 718 RSK Spyder

Engine: Type 547/4 (1,587cc) or 547/3 (1,498cc) air-cooled four-cylinder with two valves per cylinder. Dry sump lubrication (with 10-litre oil tank) with aluminium crankcase and cylinder heads and alloy barrels with chromium-plated bores. Fabricated Hirth crankshaft supported in three roller and one ball bearings. Single-piece connecting rods with deeply dished forged pistons. Two high-lift camshafts per side operated from the crankshaft by intermediate shaft and two vertical and two horizontal shafts (and using 14 bevel gears). Bosch 12-volt electrical system for dual coil ignition with twin ignition distributors driven from the ends of the top (inlet) camshaft each side and two spark plugs per cylinder. Bendix fuel pump supplying petrol to two Weber 46mm choke IDM downdraught carburettors. Vertical cooling fan with twin intakes driven by V-belt from the crankshaft. Four into one exhaust.

Capacity: 1,587.5cc (1,498cc)

Bore/Stroke: 87.5mm/66.0mm (85mm/66mm)

Maximum power: 160bhp at 7,600rpm (150bhp at 7,000rpm)

Maximum torque: 146Nm at 7,000rpm (140Nm at 6,300rpm)

Compression ratio: 9.8:1

Transmission: Hydraulically actuated single-plate Fichtel & Sachs clutch. Type 690, two-shaft five-speed 'barrel-case' gearbox (with case in magnesium alloy). Second to fifth ring synchronised with the unsynchronised first gear accessible through a locking catch. Independent rear axle with two universal (Hookes type) joints. ZF limited slip differential.

Chassis/body: Welded, cold-drawn seamless tubular steel construction space frame chassis. Front-mounted oil cooler with central nose inlet ahead of spare wheel and 80-litre alloy fuel tank. Sheet aluminium two-seater body with faired headlamps, opening doors plastic cockpit-surrounding windscreen. Cover over engine has raised cowling behind driver's head. Occasional aerodynamic stabilising fins at rear. Two leather trimmed bucket seats with front/back only adjustment. Optional roll-over bar.

Suspension and steering: Centrally located ZF worm and peg steering (2.4 turns lock to lock) with double universally jointed column to left-mounted steering wheel. Independent front suspension with twin trailing arms operating laminated torsion bars and Koni telescopic shock absorbers. Adjustable anti-roll bar. Independent rear low pivot swing axle geometry with Watt linkage, twin radius rods and coil springs over Koni shock absorbers.

Brakes: Dual hydraulic circuit to Alfred Teves twin leading shoe Turbofin drum brakes of 280mm (11in) diameter, 40mm width all round.

Wheels and tyres: 4.00J x 15in Kronprinz aluminium wheels with five fixings (nuts on to studs). Tyres : 5.50/15in front, 5.90 or 6.00/15in rear.

Weight: 530kg

Length: 3,803mm

Width: 1,480mm

Wheelbase: 2,100mm

Track (f/r): 1,290mm/1,250mm

Performance: Acceleration: 0 to 60mph (96.5kph): N/A

Maximum speed: 160mph (257kph) (Avus 1958)

basic specification as the Formula One engine with four twin choke Weber carburettors. The two spark plugs per cylinder were fired from no fewer than four Bosch HT ignition coils. The air-cooled engine is also noteworthy for its pioneering use of glass fibre for the cooling air ducting.

For the '62 Targa Florio, one of the RS61 coupés (as well as the veteran W-RS) was rebuilt to take the eight-cylinder and the new six-speed gearbox (also developed with the F1 programme). Reverse gear on these cars was selected by a separate lever beside the driver's seat and, by means of a Bowden cable, operated the gear mechanism which itself was mounted in an extension housing outside the main gearbox. Dunlop-Porsche disc brakes were fitted all round. Barth had tried discs at the Le Mans test weekend in April 1961, but it took another year of pad development before they were durable enough for endurance racing. By this time, the W-RS had shed its 'GT' bodywork and became a completely open spyder with a low plastic windscreen and no high fairings behind the driver. Towards the season's end this car featured a proper roll-over bar and glass fibre doors and bonnet.

The eight-cylinder cars were revised again for 1963 and most importantly, the front torsion bar suspension was replaced by a double wishbone front suspension with coil springs as developed for the GP cars. By the time of Bonnier's memorable victory with the coupé on the Targa Florio, the eight-cylinder engine was good for 225bhp – it was a long way from the 718 RSK's original output of just 135bhp, a full seven seasons before.

MISTAKEN IDENTITY –
804 F1

MOTOR RACING IN EUROPE went through a major philosophy change during the late 1950s, with a shift towards small capacity engines in the open-wheeled racing formulae. For 1957, the engine capacity allowed in Formula Two was restricted to 1,500cc and at the same time it was declared that from 1960, Formula One would be restricted to the same capacity (with F2 dropping to 1 litre). It was not difficult to see why the rule changes had the voiturette manufacturers collectively reaching for their slide rules. The lure of being able to compete in the sport's top formula was almost irresistible, and there were plenty of new contenders. The British Cooper and Lotus teams already had rapid monoposto machines for the fast, but still unreliable Coventry-Climax FPF, while Ferrari meanwhile wheeled out his elegant 156 V6-engined Dino. At this time, Formula One still permitted cars with all-enveloping bodywork and as a result, the changing regulations were also attractive to the small-capacity sports car builders. Because of their larger size, the sports-derived cars would always be carrying a weight penalty, but they did have two important advantages – the aerodynamic low drag of their all-enveloping bodywork, and reliability.

Only when the sports cars came out against the thoroughbred F2 cars did the size of the challenge become clear. The July 1957 F2 race at the Reims Speed Week saw sports car entries from Lotus, Cooper, Osca and Geothals' private 550A facing the purpose-built machinery. It was no contest. In a typically thrilling Reims slipstreamer, the monoposto Coopers driven by Jack Brabham and Roy Salvadori battled with Maurice Trintignant's Dino. Over the 304km event they just left the two-seaters standing. Although Goethals finished fifth, he was a full two laps behind the victor Trintignant by the end.

Another opportunity came at the German Grand Prix that year, which included a class for Formula Two. This time the works entered 550A Spyders for Umberto Maglioli, Edgar Barth and Dutch aristocrat Carel de

804 Formula One
Rouen, France
Dan Gurney
1962

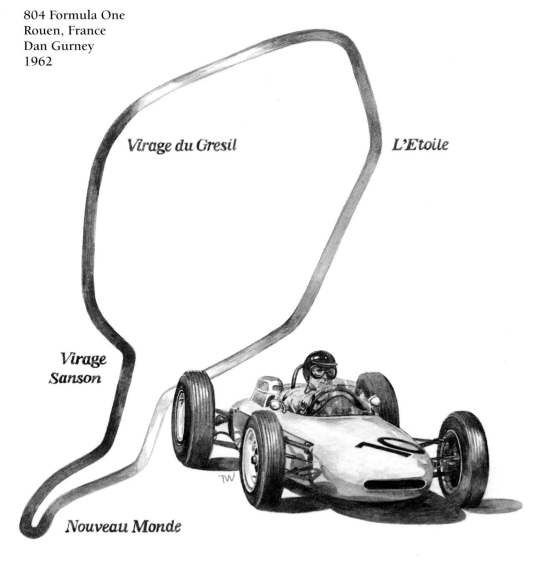

L'Etoile

Virage
Sanson

Nouveau Monde

MISTAKEN IDENTITY – 804 F1 / 37

Although Dan Gurney's best practice time at the Dutch Grand Prix was fully one second better than the previous year, the team was dismayed to find the time was two seconds adrift of the pole position time.

Beaufort. Maglioli retired but Barth set fastest time in practice around the course he knew so well. After a wheel to wheel dice with Salvadori's Cooper ended with the Cooper breaking a rear wishbone, Barth cruised to the class victory, with de Beaufort third. Barth finished 12th overall in this memorable race, one lap down to Fangio's winning Maserati.

The only change to the spyders entered in that grand prix was the removal of the headlamps, but by the time the Speed Week at Reims came round again in 1958, the new RSK model was fully defined. One of the Le Mans cars was converted to a central, single-seat cockpit and fitted with a streamlined fairing behind the driver's head. After practice, grand prix driver Jean Behra found the Porsche was the fastest car on the long straights, but because of its extra weight and slightly wrong gear ratios, was slow out of the crucial hairpins at Muizon and Thillois. He lined up for the start 1.6 seconds behind Stirling Moss in the Cooper-Climax and 0.7 seconds slower than Peter Collins's Ferrari Dino. But there was a surprise in store for the F2 regulars. To quote Denis Jenkinson from the August 1958 edition of *Motor Sport*: 'his car was nothing more than a converted sports car and he was pulling away from the might of the proven Formula Two runners'. Behra won by 20 seconds from Collins, after Moss had retired. In Jenkinson's words, 'it was an embarrassing shock to the Scuderia Ferrari and a real shaker for the British F2 boys, who thought they had got this type of racing all sewn-up'. Jenks (by this time a confirmed fan of the 356 and its air-cooled motivation) closed his report by saying the result was 'the finest thing that could have happened'.

Another to catalogue this race was Richard von Frankenberg, who noted that Behra's winning speed was as high as Fangio's in the 1954 Formula One Mercedes. He says, 'such comparisons show clearly the technical advance in motor engineering'.

A wave of confidence swept through Porsche that the 547 engine in a purpose-designed chassis could be even more competitive. August's German Grand Prix again offered an opportunity to use the car's (and Edgar Barth's) strengths.

Despite practice lap times that were over 20 seconds faster than he achieved in the 550A the previous year, Barth was beaten by a remarkable performance from a young Bruce McLaren in a Cooper. It was the New Zealander's first ever appearance at the daunting German course and in winning the Formula Two class, he finished a remarkable fifth overall in the grand prix.

Porsche pride was restored later in the year when a streamlined RSK driven by American Masten Gregory triumphed in the Formula Two Avus races. Gregory positively flew to victory at an average speed of no less than 126.08mph (202.86kph), overcoming class opposition from Jack Brabham and Britain's Jim Russell.

These high placings in Formula Two had a profound effect on Porsche's stature as a racing car manufacturer in a way that sports car racing could never have achieved. As von Frankenberg noted at the time, 'the more successful

Porsche became in the general classification of the big races, the more did the grand prix drivers want to drive them'. In turn, Huschke von Hanstein also appreciated that as the speeds rose, the more he needed to have the best drivers in his cars.

Over the winter of 1958–59, Porsche decided to build a monoposto for Formula Two. The car was still type 718 and the tube frame chassis retained the twisting-leaf spring front suspension. A wishbone-type rear suspension was designed and the 547/3 engine was further tweaked with larger Weber carburettors to produce around 150bhp. The useful rev range of the air-cooled flat-four was confined to between 7,500 and 9,000rpm and to make best use of this, a new six-speed gearbox was developed. Remarkably, the car still used drum brakes, at a time when virtually every other major manufacturer had adopted disc brakes (even Ferrari changed to discs for his 1959 racing cars). The new car first appeared at the Monaco Grand Prix and was driven by rising German driver, Wolfgang von Trips. A surprise entry was another Porsche-engined car by Jean Behra.

Also during that winter, Behra had commissioned ex-Maserati engineer Valerio Colotti to design and build a Formula Two car to take the Porsche 547 engine. Colotti's Tec-Mec Modena-based concern was making a name for itself for the gearboxes fitted in Rob Walker's Coopers (driven by Moss and Trintignant). The Behra-Porsche kept the RSK's engine and suspension and fitted these to a narrower single-seater space-frame chassis. Driven by the inexperienced Maria de Filippis in Monte Carlo, the attrac-

tive car failed to qualify. The works car was driven by von Trips and looked much more promising. However, in the race the German collided with two other cars and retired.

Behra ran his car in Pau, but was outclassed by the dominant Coopers. The next time the pair came out together was at Reims in July and at this fast course the two Porsche single seaters were on terms with the Coopers and the Ferraris. The Behra-Porsche was initially driven by Colin Davis, but it was taken over by Hans Herrmann who put

Dutch aristocrat Carel de Beaufort drove this centre-seat 718 RSK in his home grand prix at Zandvoort in 1959. He finished tenth and last, seven laps behind winner Jo Bonnier in a BRM.

The 1960 German Grand Prix was a non-championship Formula Two event. Hans Herrmann leads Count Wolfgang von Trips, eventual winner Jo Bonnier, and Dan Gurney in a race that was run on the short, south loop of the Nürburgring. (LAT)

the car on the front row alongside Moss in the Cooper and Cliff Allison in the Dino. Jo Bonnier trailed in the rebuilt works F2 car as did von Trips in a factory-entered RSK streamliner with the new double wishbone rear suspension.

In the race, Herrmann had a wheel-to-wheel dice for the lead with Moss, the Cooper being faster through the turns out to Muizon while Herrmann would have the advantage under braking and on top speed. The dice was resolved only when Herrmann had to take to the escape road at the Thillois hairpin. Bonnier in the works car came home a lucky third after Allison's Dino blew up while in third place, von Trips finished fifth to demonstrate that although the RSK might have now been out-dated for F2, it was still reliable.

Based on these strong results, it is not surprising that Porsche decided to focus their principal effort on formula racing for 1960. They had the engine and they had proven they had the basis for a competitive chassis. Huschke von Hanstein agreed terms with Jo Bonnier and Graham Hill to drive the two works cars while a third car was run by Rob Walker for Stirling Moss to drive.

It was Moss who brought the first results of the year, winning the first heat of that April's Brussels Grand Prix and then the Aintree 200 (ahead of the works cars of Bonnier and Graham Hill). John Surtees had a go in the Walker car (after Moss was sidelined by injury) at the Solitude Grand Prix – the pretty course overlooked by the Schloss Solitude, just a few kilometres outside Stuttgart.

The race turned into a close dice between the new rear-engined Ferrari Dino of von Trips and local hero Herrmann in the Porsche. Von Trips won with Herrmann, Bonnier, Hill and Dan Gurney snapping at his heels. Surtees, still making the change from two wheels to four, retired after finding the Porsche's (already notorious) gear-change very tricky.

That year's German Grand Prix was a Formula Two-only event on the *Südschleife* course of the Nürburgring. Run in rain and mist, Bonnier capitalised on his knowledge of the track to win from von Trips (in a Porsche this time). Both Moss and Bonnier won non-championship races later in the year.

An equal first (with Cooper) in the Formula Two Manufacturers' Championship was a great result for Zuffenhausen in their first year of serious competition and with the rules for Formula One changing to a maximum capacity of 1,500cc for 1961, it was perhaps not surprising that the way was open for a challenge at the highest level.

Preparations began in earnest. Both Bonnier and Gurney left BRM to become Porsche factory drivers in the 1961 Formula One World Championship. Gurney had first competed in F1 during 1959, when despite a late season start, he finished seventh in the world championship driving a works Ferrari. He was attracted to BRM for 1960 and after a frustrating season of unreliability and mishaps was persuaded by Porsche team manager Huschke von Hanstein to join Porsche's new F1 team for 1961. Gurney would thrive at Porsche. The lack of politics and the raw enthusiasm of the small, but dedicated racing team was the kind of environment that allowed the popular Californian to apply his driving skills and dogged persistence to the full.

During the winter of 1960–61, a new flat eight engine was designed as was a longer wheelbase chassis to take the larger engine. But there was disappointment in store. When the new engine was run on the test bench, it failed to develop anything like the power expected. The projected 180bhp maximum output turned out to be closer to 120bhp. For the new effort in 1961, there was little choice but to fall back on the bulbous 718-derived F2 cars from the previous year. But Porsche were not the only ones who were unready for the new formula.

Ever since the announcement that F1 was going to be reduced to the new engine capacity, the British teams had put up a fierce opposition, hoping that the limit would remain at 2.5-litres and so extend the life of the doughty Coventry-Climax four-cylinder. At this time there was even talk of staging an alternative Intercontinental Formula, with a top capacity limit of 3-litres. It was said this was a capacity more in keeping with motor racing's top class.

Stirling Moss in the Rob Walker-entered monoposto F2 car headed a 1–2–3 for Porsche in the 1960 Aintree 200. (LAT)

The Intercontinental Formula never happened. Through the spring of 1961, it became clear that the rules were not going to be changed away from 1.5-litres and completely unprepared, the British constructors – Lotus, Cooper and BRM – had to cobble together what they could using the dated 1.5-litre Coventry Climax engine. Ferrari was the only team that was ready and came to the first championship race in Monte Carlo in May 1961 with the stunningly compact shark-nosed Dino 156. The powerful Vittorio Jano-designed 185bhp 65 degree V6 had the legs on everything else in the field, its power delivery and reliability having been honed during the course of the previous year's F2 season. Such was the momentum Ferrari brought to that first race of the new formula, that Richie Ginther also debuted a brand new 200bhp 120 degree V6 in his 156.

With the four-cam four-cylinder engine developing around 160bhp – about the same as the Climax four-cylinder – the Porsches found themselves able to stay with the British constructors at the start of the season, even though they were invariably out-classed by the Ferraris.

Surprisingly, Bonnier had won the first heat of the first F1 race of that year, the non-championship Brussels Grand Prix, while Gurney chased Giancarlo Baghetti, making his first grand prix appearance driving a Ferrari, all the way home in the post-Monaco Syracuse Grand Prix. But it was beginning to look as though the Ferraris would have it all their own way throughout the season. It was also clear that the Lotus was gaining speed at every event in the hands of Moss and the works team's gifted new driver Jim Clark. The Porsche chassis found itself simply out-distanced by the pace of development, particularly as the experiments with Kugelfischer fuel injection and a new chassis went nowhere. The eight-cylinder engine – although reputedly coaxed to 160bhp – was still not strong enough for competition.

The races became Ferrari processions, especially once the new 120 degree V6 was fully competitive. Fortunately, there were two notable upsets to the form book. The first championship race of the year had provided one when Moss flailed the Ferraris in his under-powered Lotus 18.

The French Grand Prix at Reims would provide the second twist of unpredictability to an otherwise predictable season. For this event, Porsche entered three 1960 F2 cars in a last ditch attempt to secure some results. Bonnier and Gurney were joined by Carel de Beaufort. Perhaps it was the blistering heat that resulted in the pace-setters all retiring – Phil Hill, von Trips and Ginther in the Ferraris and even Moss's Lotus. It left Bonnier and Gurney to fight it out with the inexperienced Baghetti (whose car was fitted with one of the less powerful 65 degree Dino V6 engines).

The Porsche Formula One team for 1961 and 1962 was centred around drivers Joachim Bonnier (left) and Dan Gurney. They are seen here talking to team manager Huschke von Hanstein.

Dan Gurney chased F1 newcomer Giancarlo Baghetti all the way home in the non-championship Syracuse Grand Prix in 1961. Following the disappointing performance of the new eight-cylinder engine, the team was forced to use the four-cylinder cars for the rest of the season. (LAT)

The nail-biting close finish to the French GP at Reims in 1961 saw the novice Baghetti (50) out-smart the experienced Gurney (12) with a brilliant pass just a few metres from the chequered flag. Bonnier (10) would drop out only two laps from the end. (LAT)

The race developed into one of the most exciting grands prix of all time, with the lead changing virtually every lap. Baghetti, apart from his fortunate victory in the Syracuse GP, could only call upon his previous Formula Junior experience while Bonnier and Gurney were by this time seasoned grand prix competitors. The blistering heat took its toll on Bonnier only two laps from the end and as they crossed the line to start the last five miles, it was just Gurney and Baghetti mere metres apart. Gurney held the advantage over the last lap and as they scrambled into the final hairpin at Thillois, the Ferrari was glued to his tail. They faced a half-mile dead straight drag from Thillois to the finish and Gurney held it until just 300 metres from the line, when Baghetti dived out of the Porsche's slipstream. The Ferrari won by half a length. It was a remarkable display of driving coolness by a complete newcomer to Formula One.

Far from disappointed, the Reims result buoyed the Porsche team and partially salvaged a somewhat tarnished reputation. For the British GP, Bonnier was on the front row with a practice time that equalled exactly the time set by the three Ferraris (the four equal best times being a feat unequalled before or since). But that was as close as the Swede would get. He finished fifth (behind Brabham) and Gurney was seventh.

Over the remaining three races, it was Gurney who achieved most. Still committed to the four-cylinder car, the American made up for a dismal seventh in Germany by taking second place at both Monza and Watkins Glen. The race for the world championship focused predictably on the Ferrari team drivers. When world championship favourite Wolfgang von Trips was killed at Monza, a somewhat lucky Phil Hill claimed the title for the red cars.

For Porsche, the taste of 1961 was bittersweet but there were some encouraging results. Gurney was third equal (with Moss) in the drivers' championship, while Porsche took third in the constructors' competition. Bloodied, but not defeated, Zuffenhausen was convinced that their flat eight, in a state-of-the-art chassis could yet achieve far more.

Race record

It was hardly surprising that a sound – if not winning – result awaited Porsche at the end of that season. Aside from the dominant Ferraris, the invariably unreliable efforts to extract more power from the Climax four allowed the 718-derived cars to score consistently. The mistake was to assume this was a normal F1 year. Even the Reims result should have sounded a warning that over-confidence for the following year was dangerous.

The slim new 804 was first run in February 1962, but its testing was cut short by internal argument over whether Porsche should in fact be competing in Formula One. Bad weather and then a crash which wrote off the first car stunted development further. Ferry Porsche had taken a decision that the four-cylinder would not be run again, despite the engine now running on fuel injection and delivering a reputed 180bhp. All the effort went on the eight and as brought to the opening round of the 1962 World Championship – the Dutch Grand Prix at Zandvoort, the engine was good for perhaps 178bhp. Practice showed the cars to be skittish and Bonnier in particular found it difficult to settle the car through the often sand-covered sweeps in the Dutch dunes.

Ferry Porsche was appeased however, when a gritty lap by Gurney resulted in a time that was fully one second faster than his previous year's best in the 718-based car – enough for a third row position on the grid. It was, however, two seconds off John Surtees's pole time (in a V8 Climax-engined Lola). The boss's presence at Zandvoort reflected his serious concern about the progress of the Formula One effort. The problem was that although the team was making rapid progress, it seemed others were advancing at an even greater rate. Even Ferrari were left gasping with their now out-dated V6.

A sparkling start by Gurney saw the Porsche in third place behind Clark and Graham Hill until the gear linkage broke. The resulting pit stop cost six laps and the linkage broke again some time later. Bonnier fared no better, having been consigned to one of the old F2 cars. He finished

Jo Bonnier found the new 804 a real handful around the sandy expanses of Zandvoort. (Günther Molter)

Dan Gurney began the season with a respectable, if not race-winning 180bhp from the 753 eight-cylinder, compared with perhaps 190bhp from the early Coventry-Climax V8s.

seventh, five laps down on winner Graham Hill in the new P57 BRM.

Ferry Porsche wanted the team to spend some time testing the cars. They had to find more speed and reliability before another outing. But the next race was the Monaco Grand Prix and both Gurney and von Hanstein wanted to learn more by racing the car. As a result of their pleas, a lone 804 was sent to Monte Carlo. Gurney wrung a very good second row grid position from the car, but in the melée of the first lap the Porsche was shunted from behind by Ginther's BRM at the Gasworks Hairpin. A wrecked gearbox resulted in an immediate retirement. Bonnier, again in a borrowed four-cylinder car, soldiered to fifth place, this time seven laps behind winner Bruce McLaren. Although

the Monaco crash was not Gurney's fault, Ferry Porsche insisted the team miss the Belgian Grand Prix and spend the next month testing.

Two weeks later, and after a very detailed review of the car, the team held a test at the Nürburgring, with the objective of going a whole grand prix distance without problem. During this successful test, Gurney was able to record the fastest lap ever (8 minutes 44.4 seconds) around the *Nordschleife* – the longer northern sector of the course that was used for the grand prix. The fastest lap in the previous year's GP had been claimed by Phil Hill in the Ferrari 156 at 8 minutes 55.2 seconds so not surprisingly, spirits were significantly boosted by this.

The next grand prix was the French, but instead of the ultra-fast Reims, the location was the twisting road circuit at Rouen-Les-Essarts, just two miles south of the centre of this bustling north-eastern French city. Compared with the *'vitesse et champagne'* image of Reims, Rouen is *'vin et baguette',* a workmanlike, but pretty circuit set in dense rolling woodlands that took far more from the drivers than they would care to admit.

Today the course at Les Essarts is difficult to find. Such has been the rapid expansion of Rouen, the little village has been engulfed by the city's urbanisation. But the pits and grandstands are still there, the course having been used for French national racing until the early 1990s. Go south towards Grand Couronne and Elbeuf on the main N138 passing the turning to Paris on the A13 autoroute and look for the signs to Les Essarts. You will invariably join this challenging road course at the last corner before the pits. After a fast straight past the grandstands, the road falls away in a series of very fast right-left-right sweeps with a forbidding embankment on one side and an unguarded drop on the right. The road runs down into the base of the valley and at the Elbeuf crossroads, does a full 180 degree hairpin reversal at the virage Nouveau Monde and back up the other side of the valley. In 1962, this bend was cobbled and in the 1990s, these could still be seen through the patches of worn asphalt. Indeed one of the drivers' main criticisms of Rouen was its generally poor surface. All around this section the valley sides rise quite steeply and the spectator seating is still there, albeit now covered with mature trees. The climb up the hill from Nouveau Monde was fast until the sharper left-hander at Sanson. This slowed the momentum up the hill which continued until the course opened out on to the level Gresil straight. The road joined the much better condition N138 Le Mans to Rouen road in a fast right-hand bend and followed this until Les Essarts village, where it turned right again for the startline. The course was 4.08 miles (6.56km) long.

Carel Godin de Beaufort campaigned a 718-derived four-cylinder car throughout the 1962 season. His best results were sixth place at both Zandvoort and Rouen. He is seen here (number 18) at the Solitude GP.

The French Grand Prix had twice been held at Rouen in the 1950s and after 1962 would be held twice more as the French Grand Prix wandered in search of a regular home. Rouen, like many of the courses that demanded the best of that era of racing drivers, succumbed to rising concerns about safety. The ultra-fast sweeps downhill after the pits became fearsome in the late 1960s' breed of Formula Two and Formula One machines. When Frenchman Jo Schlesser came to a horrific end there during the 1968 event, it sealed the fate of Rouen at the top level.

The twists and turns of Rouen promised to obscure the power disadvantage the Porsche flat eight suffered over the Climax and BRM engines, while championship-leader Phil Hill was forced to sit the race out since Ferrari was unable to send any cars as a result of a dispute with his staff. Several of his leading engineers subsequently departed for the new ATS team.

Dan Gurney had never raced at Rouen before. He came to the event with influenza, but was pleased to be back among the action. The 804 was showing obvious signs of its month away from the scene although, as it had been all season, the press attention was centred on Clark's remarkable Lotus 25 (which had won the earlier Belgian Grand Prix). Practice was not inspiring for Zuffenhausen, with Gurney lining up in sixth position – 1.7 seconds behind Clark's fastest lap. But such was the pace of progress that de Beaufort in one of the old F2 cars was the slowest of the field, a full 11.7 seconds behind.

After a typically chaotic and crowd-filled start, the 17-car pack roared off in a 100mph wheel-spinning, smoking gaggle down the hill. Reflecting the danger that lay just millimetres either side of the asphalt, there was no contact as

the field sorted themselves out into an impatient, but obedient single file around Nouveau Monde. As they began the haul up the hill it was Clark, from Graham Hill and Bruce McLaren.

For ten laps this was the way it remained until Clark's handling went off, letting Hill and Surtees pull away. Behind Clark came McLaren, Brabham and Gurney, the Californian uncomfortable in the new-style 'lay-down' cockpit of the 804. McLaren was the first to go, spinning off at Sanson as he struggled to find gears. Brabham pulled off with broken suspension and in the July heat, Surtees

After a month away from the racing in 1962, Porsche came back at Rouen with cars that were significantly improved. Gurney rounds the Nouveau Monde Hairpin on the way to victory. Note his more reclined position compared with the Zandvoort views. (Porsche Archiv/Günther Molter)

A week after Rouen there was a non-championship F1 race at Porsche's home circuit in Solitude. Jim Clark in the ground-breaking Lotus 25 (left) gets the drop on Gurney (10) at the start. The Scotsman later spun and Gurney led Bonnier home for a Porsche 1–2.

have it punt him in the rear going into the corner. This let Clark through until Hill once again retook the lead. Shortly after, Clark pitted to retire with bent steering. Hill was now 30 seconds ahead of Gurney, who was a full lap ahead of Surtees. But Hill stopped on lap 42 with faulty fuel injection and with 12 laps remaining Gurney could cruise to the finish. Consistency won the day for Porsche.

A week later, the team was in Solitude for a non-championship race. Again there were no Ferraris, but Team Lotus headed the rest of the strong field. On a course he knew very well, Gurney led the 25-lap race from start to finish. When Clark spun and retired, Bonnier came home second in the other Porsche eight.

It all looked so good at this point. The testing had apparently paid off and it was easy to ignore the fact the eight was producing a mere 175–180bhp (when the new Climax could call on at least 190bhp).

The illusion came to an end at Aintree. Jim Clark simply drove away from the rest to win the first of what would be five British GPs in the coming six years. The championship was developing into a stirring battle between the Scottish driver and Graham Hill in the BRM. The German Grand Prix demonstrated Gurney's fine skills and proved to be frustrating, rather than disappointing. Although his time was some three seconds slower than his testing best, Gurney claimed pole position. In typically streaming wet Eifel conditions, the Porsche led initially, but was soon overhauled by Hill. When Gurney's cockpit-mounted battery became loose, Surtees squeezed by for second.

Gurney speeds past the pits at Solitude. This would be the last victory for the 804. (Porsche Archiv/Günther Molter)

was slowed by fuel vaporisation. So by half-distance it was Hill, from Clark – still unhappy with his handling – and Gurney. The Porsche was running well, if not at all on the pace of Hill and Clark. But then Clark came round ahead of Hill. Graham had passed a slower car under braking only to

The British Grand Prix at Aintree was a jolt back to reality. Just six days after the Solitude race, the Porsches had to watch Jim Clark's mastery from a great distance. Bonnier gets inside Roy Salvadori, but both would retire. (LAT)

Wedging the battery with his legs, Gurney fought back but was unable to re-pass in the very difficult conditions. At the chequered flag, just 4.4 seconds separated these three drivers after 2 hours 38 minutes of racing. Clark was the spectator in this one, finishing fourth, some 40 seconds behind after the full 15-lap distance. Bonnier, enduring a wretched season in the second Porsche, just missed a point with seventh place.

Only the road course was used for the Italian Grand Prix at Monza and the event proved to be a benefit for the two BRMs of Graham Hill and Richie Ginther. This time it was Bonnier who scored for Porsche, with a single point for sixth place (but a lap down), to add to the two he had achieved at Monte Carlo. Gurney retired with a failed crown wheel and pinion (the same failure as befell Bonnier at Aintree).

Porsche's final grand prix entry of 1962 came at Watkins Glen. Gurney qualified 1.1 seconds slower than Clark and the race proved to be a British benefit with Clark winning from Graham Hill. Gurney was third at one stage, but fell back to finish fifth a lap down. Bonnier struggled home 13th (and last) after he spun and hit the Glen's guard-rail.

So that was it. The team declined to go to the South African Grand Prix at the end of December and retreated to Zuffenhausen to contemplate its racing future. The grand prix adventure had been a chastening experience, but it was far from being a failure. As a production car manufacturer, Ferry Porsche was not prepared to sacrifice the business he had established to fuel the obsessive lust for development that Formula One demands. There were many more factors to be taken into account than what had been a fortuitous change of the regulations. Porsche's hope that their success in sports car racing would carry them through was misplaced. All the evidence was there at an early stage to suggest it would not happen without a very serious and dedicated effort, funded by an unconstrained budget.

The 48th French Grand Prix remains the only Formula One championship race to be won by a car carrying the Porsche name.

Engineering

The participation in Formula One marked a very significant change in the pace of engineering progress at Porsche. Up to this point, the racing cars had followed a process of steady evolution, which had originated with a set of chassis and powertrain components based on the four-cylinder Volkswagen car. The 550 racer and the 547 four-cam engine that followed were brilliant adaptions from the basic theme and through the 1950s, Porsche gained a strong rep-

Jo Bonnier rounds the Karussell at the 1962 German GP. The 1960s would see a culture change overtake motor racing. The days of the polo shirt were numbered even in 1962, but seat belts and effective roll-over bars would take a few more years yet. (LAT)

utation for following their own path, yet producing fast and reliable cars. That philosophy worked for the racing sports cars and by dint of considered evolution and experience, the results followed. But F1 proved to be very different.

The conditions that confronted Porsche in Formula One in 1961 were unique. Faced with no suitable powerplant for the new 1.5-litre formula, the British constructors fell back on the four-cylinder Climax. To find speed, they had to use all their ingenuity to minimise aerodynamic drag and improve cornering performance. As a result by 1962, these *garage-ists* (as Ferrari somewhat disparagingly called them), were markedly ahead in their thinking on the development of chassis that extracted the best from an under-powered engine.

From the moment Porsche decided to run a Formula One programme, it was thought all that was needed was a suitably powerful engine. Ferrari was also thinking along the same lines. And both manufacturers began – in total secrecy – to develop new designs from 1960. The design of the new engine became the responsibility of Hans Hönick, who had worked with Ernst Fuhrmann on the four-camshaft four-cylinder. Supporting him was a young engineer who would bring a new level of innovation to engine design at Porsche – Hans Mezger.

The engine was laid out in both 1.5-litre and 2-litre capacities, so that it could be used in sports car racing and

Although the 804 was a diminutive car when viewed from the outside, there was a great deal of complexity beneath the skin. The installation of the flat eight-cylinder engine was notably tidy. This car is prepared for the Italian GP at Monza, complete with taped-off wishbones and, just visible, covers on the wheels in an effort to reduce aerodynamic drag.

F1. The 1.5-litre was typed the 753, while the 2-litre became the 771. It was air-cooled – of course – because experience had shown there was no reason to change away from this simple method of cooling, which also offered a minimum weight design. It was expected that 180bhp would be required, but that within a short time as much as 225bhp would be essential for a front-running engine (by 1964 this was the case). The only way to have the potential for that level of specific power was to use multi-cylinders to permit high revolutions. The layout chosen was a 180-degree eight-cylinder. A forged crankshaft ran in nine shell-type main bearings – each rod having its own crank journal) – with the rear being a roller (as in the 547). The crankcase was cast magnesium alloy with the heads and the chromium-plated cylinder barrels in alumnium.

At 54.6mm and 66mm, the bore and stroke reflected the primary need for high rpm potential, but also to obtain an

engine with as small a frontal area as possible. The tiny 126mm forged steel connecting rods ran in plain Vandervell bearings – it being a big decision at the time to forgo the fabricated Hirth crank and needle rollers. Tests had shown there was no perceptible loss of power using the plain bearings and the whole assembly was lighter. The big end bearings themselves notably had no circumferential groove for lubricating oil feed, which allowed a narrower bearing shell and, as a result, a shorter engine. Instead of the usual splash crankshaft lubrication arrangement, Mezger was able to feed oil through a central axial drilling in the crankshaft and out to the big ends. Over the coming years this oil feed method would be effectively developed into the innovative low pressure system used on the 908 and 917 engines.

Bronze little-end bushes supported the forged aluminium pistons. A 90-degree included angle was chosen for the (two per cylinder) valves and to achieve the high 10 to 1 compression ratio, the pistons had sharply domed crowns with cut-outs for the valves. It was considered that the larger valves this layout offered would improve engine breathing. The head design would prove to be the engine's weak point.

The four overhead camshafts were driven by two inter-mediate shafts (one above and one below the crankshaft) and bevel gears. The glass fibre-reinforced horizontal cooling fan and the two Bosch distributors were gear-driven from the top intermediate shaft. The lower intermediate shaft (which drove the exhaust valves) also drove the pair of oil pumps.

The 753 was ready for bench testing in December 1960, but the first runs produced a mere 120bhp, which by the spring could only be edged up to 160bhp. With the 120-degree Ferrari V6 engine good for 180bhp and even the 547 four producing a reliable 160bhp, the eight would remain on the test bench for the 1961 season.

The main area for development centred on improving the 90-degree valve arrangement and the shape of the combustion chambers. This work was driven forward by Hans Mezger and the young Ferdinand Piëch, Ferry Porsche's, nephew, and these two very bright engineers studied head designs with included angles of 84 and 73 degrees.

The development on the eight continued through the year but as an insurance policy, Swiss engineer Michael May was employed as a consultant to further develop the four. Starting in the summer of 1961, he completely revised the 547's breathing, fitting a four plunger Bosch mechanical fuel injection pump and a slide throttle arrangement. Power rose to an impressive 185bhp and although the output was reliable, it was available only over a very limited

revolution range. But with much public attention focused on the eight however, May's four would not be raced by the works.

Meanwhile, Ferry Porsche also authorised the design of a completely new chassis, which first ran in February 1962. The 804 was a product of Porsche's single year in Formula One during 1961. The design was clearly influenced by Colin Chapman's Lotus 18 and the Carlo Chiti-led Ferrari 156. The most noticeable difference between the new car and the old 718 monopostos was the very low stance.

The 804 used a multi-tubular steel space-frame chassis, which was much slimmer than the previous 718 F2 designs, but still lacking the compactness of the best British designs. Following the lead set by Colin Chapman in the search for lower frontal area, the driver in the 804 lay back much more than previously and was surrounded by a sculpted aluminium fuel tank (to ensure minimal weight distribution change as the fuel load lightened). Another fuel tank was positioned ahead of the front wheels, next to the oil tank. Although a layout that would not be contemplated today (on safety grounds), this aimed to counterbalance the mass of the large six-speed transaxle. The suspension was a double wishbone arrangement all round, with longitudinal torsion bars and inboard shock absorbers. F1-convention was followed with Porsche-developed disc brakes with four piston calipers, but the Rudge-type knock-off wheels favoured by the other constructors were not used, Porsche remaining loyal to the five stud hubs of the earlier cars.

Porsche's concern at the slow pace of development of the eight was no doubt heightened by the debut of the new Coventry-Climax V8 at the 1961 German Grand Prix. The new engine, fitted to reigning World Champion Jack Brabham's Cooper, claimed second-fastest time in practice but retired when Brabham went off the road. The Porsche brows must have become even more furrowed at Monza, because BRM debuted their own V8. This uncomplicated 90-degree water-cooled engine benefited from the new Lucas fuel injection and transistorised ignition. In the words of LJK Setright, the BRM's first impression was 'altogether more promising'. The Climax was soon fuel injected and sparked similarly and by the first race of the 1962 season, in Monaco, these new British V8s were probably developing close to 190bhp, eclipsing both the Ferrari V6 that had been so dominant the previous year and Porsche's still carburettor-fitted and coil-ignited flat-eight.

At a non-championship race at Pau, Lotus had rolled out its new 24 model, notable because the driver was even more reclined than the previous year's 21. But at the first round of the World Championship, there was another new

model that was to eventually eclipse all the other runners – the monocoque Lotus 25. This revolutionary machine, which used the aluminium skin as the main structural element – like an aircraft – offered a significantly more compact design. It was lighter, but no less than three times stiffer than the space-frame 21. The Lotus 25 would define the Formula One racing car for decades to come, changing the designer's philosophy away from the maxim that the engine was all-important, to one that had to consider the whole car as an integrated system.

With around 180bhp, the Porsche eight nonetheless looked a promising, if not spectacular prospect at the start of the season. After Monaco, a month of development brought improvements to both engine and chassis. Changes were made to the wrap-around fuel tank which allowed the driver to recline even more (inspired by the totally reclined position of the driver in the Lotus 25), but this was not so straightforward. Accommodating Gurney's

Gurney made a strong start to the Dutch GP and was lying third when the gear linkage broke. (LAT)

The 1962 German Grand Prix at the Nürburgring was one of Dan Gurney's great career drives. Just 4.4 seconds separated winner Graham Hill, the second-placed Surtees and Gurney in a washed-out race which lasted over two and a half hours. (Günther Molter)

tall frame meant his knees were raised beyond the dash and an additional fuel tank was added just in front of the instruments. The front suspension was stiffened by a trailing radius arm on the top wishbones and an anti-roll bar was added at the rear. The original Koni shock absorbers were switched to Bilstein units. The frame itself was made more rigid with extra tubing, while the rear track was increased with wheel spacers. So equipped Gurney was able to set his fastest time at the Nürburgring test in June and win at Rouen early that July.

The Bilstein dampers were changed back to Konis in time for the British GP, while Bonnier opted (wrongly) for Dunlop tyres at the Nürburgring. For Monza, the fuel capacity was increased (by extending the front tank right to the very end of the nose!). Strenuous efforts were made to reduce weight by careful drillings and a new front cowl was made from glass fibre-reinforced plastic. To gain more speed, the front and rear top wishbones, were given fairings and the engine cover was re-profiled. Glass fibre discs were attached to the wheels to improve drag. Hans Mezger also tried to save the 8bhp consumed driving the cooling fan. An electro-magnetic clutch allowed the driver to disconnect the drive for up to ten seconds, before the engine temperature rose to an unacceptable level. This device was used at Monza and Watkins Glen with no obvious benefit.

Hoping that the 804 might merit an occasional appearance in 1963, Mezger continued a low key development programme on the 1.5-litre engine (based on advances made with the 2-litre sports car engine). Still running on carburettors, the best output the 753 would achieve was a good 200bhp – the result of improved cylinder head design (which increased the compression ratio to 10.5:1) and weight reducing details, such as titanium connecting rods.

It is easy to say that the 804 took Porsche nowhere, but the exercise allowed the engineers – particularly the emerging new generation – to step outside the previously restricted convention of sports cars and experiment. The lessons learned would be applied to a whole generation of racing cars to come.

SPECIFICATION
1962 804 Formula One

Engine: Type 753 (1,587cc) air-cooled horizontally-opposed eight-cylinder with two valves per cylinder. Dry sump lubrication (two scavenge, one pressure pump) with magnesium alloy crankcase and aluminium alloy cylinder heads and barrels with chromium-plated bores. Forged steel crankshaft with eight main Glyco shell-type bearings and one rear ball bearing. Single-piece connecting rods using shell-type Vandervell big-end bearings and bronze shell little ends with deeply domed forged pistons. Two camshafts per side operated from the crankshaft by two intermediate shafts (one over, one under the crankshaft), bevel gears and finger-type cam followers (adjustable from outside the engine). Bosch 12-volt electrical system for dual coil ignition with twin ignition distributors driven from the lower intermediate shaft and two spark plugs per cylinder. Bendix fuel pump supplying petrol to four twin-choke Weber 38mm downdraught carburettors. Horizontal glassfibre reinforced cooling fan with twin intakes gear-driven from the upper intermediate shaft.

Capacity: 1,494.4cc

Bore/Stroke: 66mm/54.6mm

Maximum power: 178bhp at 9,200 rpm

Maximum torque: 153Nm at 7,200 rpm

Compression ratio: 10:1

Transmission: Mechanically actuated single-plate Fichtel & Sachs clutch. Type 718, two-shaft six-speed 'barrel-case' gearbox. Independent rear axle with two universal (Hookes type) joints. ZF limited slip differential.

Chassis/body: Welded, cold-drawn seamless tubular steel construction space-frame chassis. Lower tubes serve as pipes for the front-mounted oil cooler. Mid-mounted, internally baffled 75-litre aluminium fuel tank sculpted around the driver, plus additional 40-litre tank ahead of the front wheels.

Suspension and steering: ZF rack and pinion steering with flexing steering arms. Front: Double wishbones with longitudinal torsion bars with inboard Koni or Bilstein shock absorbers. Anti-roll bar. Rear: Double wishbone with Koni or Bilstein torsion bars integrated into the inner pivots, inboard shock absorbers. Anti-roll bar.

Brakes: Four-wheel disc brakes with aluminium four-piston calipers. Monobloc dual circuit master cylinder.

Wheels and tyres: 5.00 x 15in front and 7.00 x 15in Dunlop D9 or D12 racing tyres on 5J front and 6J rear alloy rims.

Weight: 452kg dry (42 per cent front, 58 per cent rear)

Length: 3,600mm

Wheelbase: 2,300mm

Track (f/r): 1,300mm/1,330mm

Performance: Acceleration: 0 to 60mph (96.5kph): N/A

Maximum speed: 170mph (273.5kph) (ref: Boschen & Barth)

STYLE AND VERSATILITY — 904

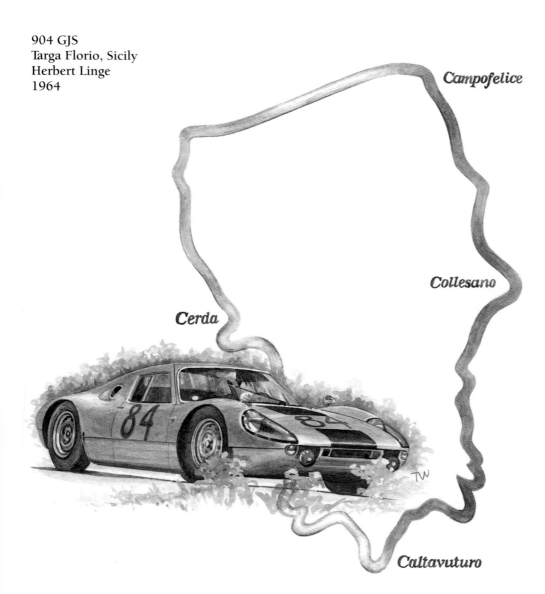

904 GJS
Targa Florio, Sicily
Herbert Linge
1964

Campofelice

Collesano

Cerda

Caltavuturo

HISTORY HAS NOT BEEN KIND to the 1960s' Porsche Formula One effort. Ferry Porsche appeared to throw in the towel after barely two seasons and just when it appeared his team was finding its pace. Or perhaps his decision was hard, but very sound – the kind of decision generals have to make sometimes in war.

Although parallels with Ferrari are never very far away when looking at the Porsche automobile business there are stark contrasts. Maranello paid for the spiralling cost of its F1 (and sports car) programme during the 1960s through production car sales. The marque is famed for its 'live to race' image, but it cost Enzo Ferrari control of his business when, in 1969, he had to sell to FIAT. On the other hand, Ferry Porsche regarded the production car business as his main activity, with the competition element there to improve the breed and take care of the marketing. He made his decisions accordingly and retained control of the company.

The Formula One project became Ferry Porsche's first big test as the managing director of a company that in little more than a decade had grown at meteoric speed. He was having to address a whole array of growing pains. The F1 programme consumed 3 per cent of the company's gross turnover in 1962, but this was not so important as the time demands being placed on his very best engineers. Formula One demanded 100 per cent of their time and more.

In the big picture at Porsche there was significant engineering support required to cope with the ever-increasing production volume. In 1962, some 8,205 356s were built, which would rise nearly 18 per cent in 1963. Who said the F1 programme brought no benefit? The following year Porsche bought the neighbouring Reutter bodyshell factory in Zuffenhausen in the scramble for space to build production cars. Stretching the small team of engineers still further was the intensive development programme on the new production model that would eventually replace the 356 and not least, there were major commitments to the company's consultancy customers (particularly Volkswagen). The F1 effort was unsustainable without external funding. By walking away when he did, Ferry Porsche laid the foundation that preserved his company's independence to the present day.

Whether Porsche could have maintained the technical pace being set by the British constructors is not the issue. The engineers Ferdinand Piëch began to group around him from 1963 would prove that he and his colleagues had the essential blend of ingenuity and common sense to produce extremely capable racing cars. But such would have been the cost, the company's independence would surely have been surrendered. In the vacuum that followed the F1 withdrawal, a new direction was needed for the motor sport activity.

A new set of rules had been established in 1962 for sports car racing, perhaps more accurately termed Grand Touring racing. To qualify, manufacturers had to build 100 examples of the car, but there was also a class for GT prototypes. As proposed the FIA's new, class-focused rules did not offer a championship that would result in an overall winner. It was the Le Mans organisers – the Automobile Club de L'Ouest – who glued the concept together into a workable championship and brought in Sebring, the Targa Florio and the Nürburgring in the *Challenge Mondiale de Vitesse*.

On the announcement of the new rules back in 1959, Porsche had realised the complex, space-framed 718s would not be suitable, even for limited production. At the end of that year, an order was placed with Carlo Abarth of Turin for some 20 cars based on the production 356B Carrera GT. These Abarth-Carreras used the floor pan, suspension assemblies and 547 four-cam engine from the series model. The Abarth-Carrera was lighter than the regular production car and its very pretty coupé body was better aerodynamically. An Abarth-Carrera won its class in the 1960 Le Mans and the car became a popular choice for customers. Through 1961 and 1962, Abarth-Carreras formed the successful mainstay of Porsche's representation in GT racing as the factory concentrated on Formula One.

The GT rules continued to evolve during 1963 and as manufacturers came to terms with the new environment, more names began to appear. Ferrari dominated that year with the 250GTO, but the large capacity scene was livened up by the introduction of new prototypes such as the lightweight Jaguar E-Type, the Shelby Cobra and the attractive Lola GT. In the smaller classes, the Carreras held Porsche's reputation against opposition that had only begun to strengthen that year. Alfa Romeo returned with a new 2-litre model and Carlo Abarth himself entered a new car powered by a 2-litre Simca four-cylinder engine.

Porsche team manager Huschke von Hanstein wanted to kick-start the factory racing effort once more with an idea for a new challenger in the up to 2-litre GT class – a racing proposal based firmly on known territory for Porsche and which could be turned into a useful revenue earner from customer sales. But what would be the basis for the new car?

The reasoning behind the decision to contract Abarth back in 1959 was still sound in 1963. The 718 sports car was not the way forward for a limited production grand tourer because it took so long to build. The traditional space-framed, aluminium-bodied racing car provided the necessary light weight and stiffness for a thoroughbred racing car, but because they needed to be hand-built, were completely unsuited to series production. The conventional option for production was a steel-bodied car, but this was

The factory-entered 904 Carrera GTS of Herbert Linge and Gianni Balzarini had a strong run to second place in the 1964 Targa Florio. (LAT)

too heavy for racing and required very expensive tooling. If 100 cars were required then an alternative, more production-friendly lightweight design was needed.

Porsche's technical head of the time was Dr Hans Tomala. In the studies for a new GT racing car, Tomala must have been influenced by the progress made by another marque – and one that had been a thorn in the side of Porsche's racing activities for many a year. In 1957, Colin Chapman had stunned the motoring world with the new Lotus Elite. The style-setting Elite was to spearhead Chapman's desire to offer an upmarket GT as a road car, yet have the basis of a class-winning prospect for both Le Mans and the Monte Carlo rally. Chapman turned to the possibilities of using glass fibre-reinforced epoxy resin, a composite material used in aviation and for boat construction. Typically, the Elite embraced the new technology wholly, with the entire unitary body comprising glass fibre and steel sub-frames only being used to carry the suspension and engine. After an unsatisfactory spell working with a small pattern-making business, Lotus turned to the Bristol Aircraft Company to manufacture the bodyshells. Porsche may have mixed it in 1959 with Ferrari and Aston Martin in the Sports Car Championship with the 718 RSK, but this was also the year when the Elite won the 1,500cc class at Le Mans. The glass fibre car had proven it was a race winner.

A few pivotal years passed, during which racing car design was gripped by the rear-engine revolution. It was fortuitous for Porsche. Tomala and his engineers found that the rich experience with the mid-engined 718 coupés over the previous two years would provide all the essential layout information for the new car – including wheelbase, track and suspension data. And there was also a new engine. When the decision was taken to produce a new car in late 1962, Tomala initiated a design that would use the new six-cylinder engine and five-speed gearbox from the forthcoming production 901 model. In fact, the engine bay was designed so that as well as the six, either the existing eight or four-cylinder engines could be fitted.

Ferry Porsche's eldest son, Ferdinand Porsche was given the brief to design a suitable bodyshell for the new car. Resting on the shoulders of the 28-year-old Butzi was the knowledge that he was the eldest son and heir of the Porsche dynasty. It was a weighty responsibility, especially as he did not have the inclination to become a business leader in the mould of his father or an automobile engineer as his grandfather. Butzi's fascination was product design – the artistry of form rather than function. With his father's blessing he had established a small styling studio in Zuffenhausen and as well as the revised RS60 and RS61 sports cars, he had drawn the lines of the sleek 804 Formula One car. In the 718 coupé that first ran in 1961 he demonstrated the attractive design cues of a pointed nose, deeply raked windscreen and doors which over-lapped into

One of the three 904 prototypes built in 1963. The doors which overlapped into the roof line significantly helped access to the car and at the same time were a brilliant styling feature.

the roof section that would prove so successful on the new model.

Perhaps the least successful aspect of that 718 coupé had been the tail, and on the new model, Butzi would follow the contemporary fashion for a cut-off Kamm-type tail (as integrated so successfully by Ferrari on the 250GTO and 250P, but keeping the cut-away rear deck for improved engine breathing and cooling. This latter, elegant, solution to both function and rearwards visibility would be much-copied by others in later years. During this period, there was no time to develop new body profiles in the wind tunnel. Body forms were evolved rapidly as a result of experience and intuition. It is perhaps because of this – and Butzi Porsche's artistic eye – that the new model emerged as arguably the most attractive Porsche ever.

The new car was first shown publicly in November 1963, but with a modified version of the four-cylinder engine (the

six was still far from ready). The new model, which until this point had been given the type number 904, would be sold as the Carrera GTS.

Race record

The first 904s were shipped directly to the USA and it was there that the type made its first competition appearance in February 1964. Previously a 3-hour race, the Daytona Continental was extended to a 2,000km event. In a race notable more for the dominance of the Ferrari 250GTOs and the first appearance of the striking Carroll Shelby-entered Daytona Cobra, the single 904 retired. The 12 Hours at Sebring in March brought a more productive result. Still running as a prototype, American racing legend Briggs Cunningham and Lake Underwood won their class with the 904 and were ninth overall, in what was another Ferrari demonstration.

A very new-looking 904 swings through the Karussell during the 1965 Nürburgring 1,000km. It is not difficult to understand why many consider this to be the most elegant of Porsches. (Porsche Archiv/Günther Molter)

The 904s competed in both early season American endurance events in 1964. At Sebring, the 904 of Briggs Cunningham and Lake Underwood played a supporting role to the mighty Ferraris and Cobras, but finished ninth overall. (LAT)

The eight-cylinder had its first race at the 1964 Targa Florio in the hands of Umberto Maglioli and Edgar Barth. After leading for five laps, Maglioli had a spring mounting break and he spun into a wall. He eventually finished in sixth place.

A month's development following Sebring (including the Le Mans test weekend) was all the time available to bring the still-new 904 to readiness for the Targa Florio. The Sicilian road/rally was a near-perfect demonstration of Porsche's command of this tough event, which was run in sweltering Mediterranean heat. Admittedly the entry was weakened because Ferrari had chosen to give the Targa a miss, but there were a pair of strong GTOs and the works Shelby Cobras to provide some impedance to the Porsche attack.

Of all the endurance races where Porsche have succeeded over the years, the Targa Florio is unique. Actually avoided by other manufacturers if at all possible, because the 44.7-mile (72km) course brought so many unexpected challenges – and dangers – it became an obsession for Porsche. The drive down through Italy was demanding enough and itself would often be used by the racing team to evaluate some new modification idea for the production cars.

Even in the 1960s, the Targa course was incomparable with any other in racing. It was made up entirely of public roads – of course – and amounted to more of an asphalt rally than a race, where the competitors set off in timed intervals rather than altogether in a conventional start. Learning the route was a major challenge and for days before the event, many an unsuspecting rental car would be seen pounding the course. But practice would only familiarise the driver with which way the road turned, and over 44 miles it was easy to forget that! The unpredictability of the Targa came from the changing road surfaces, the slickness of the village streets and the hazards that awaited the driver on the open road. It was not unusual to confront a truck or car coming out of the dust or to find the road surface completely broken up in the often searing heat. The hazards were everywhere, from the enthusiastic Sicilian crowds who cheered on each car from the very roadside to the unforgiving walls, posts and sheer drops that were to be found all along the route.

The *Piccolo Madonie* (there was a longer course used before the Second World War), can be found mid-way between Messina and Palermo on the northern coast of Sicily. Race headquarters was always based in the seaside town of Cefalu, but the start area was just off the main coast road, the SS113, on the SS120 road to Cerda and Caltavuturo. Going away from the coast the dusty, narrow road winds up towards Cerda through peaceful olive groves, sun-parched fields and clusters of red-tiled farm buildings. The drive through Cerda is exhilarating, if only because you can immediately sense the thrill it must have given the drivers to blast through the crowded town streets in their big, noisy racers. But out of town the road begins to climb into the mountains and the twists and turns become ever more demanding. The road follows the rising side of a wide valley, through which a great Autostrada has since been swaged, but the drive itself is still uncut, pure driving pleasure. It is not difficult to understand why the likes of Bonnier, Maglioli and Barth always chose the spyders for this course. Good visibility from the cockpit is essential as you need to see right across the sharp hairpins and spot the many pot-holes, ruts, bumps and loose gravel that litter the winding road.

Caltavulturo is one of those uniquely picturesque southern Italian villages that seems to nest on a hillside. The track dips across the valley to the village and rushes up to the summit of the same name. The countryside is now very rocky, but the climb combined with the never-ending twists demand the best from any car. The descent from Caltavuturo is faster and brings the driver to the place where Porsche used to site their refuelling and halfway pits. Bivio Polizzi, near the village of Scillato where the Autostrada intersection now cuts the scenery, is deep in the mountains. It must have been a long hot day up there, waiting for the cars to come through – but also great to listen to the sound of a racing V12 echoing off the sometimes sheer rock faces. There is more turning, climbing, exhausting driving yet as the course climbs again to Cervi and down to the next village at Collesano. The coast is a refreshing sight after the demands of the mountains and the old main road between Campofelice and the return to the start is a 3-mile straight – the only place where the drivers could really open up their machines. The race covered ten laps and it was a day's

work, with the first departure at 8 o'clock in the morning. Winners Davis and Pucci took over seven hours to win in 1964 and their fastest lap took no less than 41 minutes 10.8 seconds – that is an average speed of just 65mph (105kph). It was that twisty.

The course remains one of the most important relics of motor racing's heritage. To win here required more than simply an agile and balanced car. The drivers required skill, courage, a good memory and astute mechanical sympathy. The Madonie is a quite astonishing place to contemplate and totally out of place as a modern racing venue. It is breathtaking in its geographic setting and unmatched as a driving challenge.

Colin Davis, son of 1920s' Bentley driver Sammy Davis, partnered Baron Antonio Pucci to victory in the 1964 event – Porsche's second successive Targa and fifth in total. Herbert Linge and Italian driver Balzarini finished second in another 904 and there were four Porsches in the top eight finishers. Edgar Barth and Umberto Maglioli were entered in a new 904 powered by the eight-cylinder 771 engine, while Jo Bonnier and Graham Hill were in the veteran W-RS Spyder. Maglioli crashed while leading after a spring broke, but at least the car finished (in sixth place). The W-RS, driven from the start by Bonnier, broke a drive shaft coupling on the second lap and retired. The big Cobras were out of place on the twists and turns of the *Piccolo Madonie*'s mountain course and suffered with various chassis breakages. One of the GTOs led after Maglioli crashed, but this too retired with a broken rear axle.

The next race on the calendar was the Spa 500km, a quite different challenge to the Targa. Instead of agility, Spa required speed and totally confident high speed cornering performance. It was not surprising then, that Barth could not keep up with the works GTOs – the red cars even left

Pressing on during the Spa 1,000km in May 1964. This revealing high-speed cornering photograph illustrates the large amount of body roll typical on a 1960s racing car. It would be at least another five years before tyre technology allowed greater roll stiffness.

The Porsche System team at the 1964 Nürburgring 1,000km. Watched by Gerhard Mitter (sitting on the pit counter, wearing sunglasses), Jo Bonnier climbs in. Discussing progress to the rear of the car are, from left to right: Colin Davis, Huschke von Hanstein, Edgar Barth and Richie Ginther.

carnage and many cars crashed during the qualifying, including Barth in one of the eight-cylinder cars and three production 904s. The driver of one – Randolph Moser – was killed (as was another driving an Aston Martin). The race fell to the controversial 3.3-litre 275 LM-bodied Ferrari. Controversial because the FIA refused to accept it was derived from the 250P that was homologated! Ben Pon and Gunther Koch claimed third place in a production 904, with Bonnier/Ginther recovering from a sticking throttle to finish fifth.

The Ford GT40 had retired with fractured rear suspension at the Nürburgring, but at Le Mans the crowd witnessed the first big Ferrari-Ford battle. This rather put in the shadow the fact that all of the five four-cylinder 904s which started also finished (the highest, driven by Buchet/Guy Ligier, finished seventh overall). Both factory eight-cylinder prototypes retired. At the front, Ferrari crushed Ford with Graham Hill and Jo Bonnier earning a deserved victory.

The last big international event of the '64 season was the Reims 12 Hours, held in July. After the traditional running midnight start, the Fords succumbed again and once more, the 275LMs swept the leader-board. A single eight-cylinder 904 prototype was entered for Barth and Colin Davis and joined no less than eight production 904s. Predictably, the eight-cylinder car retired, while production 904s claimed a resounding fifth, sixth and seventh places with eight Porsches in the top 20. As far as the customers were

the Cobras and E-Types for dead on the long straights of the Ardennes course. Barth dominated the 2-litre class and after many of the top runners retired, claimed fifth overall.

A maximum effort from Zuffenhausen came at the Nürburgring 1,000km. The race became a triumph and a tragedy. While the brand new Ford GT40 brought a fresh challenge to the top class, Porsche rolled out two eight-cylinder 904s for Bonnier and Richie Ginther – at the time also an F1 driver with BRM. Practice was nothing short of a

Type 904s lined up outside Werk 1 in Zuffenhausen, with more just visible in the workshop.

concerned, the 904 was a star, and Porsche emerged as the winner of the *Challenge Mondiale de Vitesse* that year.

October's Paris 1,000km at Montlhéry closed the season on an up-beat note for the factory prototypes, with Barth/Davis claiming third overall. This was also the race where the new six-cylinder engine was first tried in the 904. It retired with broken rear suspension.

Early in 1965, the 904 demonstrated its versatility when a four-cylinder car was entered in the Monte Carlo Rally. Eugen Böhringer and Rolf Wütherich managed to survive snow, hail and ice to finish second overall.

The new racing season began soon after, with the Daytona Continental event at the end of February. A customer 904 finished fifth overall and first GT behind a train of now-reliable Ford GT40s and Cobras. A single factory eight-cylinder was taken to the Sebring 12 Hours a month later. This event was notable for a typical Florida deluge around mid-distance. The conditions, which flooded the track for more than an hour, allowed the 904 of Underwood/Klass to catch the GT class-leading Shelby-Cobra. Hopes were raised, but when the sun came out again, the track quickly dried and the Cobra was able to pull away once more. There was satisfaction for the small factory team also, because Gerhard Mitter and Herbert Linge's eight-cylinder made it to the finish in ninth place. It was rich reward for the team's hard search for reliability over the winter. Ben Pon and Rob Slotemaker opened the European season with a resounding fourth place at the

Monza 1,000km behind only the two winning Ferraris and a GT40.

That year's Targa Florio saw another maximum attack by Porsche. As well as an eight-cylinder prototype coupé for Jo Bonnier/Graham Hill, there was a six-cylinder car for Maglioli/Linge and a completely off-the-wall open-bodied prototype 904 for Davis and Mitter. This latter car looked like it was some kind of test mule and was originally intended for Bonnier and Hill. These drivers declined the opportunity however as they found the car very skittish in its handling. A fourth Porsche System Engineering entry was perhaps the benchmark for all these prototypes – a regular four-cylinder 904 for Pucci and Klass. Unlike 1964, Ferrari was out in force with three of the new 350bhp 3.3-litre 275/P2 open prototypes. It was a race in which Ford knew they had little chance, so only a single open GT40 was entered. Local driver Vaccarella hared off into the lead in his 275 in very hot and humid conditions. Within a few laps he had broken the lap record, but the sister car of Scarfiotti and Parkes crashed. When Baghetti was stopped by faulty electrics beyond Cerda, hopes rose in the Porsche camp that Stuttgart reliability would win the day. At one point the open 904 and the six-cylinder car were lying second and third, but Bonnier in the eight-cylinder coupé was delayed by throttle cable problems (a common 904 fault). Unfortunately, the lead car did not falter and Vaccarella and Bandini took Ferrari's sixth Targa victory. Porsche's tally in this event numbered five. When the race

The 904 soon became popular with racing customers, who found the new glass fibre coupé to have more than capable performance. This is the brand new car of Günter Selbach and Herbert Schulze at the Nürburgring 1,000km in May 1964.

The 904 quickly became the car to have in international grand touring races during 1964. With around 180bhp in racing trim, the car was a regular winner.

times were calculated, the Davis/Mitter open 904 finished just four minutes behind the Ferrari after the seven-hour trial.

This was as close as Porsche would get to the winner's laurels in 1965 which, spurred by the threat from the Ford GT40, turned into a demonstration of Ferrari's strength as a sports car manufacturer. Even at the Nürburgring 1,000km, the 275/P2 blitzed the opposition and showed that Porsche needed to rethink their approach. What shocked the Zuffenhausen team most at the 'Ring was the speed of the new 166SP Ferrari Dino driven by Vaccarella and Bandini. While the Dino was able to mix it with the leading group of 275s, the lone GT40 and the Cobras, the Bonnier/Rindt eight-cylinder 904 trailed. After just a year and a half at the top level of international sports car racing, it seemed the 904 had met its match.

With the team now being driven relentlessly by Ferdinand Piëch, Porsche competition efforts turned instead to the European Hillclimb Championship. In a

competition where there was no minimum weight and an upper engine capacity of 2-litres, it was a perfect laboratory for Piëch's emergent team to study the limitations of the 904. They would focus on the car's unconventional construction, the relatively high unsprung weight of the suspension assemblies and the importance of braking efficiency. And most of all, they would focus their attention on the art of racing car weight reduction.

The legacy of the 904 was that it served as a beacon for Porsche through a time of intense change at the family-owned company. Against a background of rapid expansion in the production car business and of Ferry Porsche being pulled too many ways by demands for expenditure, the 904 was a famous success.

Engineering

The 904 is a rare bird in the history of the Porsche racing car. It is notable first because it was not a development of an earlier model (although the engines were carried over) and secondly, it adopted a very innovative form of chassis construction. For a customer racing car, there are constraints placed on the engineer that do not exist when laying out a very short run prototype. Among these, it is most important the finished car is structurally reliable and maintainable.

In laying out the 904, Dr Tomala's engineers undoubtedly drew inspiration from Colin Chapman's Elite, and were also able to call on their own experience to evolve a better solution to the challenges of using a glass fibre resin composite for a small production series bodyshell. The Elite was a very stiff, lightweight structure once its three major elements were bonded together – it was a great racing car – but it had some major shortfalls as a refined GT. Most notable was the extreme road noise and the roar of the raucous Climax FWE was transmitted directly into the cabin.

In charge of the 904's chassis layout was Ing. Schröder, who drew out Dr Tomala's ideas for a combined glass fibre bodyshell and separate steel girder chassis. By themselves, the two cross-braced, steel box section chassis frames would have been far too flexible in torsion. Only when the glass fibre/resin composite body structure was bolted and bonded on to the steel chassis did the whole assembly achieve the required stiffness. The new structure of the 904 achieved the same torsional stiffness as the best of the 718 space-frames. Manufacturing problems meant stiffness varied considerably from car to car, not only because it was difficult to control the thickness of the laminate, but also because the quality of the chassis bonding deteriorated with use and time. But by fitting the suspension and engine to the steel structure, it was possible to partially isolate the cabin from the mechanical noise and vibration. In this respect, the design was a considerable improvement on the Elite and accepted that composite technology did not, at that time, offer the complete answer to the design problem. Chapman himself would perhaps come to accept this and in the design of the later Elan, he used a glass fibre bodyshell over a steel backbone chassis.

The Zuffenhausen engineers had experimented with certain simple glass fibre components on both the sports and the F1 cars during 1962 and 1963, but the complexity of what was required on the 904 was significantly greater. Like Lotus, Porsche turned to the aero industry to tap into experience of working with plastic. Heinkel needed no introduction as a manufacturer and they had spare expertise and capacity to deliver complete bodyshells to Porsche through the winter and early spring of 1963–64.

The bodyshell itself was made up of some 50 glass fibre components, bonded carefully together. This included the

The twin box-section steel girder chassis would have been far too flexible by itself. Only when the glass fibre bodyshell was attached did the whole car achieve the desired chassis stiffness.

main floorpan and engine firewall. Since the seat buckets were moulded into this structure (to further help with rigidity), adjustment for different heights of drivers came from a telescopic steering column and pedals that could be adjusted to one of three positions. Whereas the Elite's lay-

The bodyshell was made by aircraft builders Heinkel, in Speyer. The complete assembly was made up of some 50 separate mouldings.

up varied in thickness from 9–10mm at high stress areas down to 3mm for non-stressed parts, the 904's body averaged around 2mm, with reinforcement for the main chassis mounting points.

Early in 1963, it was obvious that the new 901 engine would not be ready for the series 904. An alternative powerplant would be required that would be able to compete on equal terms with the expected challenges from the new Abarth-Simca and the Alfa Romeo. This task fell to Hans Mezger, ably supported by among others, the young Ferdinand Piëch.

Even for a limited series production car, the 2-litre 771 eight was far too costly (although the engine would be fitted in certain of the factory cars). The only option was the 547-derived four-cylinder engine. The four had been enlarged to 2-litres in 1961 and developed for production

There was plenty of space in the engine compartment for larger power plants. This is a production 904 with the 180bhp 587 four-cylinder engine.

for the Carrera 2 road-going coupés. In this form, and known as the type 587/1, the engine initially developed a useful 130bhp. By 1963, the second development of this engine was developing 140bhp in road trim, but this clearly was not going to be enough for racing.

At 1,966cc, the 587 was as close to the class capacity limit as was feasible, so Mezger set about gaining the extra bhp necessary by increasing engine revolutions. The 2-litre engine already reflected the drive for improved simplicity within the engine. For example, the forged steel crank ran in plain main and rod end bearings.

Mezger had made a name for himself in the calculation section in earlier years, deducing improved camshaft profiles and combustion chamber volumes for the earlier fours and the Formula One eight-cylinder engines. Using this experience, he enlarged the inlet and exhaust valves, increased the overlap of the camshafts and revised the shape of the piston crowns. The Weber 46 IDM twin choke carburettors were carried over from the late-model Carrera 2's engine, but Paul Frère notes in *The Racing Porsches* that some cars were delivered with the Solex 44 P11-4 carbs that had been used on the original 1961 Carrera 2. The exhaust system used had an enormous effect on the output of these engines and the 904 fitted with the new 587/2 engine developed 155bhp in road-going (silenced) form and 180bhp with a straight-though racing exhaust. As the car could be used on the road, the engine was mounted to the steel chassis using rubber isolators.

A single-plate clutch transmitted power to the new five-speed gearbox. The internals were the same as those destined for the 901, but because the engine was turned round relative to the rear-engined model, a new casing was manufactured. A ZF limited slip differential was fitted as standard. The transmission suffered because of its newness however. Drivers complained the change was stiff and that the shift was fragile. Development would improve the feel of the gear change, but this would prove to be the Achilles heel of the 904.

The Formula One experience gave the engineers a wealth of experience in contemporary suspension design as practised by the likes of BRM, Cooper and Lotus. The 1963 W-RS and 718 coupé had been revised with a full wishbone front suspension and Bonnier had demonstrated how good the car had become on that year's Targa Florio. The suspension design for the 904 was evolved from that successful layout and featured a fully adjustable coil spring/shock absorber arrangement, with adjustable anti-roll bars front and rear. On the front, this included an element of anti-dive geometry (intended to reduce the tendency of the nose to dip under heavy braking). Like the engine, the suspension linkage to the chassis was through rubber couplings.

Testing had begun on the new Weissach turning pad in late August 1963 and there was soon a long list of other problems to be resolved. Chief among these were an erratic suspension response, overheating in the transmission, a poor gear-shift and fading brakes.

Many of the handling problems were the result of using rubber at the suspension pivots to isolate the movement from the chassis and so reduce cabin vibration. This was resolved at the front by fitting radially stiffer Silentbloc bushes, while at the rear the radius rod mounts were located by rigid spherical joints. Too-light steering was improved with extra wheel camber and castor. The engine mountings were also distorting to such an extent that the car would jump out of gear.

The initial layout of the 904 called for the same disc brakes as used on the 356C, but testing at the Nürburgring showed these to be prone to high pad wear and fading. Further analysis of the forces involved resulted in the front slave cylinders being enlarged to shift more of the brake bias to the front wheels. The brake discs were increased in thickness from 10.5mm to 12.7mm, which brought the maximum operating temperatures down significantly and reduced the fading problem. However, the 10.5mm discs were still used, to give a lighter pedal feel and efforts were made to provide an improved supply of cooling air. The openings for the fronts were either side of the oil cooler entry and for the rears, on the rear flanks of the roof.

The cockpit was spartan. The moulded buckets in the glass fibre undertray were covered with a thinly padded leather upholstery. A classic 1960s three-spoke wood-rim steering wheel was backed by a pronounced cowling containing the now standard basic Porsche instrument display – a speedometer, tachometer and a combined oil temperature and pressure gauge. A Webasto petrol heater was an option for those cars that would be used on the road.

More than 100 cars were built between November 1963 and April 1964, to qualify for the FIA's GT category. Such was the demand for the 904, plans were started for a second series of 100 later in the year.

The 587/3 four-cylinder was uprated to 185bhp by revising the camshaft timing, adopting larger inlet valves and a new exhaust system. By this time, all 1964 cars that came back to the factory for work received detailed chassis strengthening improvements (particularly around the suspension pick-ups). The detail tuning continued with an option for a remarkable 75 per cent locking limited slip differential for twisty courses, a new, more positive feel rack and pinion steering, stiffer lower front wishbones and alloy

wishbones for the rear suspension. Efforts were made to improve the generally disliked gear change and a catch tank was added to the fuel system to prevent the engine cutting when cornering with low fuel.

In April 1964, a 904 fitted with the eight-cylinder 771 engine appeared at the Le Mans test weekend, differing visually by larger front brake air ducts and the open inlet for the horizontal cooling fan. Later that summer, a 904 introduced the new racing version of the six-cylinder engine. Initially good for 190bhp, by 1965, the 901/20 was developing 210bhp (the same as the eight in endurance racing trim) using Solex carburettors and two spark plugs per cylinder. It was not difficult to understand why the engineers preferred the simpler six to either the frenetic four or the temperamental eight.

A durability test (led by Ferdinand Piëch) at a chilly and wet Monza in December 1964 resulted in further improvements for the still-planned second series of 904s, this time powered by the six-cylinder engine. However, the FIA changed the number of cars required to be built to qualify for the production GT class from 100 to 50 and so only around ten 904/6s were built from a second batch which numbered just 20. The new rules, and increasing competition, forced Porsche to accept that although the 904 was still successful in 1965, it was likely to be outclassed during the following year by cars designed more for racing than production.

The 904 was designed to accept the eight-cylinder, 2-litre type 771 engine. The car was first run at the April 1964 Le Mans test weekend.

The small number of sixes and eights meant whenever the cars raced they were classified as prototypes. Through 1965, the sixes ran with Weber carburettors (these had been tested at Monza the previous winter). To maintain the competitiveness of the 904, Piëch began to experiment with many significant lightening modifications. In 1964, there had been a remarkable magnesium 901 engine (the camshaft housings were the only aluminium castings), while the 1965 Targa Florio marked the debut of a light-weight open-bodied version of the 904.

Two of these open prototypes were built during the winter of 1964–65 – one being fitted with a six and the other with an eight. These prototypes made no concession to elegance in their search for functional efficiency at the

Opposite: The 904 Carrera GTS with the 210bhp twin-plug, six-cylinder engine ran during 1965. This engine was far simpler to maintain than the earlier four-camshaft four-cylinder.

During the summer of 1965, the efforts to lighten and stiffen the 904/8 resulted in possibly the ugliest Porsche ever. Nicknamed 'Kangaroo' (because of its earlier cornering performance), Gerhard Mitter nonetheless won the sports car race at the Norisring in early July.

For the Trento-Bordone hill-climb in July, two new spyders were built with extra frame stiffening and more attractive, white-painted bodies. The cars proved not to be enough against the Ferrari Dino. This is Gerhard Mitter at the later Freiburg hill-climb in August. By this time a new space-frame car was well advanced.

SPECIFICATION
1964 904 Carrera GTS

Engine: Mid-mounted type 587/3 air-cooled four-cylinder with two valves per cylinder. Dry sump lubrication (with 10-litre oil tank), aluminium crankcase with cylinder heads and alloy barrels with chromium-plated bores. Forged steel crankshaft supported in three plain and one ball bearings. Single-piece plain bearing connecting rods with high crown forged pistons. Two extended overlap camshafts per side operated from the crankshaft by intermediate shaft and two vertical and two horizontal shafts (and using 14 bevel gears). Bosch 12-volt electrical system for dual coil ignition with twin ignition distributors driven from the ends of the top (inlet) camshaft each side and two spark plugs per cylinder. 450 watt DC generator. Bendix fuel pump supplying petrol to two Solex 44 P11 4 downdraught carburettors. Vertical cooling fan with twin intakes driven by V-belt from the crankshaft. Open racing exhaust.

Capacity: 1,966cc

Bore/Stroke: 92mm/74mm

Maximum power: 185bhp at 7,200rpm

Maximum torque: 201Nm at 5,000rpm

Compression ratio: 9.8:1

Transmission: Hydraulically actuated 201mm diameter single-plate Fichtel & Sachs clutch. Type 904, two-shaft five-speed 'barrel-case' gearbox (with case in aluminium alloy). Second to fifth gears synchronised, first and reverse outside case. Independent rear axle with two universal Nadella joints. ZF limited slip differential.

Chassis/body: Pressed steel box section, with twin longitudinals and smaller box-section transverse cross-members. Moulded glass fibre resin composite bodyshell bolted to the steel chassis. Seat forms moulded into structure with adjustable steering column and pedals. 110-litre front-mounted fuel tank. Optional Webasto petrol heater.

Suspension and steering: ZF rack and pinion steering (with 2.1 turns lock to lock) with two universal joints and rubber coupling in column. Independent front suspension with unequal length double wishbones using Silentbloc rubber bushes and with anti-dive geometry. Coil springs over telescopic shock absorbers and adjustable anti-roll bar. Double wishbone rear suspension with top unit apex inboard and twin forward mounted radius rods. Coil spring over telescopic shock absorber. Adjustable anti-roll bar.

Brakes: Dual hydraulic circuit to Alfred Teves-Dunlop disc brakes all round. 274mm front, 285mm rear. Handbrake operates on small drums in rear hubs.

Wheels and tyres: 5J x 15in light alloy rims with five stud fixings. Dunlop SP 165/HR15 (185/HR15 optional) tyres. Later options include 5.5, 6.0 and 7.00in rims.

Weight: 650kg (42 per cent front/58 per cent rear empty)

Length: 4,090mm

Height: 1,065mm

Wheelbase: 2,300mm

Track (f/r): 1,316mm/1,312mm

Performance: Acceleration: 0 to 62.5mph (100kph): 5.5 seconds (source Boschen & Barth)

Maximum speed: 157mph (253kph)

lowest possible weight. The minimalist body failed to even cover the oil cooler at the front. The search was for lightness and the hand-laid laminate was very thin. Development engineer Peter Falk says the sun could be seen if you looked up through the wheel arches! From the cockpit back, the car recalled the Elva chassis that Porsche was also using on the hills around that time, with a low wrap-around plastic windscreen and air scoops at waist level to cool the rear brakes. The open body contributed little to the overall chassis stiffness and by itself, the girder chassis was not considered acceptably rigid. The result was a frame stiffened with bracing tubes supporting the suspension mountings and the floor.

The wheel rim sizes were progressively widening by this time, to get the best from Dunlop's new racing rubber. The production 904s used 5in wide rims, but on the 1965 hill-climb cars, these had increased to 6in on the front and 7in on the rear. The problem was that tyre fashion had moved on from the 15in diameter rims that Porsche used. By this time, most Formula One teams were using the smaller 13in wheels.

A new, slightly more elegant body appeared in May with more attention paid to the integration of the oil cooler into the front bodywork. The struggle to find competitiveness in the hill-climb championship focused on continuing effort to make the open 904 as light as possible, since the regulations limited engine capacity to 2 litres. But despite the enthusiastic efforts of Piëch's emergent team of engineers, Gerhard Mitter's contest against Hans Herrmann in the Abarth Spyder and Scarfiotti's Ferrari Dino again proved the 904 had found its match.

A pair of brand new open 904s were built in July 1965 with further stiffened chassis. These 650kg cars ran the eight-cylinder engine (which in hill-climb tune was good for up to 260bhp) and more rounded rear bodywork. To measure the success of the weight-saving efforts, it is worth noting these cars weighed about 50kg less than the earlier four cylinder 904 coupés, except that the 771 engine weighed some 145kg to the four's 139kg. These two cars are symbolic since, although they failed to dislodge the competition, they were turned out in white, not Porsche's traditional silver. This recalled the colours adopted by German racing cars in the first 25 years of the century and rather turned a back on the 'silver arrows' responsibility that Porsche became saddled with in the late 1950s and early '60s.

By the end of July 1965, Piëch had taken the decision to start again and the 904, the instrument of Porsche's recovery from the grand prix adventure, had merely become the discarded instrument of burning ambition.

A NEW DIRECTION – CARRERA 6

I T IS OFTEN SAID THAT THE greatest achievements are made by those with a vision of how the end result should be. When the 26-year-old Ferdinand Piëch joined his uncle Ferry's company in 1963, he had a vision. The young Piëch was intent on becoming the head of the Porsche company and taking it to the very top of the motor industry. For a young ambitious man, who had grown up surrounded by automobiles and who had not long completed his engineering diploma, early and high profile success was essential. There is little doubt that Piëch realised early on that racing offered the opportunity for that recognition.

He joined the test department and was soon immersed in the development of the new six-cylinder engine for the forthcoming 901 model and improving the pretty 904 coupé for competition. But Piëch's family link gave him the kind of advantage in the organisation that only a close member of the business's owners could have. He used that link – and power – with remarkable skill to further his own position. He seemed to have little time for the traditional methods that were in place at Porsche, even though those methods had only evolved over the short 15 years of the company's existence as a car manufacturer.

He teamed up with Hans Mezger, who had made a name for himself initially as a camshaft designer and then for his work on the Formula One eight-cylinder engine. Mezger had become concerned at the complexity of the four-camshaft four and eight-cylinder engines (the eight took no less than 220 hours to build) and their unpredictable relia-bility. He concluded that to be inherently reliable, future Porsche engines – whether for competition or production – had to be simplified to require as little skill as possible to assemble. In the new six-cylinder engine being developed for the 901 road car, he proposed his ideas on simplicity and for changes to the design to enable its adaptation to racing. He found an enthusiastic champion in Piëch, and ignoring the traditional constraints of engine design and

Carrera 6
Daytona Speedway, USA
1966

The Carrera 6 driven by Jochen Rindt and Nino Vaccarella for the 1966 Nürburgring 1,000km had the 2.2-litre eight-cylinder engine in an attempt to get on terms with Ferrari's Dino. The car fell back with a slipping clutch and then ran out of brakes. (Porsche Archiv/Günther Molter)

manufacture, set about extensively revising the new six-cylinder. It caused uproar in the still-small Porsche company, especially as Piëch and Mezger wanted to make these changes after the car's announcement (in September 1963). Tooling lead times for major components like castings could take more than six months just to produce the first-off parts. Many parts were already (and expensively) tooled. But because of Piëch's influential position, it happened.

The new six came to production with such features as dry-sump lubrication, a seven-bearing crankshaft and the use of aluminium for the crankcase, barrels and cylinder heads. The heads themselves featured a completely revised overhead camshaft layout and a hemispherical combustion chamber design. These were very advanced features for an early 1960s production engine and was a significantly

higher specification than even the 1963 Frankfurt show car enjoyed. And in the final design, as found in the 1965 production models, Mezger also achieved his goal in reducing assembly time – the new 901 engine took just 15 hours to build.

The car that began to roll off the Zuffenhausen production lines in the autumn of 1964 would astonish the world. Such was the forethought that had gone into the design the new six-cylinder engine would form the basis for Porsche racing cars almost to the end of the century. Ferry Porsche's nephew had made his mark with a bang at Porsche. But there was much more to come.

By early 1965, Piëch had virtually taken over the test and development department, sweeping away those who did not agree with his ambitious thinking and introducing new, highly talented engineers who could share his dreams.

With the six-cylinder engine now in a form that Mezger could work with, Piëch's attention turned to the current racing car – the ground-breaking 904. Although the 904 had won the European GT Championship in 1964, the following year it came under severe pressure from the new Ferrari Dino and the new 2-litre Abarth. Nowhere was this increased competition more evident than in the European Hillclimb Championship. In the mid-1960s, this series was extremely prestigious, ranking alongside the FIA's GT Championship.

Porsche factory driver Gerhard Mitter competed in two early season climbs in an eight-cylinder 904 fitted with an ugly, but lightweight open spyder body. He had come second to Hans Herrmann in the Abarth at the first and had won the second. After this, Mitter and Colin Davis had taken an unexpected second on the Targa Florio, but had then written off a brand new six-cylinder spyder at the Nürburgring 1,000km in May.

After Le Mans in June, Porsche returned to the hills, but so did Ludovico Scarfiotti in the very nimble 2-litre Ferrari Dino. The Dino had the edge on Mitter, who was driving another new six-cylinder 904 spyder. This open-bodied Porsche had a fidgety reputation, leading to it being nicknamed 'Kangaroo' – which gives a clue to its cornering performance. The main problems were a lack of torsional stiffness and keeping the wheels of the extremely light car on the ground. This latter problem was made worse by the sometimes very rough surfaces of the roads used for hillclimbs. Reducing unsprung weight became a major priority.

Compared with the early season events, the body of the 904 spyder had been revised and extensive cross-bracing had appeared in the open cockpit area to provide additional torsional stiffness. At the same time Piëch was also running a British Elva space-frame sports racer fitted with the eight-cylinder engine for Tony Fischaber. This car was better behaved and provided a benchmark for the team, but still lacked the handling predictability of the closed 904 coupé (which itself was too heavy for the hills). The experiments continued and in the relentless quest for improvement, two brand new, further modified 904 spyders were built for the Italian Trento Bordone climb in early July. These were the cars which broke with the traditional silver and were painted white. But the new cars were still not enough. Scarfiotti was victorious in Italy and Herrmann in the Abarth was second ahead of a trailing Mitter. The Ferrari would win the following two climbs. At the end of July, Piëch decided to build a completely new car – to be ready for the next event at the end of August. It was a mammoth undertaking for the very small Porsche racing team, but such was Piëch's motivational energies on his band of

The six-cylinder engine was a neat fit in the new space-frame chassis. Note here the large FIA-regulation luggage compartment.

young engineers, the car was ready in just 20 days.

The new Porsche that rolled off the truck at the Swiss Ollon-Villars hill-climb was a full space-frame machine, fitted with the eight-cylinder engine and lightweight suspension and wheels bought from the Lotus grand prix

The long-tail bodywork gave the Carrera 6 a top speed of around 175mph (282kph) on Le Mans's Hunaudières Straight – probably enough to be an irritation to the big Fords and the Ferrari P3s, one of which follows the Udo Schutz/Peter de Klerk car here. The Günther Klass/Rolf Stommelen and Peter Gregg/Axelsson customer short-tails follow. (LAT)

meantime there would be a dazzling series of ever-improving sports racing cars that would catapult Porsche on to front stage in the world of motor racing. Far from relaxing during the winter of 1965–66, Piëch and his engineers set about designing and developing a sports coupé to contest the new endurance racing championship for the following season. And there were quite a few in Porsche who were still waiting for the young know-it-alls to go badly off the rails.

Race record

The format for endurance racing was given a new image in 1966, shedding the GT label and now being aimed at pure-bred racing sports cars. There would be two aspects to the Manufacturers' Championship – the first being for competition sports cars (Group 4), of which at least 50 units had to be manufactured before they could be registered to race and secondly, the prestigious prototype (Group 6) category. There would be seven races in the new championship comprising Daytona, Sebring, Monza, the Targa Florio, Spa, the Nürburgring and Le Mans. The changes would herald a classic era in the history of sports car racing. The first event was the new Daytona 24 Hours, this race being significantly lengthened from its previous 2,000km to provide a very demanding test for any car.

The prototype Carrera 6 (also called the 906) had been extensively tested during the cold winter months at VW's proving ground near Wolfsburg and at Porsche's new turning pad at Weissach, about 15 miles (24km) to the south-west of Zuffenhausen. Engineer Peter Falk had developed what became known as a destruction test for new models – both road and race – and he, with development head Helmut Bott, had put many miles on the new car before it was shipped to Daytona. The car ran in the prototype class as the necessary 50 customer cars had not yet been completed.

Daytona was a big breakthrough for the young racing team under Piëch, facing criticism back home for turning their backs on the hard-won design experience of earlier years and plunging headlong with their own new ideas. Hans Herrmann returned to the Porsche driver squad after a brief time with Abarth and was teamed with the experienced development driver Herbert Linge. The new car, painted an eye-catching royal blue, caused a real stir of interest – and not least because it was so small. Who would have thought that a 2-litre machine stood a chance against the top-class heavyweights such as the 7-litre Fords, especially at a power course like Daytona?

Daytona styles itself as the 'World Center for Racing' but is best known throughout the racing world for being the

The space-frame spyder produced in August 1965 ran for the first time at the Ollon-Villars hill-climb. Gerhard Mitter was still unable to beat Scarfiotti's dominant Ferrari Dino.

Hans Herrmann talks to Herbert Linge while waiting to take the brand new Carrera 6 out at Daytona.

team. However, the new car was too new and Mitter was defeated again by Scarfiotti. The 1965 championship went to Maranello, but Piëch had completed the culture transformation at Porsche. The 1965 season was the season in which the new team used energy to overcome inexperience and a lack of competitiveness. In attempting to wring the last ounce of performance out of the unsuspecting 904, Piëch and his young engineers began to learn the essentials of racing car design – the importance of chassis stiffness, predictable suspension dynamics, unsprung weight and weight reduction. From the summer of 1965, it would take them just four and a half years to perfect the art. In the

home of the Daytona 500 NASCAR stock car enduro. Located just inland from the Beach off the 192 highway, Daytona is one of the great speedways of North America. It is a very unusual location for an endurance sports car race, let alone a 24-hour one, but its place among the classic racing events of motor racing can be attributed to its originator, Bill France Snr, who ran NASCAR and wanted to bring European racing to his facility. It has largely been a labour of love, because the media interest in the Daytona 24 Hours has always been a fraction of that of the annual NASCAR 500. But to the dedicated band of American road racers and to the visiting Europeans, Daytona has, over the years, become one of the three great classics of sports car racing (with Le Mans and Sebring). It is hardly a place one can term as romantic in the same sense as Le Mans or Monza, but the speedway does have enormous presence – derived not least from those awesome banked curves at each end of the stadium. Everyone has memories of Daytona, from its ability to destroy perfectly good racing cars, to watching from the pit garages the launching of the Apollo moonshots from Cape Kennedy in the late 1960s and 1970s.

Today, there are chicanes slowing the cars before they plunge on to the banking, but in 1966, there was no such caution. This was a pedal-to-the-metal course, 3.84 miles (6.2km) long. The sports car circuit in 1966 was most of the tri-oval, with 2½ miles (4km) of flat-out straights or the turns of the breathtaking 31-degree banking. Unlike the stock cars, the sports cars had to negotiate a twisty, second gear infield section. The art at Daytona was to build up speed after leaving the infield for the west banking and to carry that speed down the long back straight and – in the right car with not a little courage – to sweep at full throttle on to the east banking. The fastest cars ran at the top of the steep curves, to slingshot on to the start-line straight (a gently banked yet kinked section angled towards the 75,000 capacity grandstands). It was then hard on the brakes to enter the infield again. Speed is what keeps the motor racing turnstiles spinning and Daytona does not disappoint.

The surprise of Daytona 1966 was that the big Fords seemed to have found their reliability at last and the thundering Mark Twos finished 1–2–3 and fifth. There were no works Ferraris, but a North American team car finished fourth. In sixth place came the little Porsche! Proving that if it looks right, it must be right, the new Carrera 6 had run like a Swiss watch.

It was only at Sebring, a month later, that the Carrera 6 came up against the 2-litre opposition it had been designed to face. While the new 4-litre Ferrari 330P3s challenged the 7-litre Fords, Maranello's new 206S sports car faced the

Huschke von Hanstein (in hat) looks on as Gerhard Mitter climbs in at the 1966 Sebring 12 Hours – the first time the Carrera 6 came up against the new Ferrari Dino 206. This car retired, but Mitter helped Hans Herrmann and Joe Buzzetta take the other works car to fourth, overcoming the red car.

Flat out on the banking at Monza. In the wet conditions, the works car of Mitter/Herrmann finished a resounding fourth overall, beaten only by three works Ferrari P3s. (LAT)

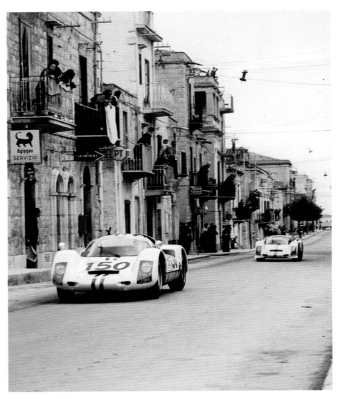

Two Carrera 6s blast through a village on the 1966 Targa Florio. The event was won by a works-loaned Scuderia Filipinetti car driven by Willy Mairesse and Herbert Müller. (LAT)

Opposite: The van Lennep family piloted the racing Team Holland Carrera 6 to a Sports class victory in the Nürburgring 1,000km. (Porsche Archiv/Günther Molter)

It could not happen today! The 1966 Targa Florio was washed out by heavy rain which turned the course into something like a rally special stage. This is the Ignazio Capuano/Ferdinando Latteri car that finished in eighth place.

Carrera 6. Derived from the hill-climb championship-winning 206SP of the previous year, the pretty Italian coupé was registered with the FIA at exactly the same (576kg) weight as the Carrera 6. Actual race weights of both cars were undoubtedly higher, with the Porsche running at around 625kg. The red car's carburettor-fitted, single-spark plug V6 was declared at 218bhp, but like the Porsche, there was undoubtedly more power available.

Only a single 206 appeared at Sebring to battle with two factory Carrera 6s, three new customer cars and five 904s. And it was the rough airfield paving that accounted for the very rapid Ferrari, losing many laps with a frozen gear linkage after easily leading the class, and even leading the whole race for half a lap at the start! After a steady run, the Carrera 6 of Hans Herrmann, Gerhard Mitter and Jo Buzzetta finished in fourth place, three laps ahead of the Ferrari. The other works car of Gunther Klass and Mitter had retired, but the private cars of Voegele and Jo Siffert and that of Ed Hugus and Lake Underwood finished sixth and eighth respectively. A 904 driven by George Follmer and Peter Gregg was seventh. Sadly a collision in darkness between Mario Andretti in the NART Ferrari and the rapidly driven Carrera 6 of Scooter Patrick and Webster resulted in the deaths of four spectators.

At Monza, the startling progress of the Carrera 6

Even in 1966, the long-tails were found to create worrying negative lift. The works cars ran with very small spoiler tabs on the tail, which barely controlled the problem at high speed.

Serious faces in the Porsche Le Mans pits during the 1966 race. From the left are Helmut Bott, Ferdinand Piëch, Huschke von Hanstein, Hans Mezger (sitting), Peter Falk and George Follmer.

continued. In streaming rain, the Herrmann/Mitter car finally finished in fourth place after the drivers found the car well-suited to the wet conditions. The Voegele/Siffert car followed in fifth, with Colin Davis/Dieter Glemser in seventh. The Ferraris faded early, the new fuel injected car being crashed by Bob Bondurant in practice and the best finisher being Lorenzo Bandini/Ludovico Scarfiotti in tenth.

The Carrera 6 was allowed into the Sports category from the start of May (Porsche would deliver some 52 customer cars during 1966, to go with its own prototype development machines). The factory cars would continue to run as prototypes all season, leaving the sports car group to their customers. The new homologation was a controversial subject among the scrutineers at the next event – the Targa Florio – and some Carrera 6s which should have been sports cars were raced as prototypes. There was a five-car

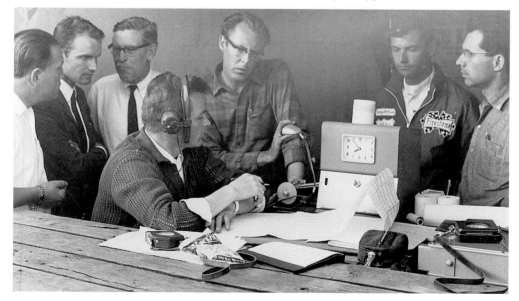

entry from Zuffenhausen. Spurred no doubt by Ferrari's progress, two of the cars were using fuel injection for the first time, while another had a 2.2-litre version of the old eight-cylinder. The principal competition on this twisty mountain course came from two Dinos and one mighty P3. Always frenzied, Sicilian ardour was not calmed any when Klass in the eight-cylinder 906 beat the P3 of local hero Nino Vaccarella to fastest practice time. What would really complicate the organisation in 1966 was the heavy rain which turned the 44.5-mile (71.6km) course into a mud and debris-strewn rally special stage. The P3 crashed and another eight-cylinder 906, driven by Davis, collided with Mitter's Carrera 6. All the works prototypes retired, but a private Carrera 6 won the race – the Filipinetti car driven by Willy Mairesse and Herbert Müller.

Next came Spa and defeat for the Porsches after they were drawn into a sprint race with the Ferraris. Calamities progressively wiped out every works car, with Mitter breaking his knee after the rear body detached on his Carrera 6 and sent him off the course. The up to 2-litre class was won by the Dino of Dickie Attwood/Jean Guichet. The Nürburgring 1,000km was no better for Porsche. Another event marked by heavy rain, the race was won by the 5.3-litre Chaparral 2D from two Dinos and the only surviving Carrera 6 driven by Bondurant and Paul Hawkins.

While the world watched the mammoth head-to-head between Ford and Ferrari at Le Mans, Porsche built their strategy at the Sarthe on maintaining a steady and consistent speed. Three long-tail Carrera 6s were entered, all with the now-trusted six-cylinder fuel-injected engines. The race was a disaster for Ferrari with all his cars, including the three Dinos, retiring. It was a 1–2–3 for Ford, but in fourth place and winning the 2-litre class were Davis and Siffert in a factory Carrera 6, followed by three more Carrera 6s, the seventh of which was the sports class-winning car of young Rolf Stommelen and Klass.

In the first complete year with their own car, Piëch's team had won the small capacity prototype class of the new Manufacturers' Championship. Three further races would wrap up the under 2-litre class in the sports car category. To complete a dazzling 1966 score sheet, Porsche also won the European Hillclimb Championship. Mitter won five out of seven events in an eight-cylinder lightweight model, beating Scarfiotti in the Dino spyder into second place.

For 1967, the fuel-injected engine was offered to racing customers and the Carrera 6 became the car to have in the up to 2-litre sports classes of both the European-based Manufacturers' Championship and the US Road Racing Championship. As had been demonstrated the year before, the Carrera 6 turned out to be perfect for hill-climbing – but perhaps this was not surprising considering its ancestry.

Over the winter of 1966–67, a new car was designed that would use yet more new ideas and learn from the mistakes of the previous season. The new 910 was the third new racing car to come from Porsche in the space of 18 months. Two fuel-injected Carrera 6s were taken to the season-opening American classics, but it would be the new machine that starred. At Daytona, and against a full complement of Fords, Ferraris and the monster Chaparral 2J, Siffert and Herrmann would finish fourth overall in the new 910 behind the three winning Ferrari P3s and 4s. Both works Carrera 6s retired, while an ex-factory car driven by Rico Steinemann and Dieter Spoerry finished fifth. At Sebring, it was a similar story with Steinemann and Spoerry scoring the best result for the Carrera 6, again behind the new 910s. Observers were noticing the pace of development at Porsche was becoming relentless. The time for the new car had arrived.

Engineering

It is easy to think the elegant form of the new Carrera 6 – typed 906 in Zuffenhausen – was the result of a stylist's eye, but nothing could be further from the truth. Although

The customer versions of the Carrera 6 were equipped with a rear spoiler and two front trim tabs to help the car's high-speed stability. Some customers removed the tabs where maximum speed was a priority, as here at Hockenheim.

The pretty lines of the Carrera 6 were a product of analysis and the wind tunnel, in contrast to the earlier intuitive form of the 904. This is the Klass/Schutz car at the Nürburgring.

the shape was pure 1960s, the 906's form was engineered from top to bottom. Wind tunnel testing had established the angular shape of the compact coupé, which featured a deeply-rounded windscreen that was bonded in place, and a cut-off Kamm-style tail section fully enclosed with a long, yellow-tinted clear plastic rear screen over the engine bay.

As well as requiring his racing cars to be as light as possible, Piëch was equally determined they would have the minimum aerodynamic drag. The new machine's most striking feature was its low pointed nose, with faired-in headlamps for better penetration, and with small openings at the front for ducts to the front brakes. The only other openings in the body were those for the oil cooler – mounted over the driver's legs and behind the mandatory spare wheel – and on each flank just behind the gull-wing doors, to cool the rear brakes and the gearbox. The quest for lowest drag (for highest top speed) would become a Piëch obsession in the coming years, but it would be some time before this objective conceded that destabilising positive lift also had to be accommodated. As a small concession to this, the eventual customer versions sported tail spoilers (as first seen on the Ferraris in 1961) to help

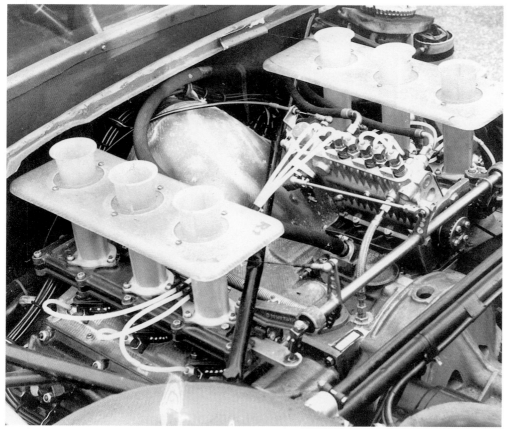

The factory Carrera 6s benefited from Bosch mechanical fuel injection during 1966. The toothed-belt drive to the fuel metering pump can be seen below the throttle linkage crossbar.

reduce the lift over the rear wheels. The wind tunnel testing also proved the worth of having two 'moustache' trim tabs at each side of the nose.

The chassis itself was brand new, but recalled the experience amassed with the earlier 718 RSK series (Ing. Hild was closely involved with the 50 'production' 906 chassis). The multi-tubular steel space-frame was complicated to build and the task was made more difficult because, to save weight, the longitudinal tubes were used to carry engine oil to the front-mounted cooler. The frames themselves were fabricated by the Weinsberg coach-builders and they built a special rig to pressure test every new chassis. It was no small task to weld up a pressure tight chassis and even more demanding for the integrity to be maintained over a season's (or more) competition.

The early six-cylinder engine was little different in appearance to that used in the production 2-litre 911, save for some important details. Hans Mezger (now in charge of the new racing design department) used his extensive knowledge to revise the camshaft and cylinder head design and introduce lightweight materials to the production-based engine. Titanium replaced steel and magnesium alloy was used in place of aluminium for many components. Typical were the magnesium alloy crankcase halves and the chromium-plated all-aluminium barrels in place of the production car's iron-sleeved items. The connecting rods were forged titanium and even the long bolts attaching the heads to the crankcase were titanium. The extensive use of aluminium produced a problem for Mezger and his engineers in that these bolts expanded far less when hot than the now wholly aluminium cylinder barrels. The new titanium bolts were covered with glass fibre to help retain their temperature, but it would not be until the development of the 912 twelve-cylinder engine that a new bolt material was evolved that replicated the expansion characteristics of aluminium. The racing six also benefited from twin spark ignition and Weber IDA downdraught carburettors and after development, Mezger was able to offer a reliable 210bhp. This was at a time when the production 2-litre 911 delivered 130bhp. In those days, it was not long before pieces that worked on the racers found their way on to the production cars – perhaps the most obvious example being the sonerous downdraught Webers for the new 160bhp 911S. If the 50bhp difference between the 911S and the 906 does not sound much, a look at the power-to-weight ratios shows the difference between the road and racing car. Whereas the 911S was typically nearly 1,100kg, the 906 was a featherweight 675kg. The resulting power-to-weight ratio of the racer was over double that of the top-of-the-range production model.

The transmission chosen for the 906 was the same five-speed unit proven on the earlier 904 and as used on the production 911. The magnesium alloy casing typified the efforts continuously being sought to use the lightest possible materials for the task.

The suspension of the 906 was effectively the same as proven on the 904. Because the 906 was a pure racer, rubber isolators were not used in the suspension and adjustable ball-joints were used. Considering that virtually every other top level racing team was using light alloy wheels, it is surprising that Porsche continued to use a fabricated wheel with light alloy rims and steel centres which dated back to the 718 sports cars. This was because all-

alloy wheels had been found to crack in long distance races. Since the 906 was a production racing car, marginal reliability – potentially dangerous in this case – was not acceptable. With the team's growing experience of racing and particularly hill-climbing, keeping all four wheels firmly in contact with what was often a rough road surface had become a priority. To reduce the unsprung weight of the bouncing wheel, hub and outboard brake assembly, Peter Falk had begun to investigate alternative materials for the brakes, the most exotic of which was chrome-plated beryllium discs. These reduced a 18.5kg cast iron disc down to just 4.6kg, but were not used for much else than hill-climbs because of their expense and concerns about

A casual scene at the 1966 Le Mans test weekend. This is one of the works prototypes, at this stage without the long-tail. (LAT)

A mud-spattered Carrera 6 accelerates past the pits during the 1966 Targa Florio. The race was further toughened by poor weather, which caught out many of the more powerful cars.

the carcinogenic dust produced during machining and use. The beryllium discs were only used at one race in 1966 – the Hockenheim 500km meeting, but they would be tried again in the coming years.

The production car's disc brakes were also the same as the 904's, except the pads were larger and brake balance was made easier with separate circuits for the front and rear. Despite being contracted to Dunlop, the development team regularly benchmarked their tyres against the improving Goodyears and Firestones. It would be some years, however, before the other brands would appear in races.

For Le Mans, the 906 was given a bodywork feature which would become much-copied in later years. The *langheck* (or long-tail) did nothing for the looks of the car, but helped edge the maximum speed upwards on the long Hunaudières Straight. To aid better penetration the nose was also extended. These long-tail 906s did not feature any movable aerodynamic devices (but a car had been tested

with moving rear and 'moustache' trim tabs). For Le Mans speed was everything and the decision was made that even moving spoilers would have reduced the overall performance (for which read top speed) given the relatively low output of the 2-litre engine. During practice the drivers complained of the tail lifting at high speed and after several trial and error experiments, the cars did race with small, but fixed, front and rear spoilers.

The 906s entered in the prototype class during 1966 were fitted with both improved six and eight-cylinder engines. The development 901/21 six-cylinder was run with fuel-injection and this gave a slight increase in maximum power (to around 220bhp), but most importantly, improved the power delivery of the engine. Fuel consumption was about 10 per cent higher in race conditions, at around 7–8 miles to the imperial gallon (35–40 litres/100km). The six-plunger injection pump was driven from the rear of the right-hand camshaft (the front on the 911, where the engine and gearbox was turned around).

Fuel metering was basic, being governed by a simple cam positioned by throttle opening. It would be a year before the cam could slide axially and take into account engine revolutions. The fuel was injected just behind the throttle slides, which themselves were mounted just above the intake ports of the cylinder heads. On later cars, the injectors were mounted right at the tops of the intake trumpets, which made for better fuel/air mixing.

The eight-cylinder was further developed for use in the 906 and increased to 2.2 litres with fuel injection. This yielded an impressive 275bhp, but despite significant progress, the reliability of this complex engine remained much poorer than the relatively simple six. The continued efforts to improve reliability would bear fruit in the coming season.

It was the 1966 Nürburgring 1,000km that persuaded Piëch to issue the instruction that from then on, all major endurance races contested by the factory would be run with new cars. During this gruelling endurance event, two cars had retired with fatigue-related problems. A half-shaft had broken on one and on another a chassis tube under the gearbox had fractured (not for the first time). It was a move intended to improve the drivers' confidence at a time when technical failure at high speed was often fatal. Much to the pleasure of the factory's customers (who would be able to buy one-race-old development machines), the policy of using new cars for each major race would persist until the advent of the very costly 917.

SPECIFICATION
1966 Carrera 6

Engine: Mid-mounted type 901/20 air-cooled six-cylinder with one chain operated camshaft per bank and two (sodium filled) valves per cylinder. Dry sump lubrication (capacity 14-litres) with magnesium alloy crankcase and aluminium alloy cylinder heads, alloy barrels with porous chromium-plated bores. Forged steel crankshaft supported in seven plain main bearings with lightweight flywheel. Single-piece titanium connecting rods with forged aluminium alloy pistons. Marelli 12-volt electrical system for dual coil ignition with twin ignition distributors driven from the ends of the top (inlet) camshaft each side and two spark plugs per cylinder. Bendix fuel pump supplying petrol to Bosch six-plunger mechanical fuel injection (continuous). Vertical cooling fan driven by V-belt from the crankshaft. Open racing exhaust.

Capacity: 1,991cc

Bore/Stroke: 80mm/66mm

Maximum power: 220bhp at 8,000rpm

Maximum torque: 208Nm at 6,400rpm

Compression ratio: 10.3:1

Transmission: Type 822 full synchronised five-speed gearbox in magnesium alloy barrel sand casting. Cable-actuated single-plate Fichtel & Sachs clutch. ZF disc-type limited slip differential. Double universally jointed Nadella drive-shafts.

Chassis/body: Multi-tubular steel space-frame two-seat coupé chassis with mid-engine location and very lightweight glass fibre bodywork. Gull-wing type doors with over-centre mechanical strut. 100-litre total capacity sill-mounted aluminium fuel tanks. Front-mounted oil cooling radiator (behind mandatory spare wheel in extreme front of nose). Adjustable seat and steering column with single tachometer in instrument display. At rear is mandatory luggage compartment with small tool kit.

Suspension and steering: Double wishbone suspension all round with progressive rate coils over Bilstein-de Carbone gas pressure shock absorbers. Adjustable anti-roll bars. Rear suspension has double forward-placed radius arms. Titanium wheel hubs with spherical bearings for suspension mountings. Rack and pinion steering.

Brakes: Dual hydraulic circuit to 10mm thick Alfred Teves-Dunlop solid disc brakes all round. 274mm diameter front, 285mm rear. Handbrake operated on small drums in rear hubs.

Wheels and tyres: 7 x 15in front, 9 x 15in rear alloy rim wheels with Dunlop R7 Green Spot (dry) racing tyres.

Weight: 625kg

Length: 4,113mm

Height: 996mm

Wheelbase: 2,300mm

Track (f/r): 1,338mm/1,402mm

Performance: Acceleration: 0 to 62.5mph (100kph): N/A

Maximum speed: around 168mph (270kph) (long-tail)

CHAPMIONSHIP FORMULA — 908

6

908
Nürburgring, Germany
Vic Elford
1971

Opposite: The 1971 version of the 908/03 featured large vertical fins on the rear body and an FIA-specification roll-over bar. This is Jack Oliver in practice at the Nürburgring. (LAT)

Bergwerk

Karussell

Pflanzgarten

Aremberg

Döttinger Höhe

Flugplatz

MARTINI
RACING TEAM

Shell   Shell

Südkehre

THE 908 IS A TRULY REMARKABLE racing car. It was the product of the relentless energies of Ferdinand Piëch's young engineering team and was built to win the Manufacturers' Championship for Porsche – a goal that had remained stubbornly elusive with the earlier – and transitional – 910 and 907 sports cars. The 908 was to totally dominate the 1969 Manufacturers' Championship and with the announcement of the 917 early that year, few would have believed the 908 had a future beyond the end of the season. But how wrong they were!

The development was taken up a gear and for the two most demanding road courses on the 1970 championship calendar a new version – the 908/03 – was wheeled out. The 908/03 was precisely the right car for the twists, turns, short squirts and sweeps of the Madonie and the Eifel. For two years running this nimble spyder replaced the goliath 917s at these courses and reliability problems aside, proved to be totally dominant. When the FIA banned the big 5-litre cars at the end of 1971, the 908 continued to show how effective a good chassis can be, even when its now-ageing 3-litre two-valve engine was outclassed. The 908 would continue to run at Le Mans until the late 1970s. It was a friendly, dependable car that got you home without drama. To many at Weissach, the 908 is the Porsche racing car that is the unchallenged number one.

The path to the 908 was an unbroken stream of racing car innovation and evolution that began with the Carrera 6 and passed in quick succession and just two seasons of racing through the 910 and 907 sports cars. Just as the Carrera 6 had made its spectacular debut in 1966 at the Daytona 24 Hours, in 1967 it was the turn of the 910. Again there was sensation as Jo Siffert and Hans Herrmann brought the brand new prototype home fourth overall, beaten only by a three-car formation finish of 4-litre Ferraris. The 910 was a racing development of the very lightweight machine that Gerhard Mitter had used to win the European Hillclimb Championship the previous year.

The 910 became the factory's main sports prototype challenger during 1967. Jo Siffert (here) and Hans Herrmann drove this eight-cylinder 910 but retired from second place. (Porsche Archiv/Günther Molter)

This hill-climb car was in turn a much-improved Carrera 6 (actually chassis No. 906-010 – hence the 910 out-of-sequence designation). The 910 used the best of the lessons learned with the Ollon-Villars spyder and the Carrera 6. Mitter had used the 2-litre eight-cylinder for the hill-climbing 910 in 1966, but the Daytona 910 adopted the endurance racing version of the fuel-injected 2-litre six-cylinder. Where the 910 made progress over the Carrera 6 was in its chassis, suspension and aerodynamics. Only the progressive rate coil springs were the same as the whole geometry was re-designed, drawing on Formula One practice and reducing unsprung weight. Porsche's own-design centre-locking 13in diameter magnesium alloy wheels were used, again copying the wheel/tyre fashion in Formula One. The smaller wheels allowed a lower, more rounded body shape to be evolved. The car is instantly recognisable over the earlier Carrera 6 by its rounded headlamp covers.

In March, two 910s had finished third and fourth in

Sebring, this time behind the winning Ford Mk 2s. It set the trend for the season, with the little white Porsches playing back-up to the pitched battle between Ford and Ferrari. At the winding Targa Florio and Nürburgring of course, the game was loaded in Porsche's favour. Using the now-reliable eight-cylinder 2.2-litre engines, Australian Paul Hawkins and Rolf Stommelen headed a 1–2–3 in Sicily and Udo Schütz and Joe Buzzetta a 1–2–3–4 in Germany. But by this time the racing community already had sight of yet another new Porsche prototype. At the Le Mans test weekend in early April, two new cars had been carefully wheeled out of the smart new maroon-coloured Porsche transporters.

Built with little compromise to practicality, the new 907 model was presented in two forms – with short and long tails. The *langheck* was a no-compromise attempt to achieve maximum possible speed on the 3.5-mile (5.6km) Hunaudières Straight at Le Mans, using the fuel-injected 2-litre six-cylinder engine. This car was a remarkable 'speed

Precursor to the 908 was the very lightweight 910 hillclimb spyder. This car used an aluminium space-frame chassis and at one point tipped the scales at just 420kg dry. Gerhard Mitter is seen here at the Sierre Montana climb in Switzerland in 1968.

special' and was a product of extensive testing at the Stuttgart Technical Institute. It remains the racing Porsche with lowest aerodynamic drag to this day. Behind a very short nose, it featured an enclosed cockpit that protruded bubble-like from the low set bodyshell. Its aerodynamic drag was fully 25 per cent less than that of the (by comparison) utilitarian 910. The most obvious other feature of this long-tail was that there were no openings in the nose. To reduce the drag to a minimum, the ducts for the brakes and driver cooling had been eliminated. The opening for the oil cooler remained, as it had been on the Carrera 6, on the top surface of the nose. This placed the hot radiator right over the driver's knees – a better-than-average cockpit heater. It put driver comfort in second place to the quest for total speed. In most other respects, the 907 was a small step on from the 910. The short-tail 907 was a more practical racing car and seemed to be a 910 that had grown up. Its body was less toy-like than the earlier car, and in detail it featured a large number of changes to improve the car's performance. The most obvious of these was that the driving position was moved to the right-hand side, since most of the courses had predominantly right-turning corners. This helped place more weight on the inside wheels during cornering.

At the April test weekend in 1967, the long-tails came face to face with the problem that had been largely overlooked with the Carrera 6 the year before. The extremely low drag shape actually had so little downforce that the car wanted to take off at speed. Barely 150mph (240kph) was possible, when the 910 with the still-preferred six-cylinder engine had been good for 167mph (269kph). By the race, a full-width rear spoiler had improved the stability, but only just enough to allow the drivers to get into top gear and press the throttle without closing their eyes. In the race the

fastest long-tail was timed at 183mph (294kph), but the most remarkable statistic of the streamlined 907 that finished fifth overall at Le Mans that year, was that it achieved an average fuel consumption average of 14 litres/100km (19.4 miles/imperial gallon).

The hill-climb championship that year went to an ultra-lightweight eight-cylinder 910, driven by Gerhard Mitter. This car took advantage of new rules which removed the minimum weight limit for the maximum 2-litre capacity cars. The engineers of the race design department had virtual freedom in the drive for low weight. As campaigned by Mitter that year, the hill-climb 910 took their ideas all the way. The car featured an elemental aluminium space-frame and was clothed in a paper-like glass fibre body painted with well-thinned paint. One car tried the beryllium brake discs again, with titanium calipers and stub axles running in magnesium wheel hubs. These exotic materials were used wherever possible and the car tipped the scales at an all-time best of just 420kg – with the eight-

cylinder engine fitted. These were the very best materials available for the task and reflected the seriousness with which Ferdinand Piëch wanted Porsche to win.

The other most important experiment during the swirl of activity that was 1967 was a new form for the six-cylinder engine. The 916 trialed the use of a double overhead camshaft arrangement to improve the revolutions potential and hence maximum power. Several engines were built and the drivers' response was universally ecstatic. There was talk of this engine going into the 911 production car, but history shows it to have simply been a stepping stone. Before the experiments had barely finished, Piëch took his engineers off in a new direction again.

Looking back, 1967 became a turning point for the engineers at Porsche. In a frenzy of activity, their knowledge and understanding of aerodynamics, low weight and engine design appeared to be working towards a climax. The prize was the World Manufacturers' Championship, one that – against all the odds – just eluded them in 1967. The racing

The long-tail 907 scored a resounding 1–2–3 win at Daytona in 1968, but drivers needed an extra helping of nerves to get the best from the car. (LAT)

budget was now into the millions of marks each year and Porsche were still contesting the under 2-litre class. Inevitably, some were asking where it was all going.

The 907s were further developed for the start of the 1968 season. The 1968 short-tail was another step on from the cars raced at Le Mans in 1967. Mezger had wrung enough reliability from the 2.2-litre eight-cylinder for this engine to be usable in the long endurance races and the remarkable experiments with the hill-climb 910s had given enough confidence to try the aluminium frame in racing. The short-tail body had the same Kamm-type cut-off tail as the 910, but the clear plastic screen over the engine bay had been replaced by a notch back rear body that exposed the inlet trumpets and cooling fan. For the fast courses, a new long-tail was available which this time was inter-changeable with the short version. At the front the oil cooler was moved to the nose and the front windscreen was now more steeply raked. The whole appearance was of a very purposeful machine. There was one other feature that the 1968 907s enjoyed. As well as the 2.2-litre eight, there was space in the engine bay for a new 3-litre engine that Mezger had been working on from soon after Le Mans the previous year.

This season turned out to be very unsatisfactory for Porsche. The spectacular Ford-Ferrari contest of 1967 had been consigned to history by an FIA rule change limiting engine capacity in the prototype class to 3 litres. The GT40s were still allowed because a sufficient number had been built for them to qualify for the Group 4 sports car class. However, no-one had expected them to contest for the overall championship. It was Porsche who were the favourites, the company was spending millions providing its team of drivers with new cars for every major race, while the opposition – principally the ageing John Wyer-entered Gulf Ford GT40s – seemed to always get to the flag first on the most frugal of budgets.

The year was a series of famous highs and lows for Porsche, but was ultimately frustrating. The highs were a 1–2–3 finish in the Daytona 24 Hours (with long-tails), wins at Sebring and perhaps rally-turned-race driver Vic Elford's greatest drive in winning the Targa Florio. The low was that despite speed there was little consistency and the Gulf GT40s won enough races (including an easy win at Le Mans) to capture the Manufacturers' Championship.

It was perhaps the competitiveness of the GT40s that resulted in Mezger's new engine being rushed into action.

Race record

The new 3-litre car was revealed in public at the April 1968 Le Mans test weekend and first raced at the Monza

1,000km the following month. The Monza course used was a combination of the old high-speed banked oval and the outer road course. Measuring around 5 miles (8km) in length, it was very fast – the average speed was more than 125mph (200kph) and the leading cars were making 175mph (282kph) on the straights – and very dangerous. The pair of new 908s lacked development and finished in lowly 11th and 18th places, after various teething troubles were made worse by the continuous hammering received on the bumpy banking.

The next appearance of the 908 came at the Nürburgring and after a period of intensive durability testing. Two cars were entered and with the Gulf GT40s making untypical strategy errors, Siffert and Elford claimed the 908's first victory with the sister car of Herrmann and Neerpasch following. For Spa, the task against the long-legged 4.7-litre Fords would be more difficult. Both 908 driver teams opted for the short-tail after the controllability of the long-tail was found to be marginal on Spa's long (and often ditch-lined) straights. The short-tail was slower, but the drivers had more confidence. But Spa 1968 was all about Jacky Ickx and Brian Redman. The Belgian grand prix driver revelled in the wet conditions and Redman surprised many by matching the lap times of his team-mate on the Ardennes

Porsche were affected by a host of problems at the 1968 Le Mans and the race was handed to a consistently driven John Wyer GT40. This is Jo Siffert at the start making for his long-tail. He and Hans Herrmann are credited with a speed of 206mph (331kph) on the Hunaudières Straight. They retired in the fifth hour with a broken clutch.

course. These two drivers simply flew away from the Porsches, despite a stirring drive from Vic Elford as he tried to make up for an early throttle linkage problem in his 908.

The student unrest in France led to the postponement of Le Mans to September that year and the next race on the sports car calendar was at Watkins Glen, in upstate New York. This was the first race at which the 908s featured suspension-controlled moving rear flaps. In response, the Gulf GT40s went to the USA with full 5-litre engines and the Fords once more showed the Porsches the way home. The 908s were defeated by a succession of mechanical problems, ranging from an over-charging alternator, another broken throttle linkage and several front wheel bearing failures. With Ford winning the American race, the championship remained wide open. It would all come down to Le Mans.

A September date, the new Ford Chicane and no unlimited capacity prototypes made for a very different 24 Hours than the previous year. Both the Wyer Fords and Porsche made maximum efforts. There were four Porsche System 908s, three supporting 907s, a 910 and even a Carrera 6 against three of the powder blue and orange Gulf cars. But mechanical trouble again hit the Porsches. The litany of problems included a broken clutch (Siffert/ Herrmann), engine cooling fan problems (Neerpasch/

The 908s return from Blanchimont on the 1968 Spa 1,000km. Torrential Ardennes weather turned the event into a benefit for rising Belgian driver Jacky Ickx driving a Ford GT40. (LAT)

The 3-litre engine put Porsche in the top class in sports car racing. The 1968 908 coupé would prove to have significant potential over the coming years. (LAT)

Stommelen) and alternator (Elford/Mitter). This latter car was disqualified after the alternator was switched – a component which, according to the rules, cannot be replaced during the race. The 907s fared little better in a race that was also badly interrupted by heavy rain. The Steinemann/Spoerry car struggled home second, well beaten by the Gulf GT40 of Pedro Rodriguez and Lucien Bianchi, with the Stommelen/Neerpasch 908 recovering to third. Ford had won the championship and Porsche had been beaten by a (very professional) private team. The season had been marred for Zuffenhausen by repeated and often unconnected problems. But perhaps the inconsistency was predictable. At virtually every race, the cars would appear with some new and usually innovative feature. The engineers were so focused on the invention of speed that durability often went missing. John Wyer identified this as early as 1967 and would capitalise on it until Porsche threw in the towel and asked him to run their racing team in 1970.

First however, was the 1969 season. Piëch made a crucial change to his team for the new year's campaign. Huschke von Hanstein, the doyen of team managers from the mid-1950s stepped back as racing team manager and his place was taken by Swiss journalist and racing driver Rico Steinemann. Von Hanstein was an aristocrat of the old school. It had become clear that he was not so comfortable as when he only had to answer to Ferry Porsche for his management of the racing team. In contrast, the ambitious Steinemann was 'on message' with Piëch and quickly became the perfect mouthpiece for the new Porsche racing culture.

No expense was spared for 1969. The 908 was extensively reworked for the new season and so many drivers were retained to drive that they became known as the Porsche soccer team.

Daytona came as usual in early February, but throughout the winter the small racing department had been working flat out on the new 4.5-litre 917. Somehow, enough resources were mustered to take no less than five new 908 *langhecks* to Florida. Once again John Wyer would form the most consistent opposition that year, with the new Lola T70 coupés providing variation and the improving 3-litre V12 Matras acoustic entertainment. All five Porsches retired with the same problem – a broken aluminium intermediate camshaft drive gear. The surprise was that the pair of Wyer Fords also dropped out to leave the win to an immaculate blue Lola entered by Roger Penske. Penske and his leading driver, Mark Donohue, had left their calling card with Ferdinand Piëch.

There were again five 908s at Sebring in March, but this

time they were brand new spyders. The regulations had been eased to allow open prototypes and Porsche took advantage of the smaller frontal area and the opportunity of a greatly improved environment in the cockpit. Lessons had been learned from Daytona and the cars used steel intermediate gears. But this time all the Porsches suffered with broken chassis on the rough airfield course and the Ickx/Jack Oliver GT40 won from the new 312P Ferrari of Chris Amon and Andretti.

Between Sebring and the next race at Brands Hatch virtually the whole of Porsche came to a standstill as the company built no less than 25 917s. This memorable effort did not stop the team from scoring a morale-boosting 1–2–3 victory in Kent. The Siffert/Brian Redman car actually succeeded with only one of its two ignition circuits operating. It was John Wyer's turn to be distracted by his Mirage project, powered by the unimpressive BRM V12. Despite both Ferrari and Alfa Romeo now fielding 3-litre cars alongside the large capacity Fords and Lolas, Porsche – with their reliability seemingly resolved – were now hot favourites for the title.

The Porsche spyder was turning into a well-loved

The 908 Spyder was first raced at the 1968 Sebring 12 Hours, Porsche taking advantage of new rules that allowed open cockpits.

machine for the drivers. The 3-litre engine may not have had the outright power of a Cosworth or a Ferrari V12, but it was reliable. It was also very obvious the 908 had matured into a supreme chassis. It is interesting to compare the improvement in Porsche lap times at Brands between 1968 and 1969, because it demonstrates the extent of the improvement achieved over the 907. Jo Siffert's pole time in the 2.2-litre 907 coupé for the 1968 race was 1 minute 34.6 seconds, while to win pole for 1969 he did 1 minute 28.8 seconds in the 3-litre 908 Spyder. The 1969 time bettered Amon in the Ferrari by a full 1.2 seconds and Jo Bonnier in the fastest Lola by 2.8 seconds.

After Brands came Monza, the last year the infamous banking would be used for an international motor race. This time it was the Ferrari that was fastest in practice, but the two Maranello cars entered lacked reliability and in the race were comprehensively beaten by the Zuffenhausen

long-tails, Siffert and Redman heading Herrmann and Kurt Ahrens.

The spyders were the obvious choice for the Targa Florio and with John Wyer giving the event a miss, Gerhard Mitter and Udo Schütz headed a 1–2–3–4 for Porsche. The pace of the open spyders on a mainly twisting course was again underlined by Madonie maestro Vic Elford (on the way to second place after an alternator belt broke) who claimed a fastest lap of 35 minutes 8.2 seconds, which compares to his very best in the winning 907 the previous year of 36 minutes 2.3 seconds – and the 1968 lap had been considered outstanding!

Spa was next and could not have been a more different challenge to the rough and tumble of Sicily. It was the turn of another new batch of long-tails – complete with moving flaps. Brian Redman has always said that if they had used the spyder at Spa, they would have been even quicker than

After crashing the 'flounder'-bodied car in practice, Jo Siffert and Brian Redman borrowed this older spyder to win the 1969 Nürburgring 1,000km. (LAT)

Opposite: Flying high at the Nürburgring 1,000km in 1970 is Brian Redman (trying one of the new Bell Star helmets). The superbly agile 908/03 had ideal dynamics for the twists and turns of the 'Ring. Siffert and Redman would retire in the race with a blown engine.

the average fastest lap of over 145mph (233kph) he set during the race. It is academic because he and Siffert finished almost a lap ahead of Rodriguez and David Piper in a 312P.

The Nürburgring was, like the Targa Florio, a course for which the spyder was supremely suited, but preparations did not go quite as the team would have liked. A new flat-topped spyder body was tried in practice, but both Siffert and Elford flipped their cars. This meant a hurried retreat to the spare cars being run by Porsche Konstruktion Öster-reich – a team financed by Ferry Porsche's sister Louise Piëch and enjoying very close relationship with the works. Once again the Gulf-Mirages succumbed to BRM V12 problems and only the Amon/Rodriguez Ferrari was able to match the Porsche pace.

The 14.27-mile (23km) *Nordschleife* of the Nürburgring is one of the great road racing courses of the world. The track requires an almost photographic memory and intense concentration to complete a fast lap. Set in the densely forested Eifel hills about 40 miles (65km) south of Bonn, the 'Ring was built in the 1920s by 2000 previously unem-ployed labourers. Their efforts produced a spectacular driver's course that was originally 17.5 miles (28km) long.

Until the circuits closure for international motor racing in 1982, the 73 corners presented virtually every kind of driving challenge, with innumerable jumps, blind brows, second-gear hairpins and heart-in-the-mouth flat-out corners. This was a course where nimble 425bhp grand prix cars easily out-paced the heavier sports cars. In 1969, Jacky Ickx in his Brabham-Cosworth, claimed pole for the Grand Prix with a time some 20 seconds faster than Siffert in the 908. But whereas the GP was over in just 14 laps, the sports car race went 44 punishing laps. It was not so much the roughness of the road surface (although the fierce winters in this part of Germany claimed a fair toll), but the hammering the engine, gearbox and brakes received on the relentlessly turning, accelerating and braking road. The 'Ring was – is – regarded as still the most demanding driver's course in the world and to be the best here was a supreme credit. Porsche used the 'Ring exten-sively for development testing and, as a result, the team's drivers were very familiar with every dip and crest.

Pit-stops gave the Porsches an advantage in the 1969 1,000km event, but when electrical problems stopped the Ferrari, the 908s were able to take the first five places. The victory gave Porsche its first International Championship of Makes title most convincingly.

Le Mans could have been a dull event given that Porsche were already champions, but the famous race turned into something special. The 100m gap between the winning Ford GT40 of Jacky Ickx and Hans Herrmann's 908 after a full 24 hours' racing – and with the two cars swapping places around the last lap – has turned into the stuff of legend. Four 908s – three long-tail coupés and a single long-tail spyder – plus two of the fearsome new 917s coupés faced a motley opposition. The main competition appeared to be the two Ferraris and three Matra prototypes. But the race did not go to anyone's plan, except perhaps John Wyer's. The Ferraris and Matras fell out, and so did most of the Porsches. The special Siffert/Redman spyder succumbed to an overheated transmission while Vic Elford and Dickie Attwood led until around three hours from the end. Their 917, which no-one expected to last that long, retired when the gearbox casing broke. That left the Herrmann/Gérard Larrousse fighting head-to head with the unfancied Gulf GT40 of Ickx and Oliver. Ickx won. It was a frustrating defeat that recalled the desperate closeness of Dan Gurney's loss in the French Grand Prix at Reims in 1961.

By comparison, the Watkins Glen 6 Hours was a carefree end of term event. Siffert and Elford chased each other around the woodlands of upstate New York, much to team manager Rico Steinemann's dismay and easily out-paced the entire field. The year had shown that Porsche under-

In the Targa Florio, the 908 matured into a highly effective machine. This is Richard Attwood in a Gulf 908/03 on the 1970 event. He and rally driver Bjorn Waldegaard finished fifth.

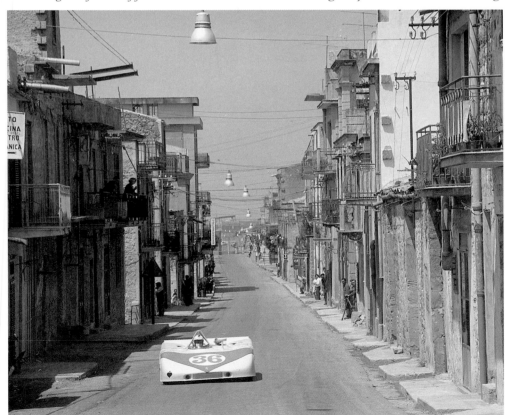

stood exactly the craft of winning sports car races and in the 908, they had perfected the tool.

If the introduction of the 917 suggested that the 908's days were numbered, then the reality was quite different. Porsche knew that the big car would be relatively unsuited to the twistier courses, particularly the Targa Florio and the Nürburgring. The development of the 3-litre car continued with engineer Manfred Bantle as the project leader, working with the guidance of Peter Falk.

The 908/03 was a major step forward and its Sicilian debut in 1970 was spectacular, not least for the vivid colour schemes devised by Porsche stylist Tony Lapine. The factory-contracted John Wyer Gulf cars were turned out with large, dramatic arrow designs and each carried a different playing card suit to identify them. This recalled the method of identification that Ferdinand Porsche had used on the Austro-Daimlers at the 1922 Targa Florio.

Siffert and Redman won the race after stirring drives by Leo Kinnunen and Elford ended with the retirement of their 908s. The factory ran all three 908/03s at the Targa, even the two Gulf-painted machines. Some spice was injected into the competition at the following Nürburgring 1,000km by allowing the Wyer team to run their own cars. Once again the /03 was the class of the field and Vic Elford claimed a brilliant victory on a course at which he – and the 908 – was making a habit of winning. The 'Ring victory again secured Porsche's second overall Manufacturers' Championship.

As in 1970, the super-light 908/03s were used in the following year's Targa and Nürburgring events. This time the cars faced an increasingly strong challenge from the rapid Alfa Romeo T33-3s. There was no doubt about the Porsche's speed, but a frightening accident to Brian Redman's car and another to Larrousse in Sicily put paid to the effort. The cars had crashed as a result of suspension failure – probably due to their extreme physical lightness. The suspensions were strengthened for the Nürburgring, and with wider rear tyres, Elford with his regular 1971 team-mate Larrousse won again. That was three wins in three years at the 'Ring for the 908.

The 908 had come to the end of its life as a factory racer at Porsche, but it was to find continuing and successful mileage in the hands of Porsche's customers. The main problem was the relatively low 350bhp power output from the two-valve 3-litre engine (at a time when a Cosworth DFV was good for 450bhp). Since 1969, Hans Mezger had been searching for a way of developing a four-valve cylinder head for the 3-litre engine, but its method of cooling (with two dimensional, top-to-bottom air cooling) was a fundamental obstacle, since the lower valves would have been

shielded. Water-cooled heads had been tested, but the development of the 917 and later the turbocharged Can-Am engine had prevented the ideas being taken further. With Ferdinand Piëch's departure from Porsche in 1971, the era of big-budget racing ended. There would be no new development of a water-cooled 3-litre. The future had become turbocharging.

Reinhold Joest achieved a good third place at Le Mans in 1972 with a 3-litre long-tail 908 (and carrying 100kg of lead to meet the new 650kg regulations). He proved the

Brian Redman shows what is meant by street racing in the 1971 Targa Florio.

car's durability by taking a third at Monza and winning the Kyalami 9 Hours at the start of 1973. Joest again ran a conventional 3-litre in 1975, picking up some useful placings in the Manufacturers' Championship as Alpine's new turbocharged car proved extremely unreliable. Joest ran to fourth place at Le Mans that year. After the Carrera Turbo's second place at the 1974 Le Mans, the durability of the more powerful turbocharged six-cylinder engine would make it an option for the 908. Joest (like several others) rebuilt his by now much-modified 908 with the tall, but short, six-cylinder – with all its plumbing – wedged into the tail.

Joest ran the 2.14-litre turbo car in the 1976. Unofficially termed the 908/04, it ran with 917/30-inspired long-tail bodywork and scored a lucky victory at the Nürburgring 1,000km against the championship series dominating Alpine-Renaults and the brand new, black-painted 936 prototype. With teething troubles cured however, the 936 would prove a more suitable chassis for the turbo engine. At Le Mans, Joest's car would run to seventh place, while the 936 scored a dazzling first-time out victory. The 908 had finally met its match.

Engineering

In its first form, the 908 could have easily been mistaken for the earlier 907. The big difference was the engine. Designed by Hans Mezger's small *Rennabteilung* (Racing Department) design office, the new 3-litre was based on the proven six-cylinder 901. It was thought the new engine might be used in a new production car at some point in the future.

Adding two cylinders with the same bore and stroke as the 901 engine yielded a capacity of 2,921cc. Where the engine differed in principle from the six was its cylinder heads. These used experience gained with the 1967 916 experimental engine which demonstrated that chain-driven twin overhead camshaft layout could have very effective benefits even with a two-valve cylinder head design. However, Mezger's aim was to develop a basically simple powerplant that avoided the highly skilled assembly of the earlier four cam engines. Initially producing around 330bhp, the new dry-sumped engine used a development of the axially-fed crankshaft lubrication system used on the earlier eight-cylinder engine, but instead of a gear-driven blower, a toothed belt was used. As was almost the norm in

Opposite: Gijs van Lennep hurls the nimble 908/3 around the Nürburgring in 1971. With Helmut Marko, he would finish third in the 1,000km race. Two weeks later the pair would win Le Mans in a Martini 917K. (GP Library)

A pit stop for the 1970 Targa Florio-winning 908/03. Brian Redman pulls off his gloves as he watches Siffert buckle in. Supervising from the pit counter are Ferdinand Piëch (in raincoat) and to his left, Helmut Bott. Behind them John Wyer observes (Porsche ran the Gulf cars at the 1970 race), while Peter Falk (seated) checks the time sheets.

Opposite: A revealing view of the 908/03 at the 1970 Targa Florio shows the pedals ahead of the front suspension line. The oil radiator must have been an excellent foot warmer.

a Porsche racing engine by this time, there was extensive use of lightweight materials, particularly magnesium alloy and titanium.

The first runs revealed various development problems. The constantly varying speed of the cooling fan and the resultant shock loads placed on the non-slipping toothed drive belt led to a single and then a double V-belt arrangement. Only when a viscous coupling was incorporated into the drive (in 1970) did the drive finally become reliable.

The main problem in 1968 was not speed, but reliability. The engine was thought to be the main source of particularly ruinous vibrations and all through the season, there was a continuous stream of broken brackets, linkages and bearings which stopped the 908 from showing its true worth. The engine was designed originally with a two-plane crankshaft which allowed each bank of cylinders to be considered as a separate engine. However, this was found to be the source of the vibrations and accounted for many of the 1968 retirement problems that the 908s experienced.

By May 1968, a new engine was running with a counterbalanced crankshaft and a new firing order to reduce the vibrations. Over the summer, this was developed into a reliable 350bhp unit. The capacity was edged right up to the 3-litre limit (2,997cc) by adding a further 1mm to the bores in time for the 1968 Le Mans.

A new six-speed gearbox was developed for the 908 which used dry sump lubrication to reduce the loss of power due to oil churning. This gearbox had been first used on the open 910 hillclimb machine, but was considered too heavy for such sprinting. The very compact diameter tripleplate clutch was located at the rear of the gearbox, with the transmission from the engine by means of a long shaft through the gearbox itself. This arrangement was said to give a faster change than a conventional layout. But the weight of this unit played heavily on the Porsche engineers' minds. A new gearbox was designed, the 916, which offered five forward speeds and reverse and used a single-plate clutch between the crankshaft and the differential. This unit used a novel jet spray lubrication system with an external gear pump as well as conventional splash lubrication.

The aluminium space-frame chassis and the coupé body of the 908 was almost identical to the 907. The first cars carried over the small 13in diameter wheels running 11.5in wide front and 13.5in wide rear tyres. At the 1968 Le Mans test weekend, the 80bhp increase offered by the 3-litre engine (over the 2.2-litre eight) yielded only 2.5mph (4kph) increase in maximum speed. This stark fact underlined the higher importance of body aerodynamics over sheer engine power on the long Hunaudières Straight, but said nothing of the courage of the drivers who achieved

these speeds in cars that were right on the edge of controllability. By the race itself, the 908s were using suspensioncontrolled flaps as had been tried previously on the hill-climb car, but these seemed to offer little in the way of confidence at high speeds.

While 1968 became a learning year for the 908s, 1969 was the year the car delivered. The minimum weight limit for prototypes was eliminated and the rule defining a minimum height for the windscreen was dropped also. With so much knowledge of reduced-weight engineering, the regulations were tailor-made for the engineers at Porsche – if they could find reliability. The American races were not encouraging. At Daytona, all the long-tails retired when an experimental aluminium intermediate shaft had broken. A month later at Sebring, the new 908/02 spyders faltered with broken rear chassis frames.

The frames were reinforced by reinstating the triangular pyramid used on the coupés, and from Brands Hatch onwards, the 908s proved to be the dominant force in 1969. The Brands Hatch race also marked the first use of Firestone tyres (rather than Dunlops), the Siffert/Redman car winning with the American tyres.

The spyder's aerodynamics were revised in time for the Nürburgring 1,000km. The new body (called 'sole' or 'flounder' around the works) had lost all the earlier car's rounded curves and featured a flat top – hence the piscine references. Top speed was increased by 10mph (16kph) at the 'Ring. But the very low drag was also their downfall and two of the three new cars were written off during official practice.

For Le Mans 1969, the three 908 long-tail coupés ran with their suspension-controlled rear flaps fixed, in response to an FIA edict banning moveable aerodynamic devices. The fourth 908 was a special-bodied long-tail version of the spyder. This car was not a full long-tail and featured abbreviated vertical fins on the rear body. The car was timed at 174mph (280kph) on the Hunaudières Straight, but retired with a 'cooked' gearbox. The new, enclosed tail had choked cooling airflow to the engine compartment. It was during the continued development of this car shortly afterwards that Peter Falk had a nasty accident in testing at Hockenheim.

It was the pressure to win the championship in 1969 and the 917, that prevented the 908/03 from being developed until the winter of that year. This was a completely revised approach to the challenge of providing an agile, very lightweight machine for the twistier courses. The late 1968 909 developed for Mitter's European Hillclimb campaign provided most of the knowledge required for the chassis, while the 3-litre engine received only detail

SPECIFICATION
1971 908/03 Spyder

Engine: Mid-mounted type 901/20 air-cooled eight-cylinder with two chain operated camshafts per bank and two (sodium-filled) valves per cylinder. Dry sump lubrication with magnesium alloy crankcase and aluminium alloy cylinder heads, alloy barrels with chromium-plated bores. Forged, single-plane steel crankshaft supported in nine plain main bearings with lightweight flywheel. Single-piece titanium connecting rods with forged aluminium alloy pistons. Bosch 12-volt electrical system with crankshaft-driven single distributor with contactless transistor ignition and two spark plugs per cylinder. Bendix fuel pump supplying petrol to Bosch eight-plunger mechanical fuel injection (continuous). Bosch alternator. Vertical cooling fan driven by twin V-belts with fluid coupling in blower hub.

Capacity: 2,997cc

Bore/Stroke: 85mm/66mm

Maximum power: 360bhp at 8,400rpm

Maximum torque: 320Nm at 6,600rpm

Compression ratio: 10.4:1

Transmission: Type 910 full synchronised five-speed gearbox with dry sump lubrication with gears placed ahead of the differential and rear axle line. Single-plate Fichtel & Sachs clutch. Half-shafts with two Hookes-type joints with a single Guibo rubber doughnut.

Chassis/body: Multi-tubular aluminium space-frame two-seat spyder chassis with mid-engine location and very lightweight PVC foam/thermoset plastic sandwich bodywork. 120-litre total fuel capacity in two sill-mounted aluminium tanks.

Suspension and steering: Front and rear double steel wishbones with rising rate geometry and titanium coil springs over telescopic Bilstein gas shock absorbers. Adjustable anti-roll bars. Rack and pinion steering. Titanium front and rear hub units.

Brakes: Drilled and ventilated steel discs with aluminium alloy calipers with two steel pistons.

Wheels and tyres: 11in wide front, 15 or 17in wide rear, 15in diameter magnesium alloy wheels with centre lock fixing. Firestone racing tyres.

Weight: 565kg

Length: 4,113mm

Height: 675mm (body only)

Wheelbase: 2,300mm

Track (f/r): 1,542mm/1,564mm

Performance: Acceleration: 0 to 62.5mph (100kph): N/A

Maximum speed: 172mph (277kph) (Porsche Museum)

improvements. The most notable feature of the new car was the layout of the major components, planned to achieve a very low polar moment of inertia. This effect can be simply described as controlling the rate at which the car wants to change direction. A very agile car will change direction quickly and this is what the racing driver seeks in the ideal car. The downside is that such a car can be tricky to drive on the edges of its handling performance.

In the 908/03, the driver was located well forward and nearly on the longitudinal centre-line of the car (with only a vestigial second 'passenger' seat) for improved weight distribution. The engine was therefore positioned around the centre of gravity and a new housing was designed for the gearbox which positioned the gear cluster ahead of the differential and rear axle line. The aluminium chassis was the minimum required to do the job and the body panels were made of a sandwich composite of PVC foam and epoxy material. Visually, the car looked very different from the 'flounder' /02. The tail was completely open and the stubby nose very short. The body of the /03 weighed a mere 12kg.

The experiments in braking systems that had continued since the Carrera 6 had led to a progressive performance convergence of the steel-based discs with the feather-light but still marginally durable beryllium units. Drilling the ventilated steel discs produced not only a worthwhile weight saving, but also an unexpected improvement in braking efficiency.

So how much better was the /03 over the 1969 spyder? In taking pole position for the 1970 Nürburgring 1,000km, Siffert knocked some 17 seconds off his pole time in the /02 spyder in 1969. It was *that* much better!

The improvements made for the 1971 outings to Sicily and the 'Ring centred on the aerodynamics. Around the lower edge of the nose, a 30mm horizontal tab (which in later years would be called a splitter) was added that was found to reduce the amount of air going under the car. At the rear, two large vertical fins improved the downforce and stability without an increase in drag. Wider 17in tyres improved the grip, while the now mandatory on-board extinguisher system was fitted along with a stronger, diagonally braced roll-over bar.

Three cars were converted to the 908/04 specification in 1975 to run in the Manufacturers' Championship and the (struggling) European Interserie. The major change was the switch to the 2.14-litre ATL engine developed for the Turbo-Carrera. The conversion involved improved gearbox lubrication and providing a very large scoop on the rear deck to keep everything cool. At the same time, the cars adopted most of the bodywork, suspension and braking components of the 917/10.

DOUBLE HEADER – 917

THE RACING WORLD WAS thrown into turmoil in 1967 when the sport's governing body, the FIA, announced from Paris that the Group 6 prototype sports car class would be restricted to an engine capacity of 3-litres from the start of the following season. Group 4 limited production sports cars would be restricted to 5-litres capacity.

Sports car racing at that time was enjoying a classic 'high' with Ford taking its second win at Le Mans with the 7-litre Mk 2s, in the face of stern opposition from Ferrari's delectable 4-litre 330P4s and Chaparral's lone ranger 2F coupé. Following that year's Le Mans, events suggest that the FIA made the decision after they learned that Ford had decided to pull the plug on their mega-budget racing effort. There was much talk that the Franco-centric governing body wanted to give their own side an opportunity to win. Both Alpine and Matra (in particular) were developing new cars for 1968.

In the event, Ferrari and Chaparral declined to continue, the Texan cars never to venture outside North America again. Despite the opportunity, the French makes failed to produce any contenders of worth for many years to come – and that would only come after more deft work with the red pen in Paris. Porsche had much to gain from a 3-litre prototype limit and although team manager Huschke von Hanstein joined others in objecting to the very short notice of the change given, he also gave his own racing department ample time to consider their options for the new class. The *Rennabteilung* immediately set to work designing a new 3-litre engine that would form the basis of the 908 sports car.

The unanswered question hanging over the Porsche strategy concerned the competitiveness of the 5-litre cars. That question was answered by mid-season 1968, by which time John Wyer's venerable GT40s had taken victories at Brands Hatch, Monza and Spa and despite Porsche's best efforts with the 907 prototypes. But there was another

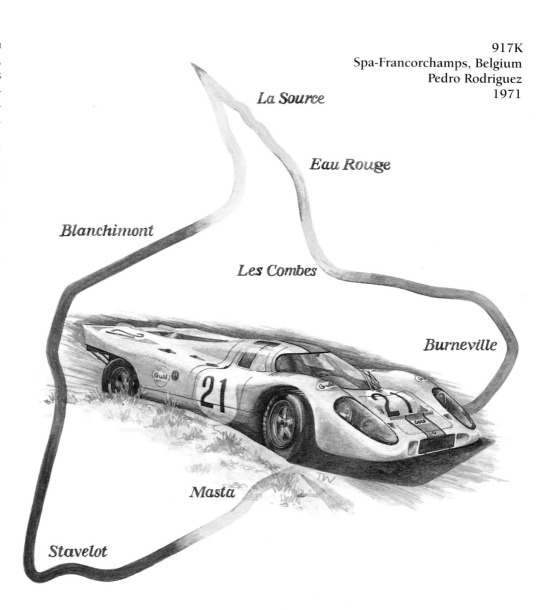

917K
Spa-Francorchamps, Belgium
Pedro Rodriguez
1971

La Source

Eau Rouge

Blanchimont

Les Combes

Burneville

Masta

Stavelot

shock in store for Zuffenhausen. Concerned with the poor calibre of the grids in the new formula, the FIA gave notice in April of that year – the same month the 908 made its first appearance at the Le Mans test weekend – that for 1969, the requirement to build 50 cars to qualify for the 5-litre class would be relaxed to 25. The intention was to make the class more attractive to smaller manufacturers of advanced sports cars.

During this time Ferrari had been keeping a watching brief on sports car racing. From Monza – in May – onwards, rumours began to circulate that Maranello were planning to build a series of 25 5-litre cars to qualify them for the sports car class. When the Wyer Fords took first and second at the Watkins Glen 6 Hours in July, Piëch needed no further persuading. Porsche would design a 5-litre car and build 25 of them. The further crushing defeat by the GT40 at the September Le Mans only reinforced the view that a 3-litre car might not be enough.

It was a spectacularly risky idea for a company as small as Porsche, especially as the intention was that the car would embody a very advanced specification. It would carve a

A peek under the rear bodywork of one of the original 1969 long-tail 917s. These cars had suspension-controlled rear flaps and the linkage can be seen in this view. Note also the mandatory spare wheel.

substantial slice out of Porsche's total turnover to undertake such a project. But Piëch used all his contacts (unsubstantiated reports allege both internal and external), plus significant resourcefulness to secure the budget his engineers would need for the task. Once budget approval had been secured, the only problem was finding the time to complete the job and ensure the new car was homologated in time for the start of the 1969 season.

Building 25 racers was not such an outrageous idea if there had been time to spread this over the course of a season and Piëch's policy of providing his drivers with new cars for the major endurance events had resulted already in these numbers of 910s and 907s being produced. More importantly for the balance sheet, there had been no shortage of willing customers for these one-race-old factory prototypes. But even if the money was no problem, to build 25 racing cars at once was an enormous design, development and logistics task.

The autumn and winter of 1968–69 at Porsche was surely one of the most exciting times in the company's history. It was a time when it seemed like the whole company was drawn in to the spirit of competition as the 917 took shape. While this was happening, it was also acknowledged that the 908 would probably still form the backbone of the new season's championship challenge – at least for the first half. It was well known that the 908 still needed more time and effort to have its reliability sorted out and be made faster.

Hans Mezger, head of the racing design department at the time says there were up to seven designers on the chassis and about the same on the new engine, with a single designer for the transmission. The design of the new car, known as type 917, was a small, highly focused exercise. It needed to be because the process had to be very short to allow all the long lead-time parts (such as castings and forgings) to be made. Mezger covered all his options during the design by ordering some key parts in several materials, or producing components with different designs. In this way he cut out (albeit at a cost) the iterative design and build process that consumes so much conventional development time.

If the motor racing community thought Porsche was reaching a climax with the new 3-litre 908 to win the 1969 championship, they would be very much mistaken. To echo another's famous words: they had not yet begun to fight.

Race record

The full kit of parts to build the first 917s was available in March 1969 and the first car was displayed at the Geneva

Motor Show that month. The sensational debut in front of the world's press was unlike that given to any previous Porsche racing car and, in typical Piëch style, placed huge pressure on his own people to get the untried car actually racing. The first trials were not encouraging. In fact, they were positively bad. The April test weekend at Le Mans showed the new 917 long-tail (or *langheck*) to be very unstable at high speed. Further trials followed at Spa but the wayward behaviour was far from understood. With the new 908 spyder proving to be a very fine racing car, few of the team's top drivers wanted to know about the 917 while they had a chance for the championship. At Spa Gerhard Mitter drove a single 917, which many years later drew a philosophical 'he was a brave man, yes' from development engineer Peter Falk, while David Piper and Frank Gardner were contracted to put some miles on the car at the Nürburgring 1,000km. The problem for Falk and the other engineers was that they had no time to give to the 917. All their efforts were focused on the 908 – improving its finishing record and chasing improved performance to keep the still-canny Wyer GT40s at bay.

Two drivers saw something in the 917 that was missed by the rest. Both Vic Elford and Rolf Stommelen wanted to drive the big cars at Le Mans. Stommelen's motives were probably only that he wanted to blitz the field and capture the headlines before walking away the hero from a smoking car. Vic Elford believed he could go much further and with a measure of mechanical sympathy, actually win the race. He convinced the chief of the Experimental Department, Helmut Bott, that the 917 should run when Bott had really only planned to run the 908s. Elford teamed up with another driver known for consistency, Dickie Attwood. The two 917s were undoubtedly the class of the field that year and true to form, Stommelen fish-tailed out of the pole slot to lead Le Mans until the car was slowed and then stopped by various problems after only a few hours. Elford and Attwood in contrast, drove their car with the lightest of touches and confounded everyone by leading all through the night and next morning. With just three hours to go, the clutch bell-housing fractured and that was that. The problem had shown up during testing, but there had been no time to fix it.

When none of the regular drivers wanted to race the early 917, David Piper and Frank Gardner were given the task. They brought the 917 home to eighth place in the Nürburgring 1,000km, despite the famously poor handling.

The 917 was brought out again for the final event of 1969 at the new Österreichring. It was August and the cars had still received relatively little development save for tweaks to improve the brake cooling and suspension. At this time it was thought the solution to the high-speed stability lay both in the suspension and in the aerodynamics. And, because Ferdinand Piëch was obsessive about his cars having minimum drag, the main work went into the suspension. Siffert and Ahrens brought the unliked car home first. But after the end of the race, Helmut Bott asked his engineers to look at the aerodynamics more closely. The small rear flaps were now set vertically and yet appeared to be useless.

At this time, development engineer Helmut Flegl was criss-crossing the Atlantic supporting Jo Siffert run an open version of the 917 called the PA in the Canadian-American Challenge. This car had been a very quick workshop conversion from a coupé, so that Siffert could compete in the Can-Am races after the July Watkins Glen sports car race. The car was run out of Richie Ginther's workshop in California and benefited immediately from the American's in-depth knowledge of the effects of spoilers on racing cars. With its 4.5-litre engine, the PA was never going to challenge the dominant McLarens for overall victory, but Siffert enjoyed a very satisfactory – and profitable – Indian summer picking up points for the minor placings. Flegl, meanwhile, received a crammer course in racing car aerodynamics, Can-Am style.

After the end of the European season Piëch announced that John Wyer would run the works 917s in 1970 and 1971. The two racing teams came together for the first time at a pivotal test session in October at Österreichring. The test resulted in the definitive body shape for the 917, gelling together the previous Ford aerodynamics experience of the Wyer engineers with Falk and Flegl's own ideas. The sharply upswept short-tail (or *kurzheck*) and a new nose profile would transform the handling and turn the 917 into the car of every racing driver's dreams.

At the first event, the Daytona 24 Hours, the two pristine Gulf 917Ks came face to face with the principal competition. Ferrari were there with their much-rumoured new 512S sports car, but so was another 917K – entered by Porsche Konstruktionen of Salzburg, Austria. The supposedly 'customer' 917K team would be a continuing irritation to the Gulf cars throughout the season.

The news that Ferrari had built their own 5-litre challenger was a huge boost for the 1970 Manufacturers' Championship. Not since 1967 had there been a serious head to head between two established constructors and here were two of the best – and with heavy-metal sports

cars as well! The 512S came with impeccable credentials and was developed under the leadership of Ing. Forghieri – acknowledged as one of the leading racing car engineers of his generation.

At Daytona, the Gulf-Porsches won first time out with new Wyer drivers Pedro Rodriguez and Leo Kinnunen heading Siffert and Redman. The Jacky Ickx/Mario Andretti 512S struggled home third, afflicted with what appeared to be a host of new car problems.

Sebring witnessed a disaster as all the Gulf 917Ks suffered failure of a new front wheel hub design, while both Salzburg 917Ks retired also. Only some very rapid driving by Mario Andretti in the 512S in the closing stages prevented actor Steve McQueen and Peter Revson winning the race in their 908 Spyder.

It may have been run in torrential rain conditions, but the BOAC 1,000km at Brands Hatch was one of those races that are fondly remembered. After an early black flag incident, Pedro Rodriguez probed the limits of his own sublime skills and the 917K's potential to dominate a race

Opposite: In a photograph that captures all the chilly dampness of an early Sunday morning at the Sarthe, Vic Elford sweeps the 1969 917 long-tail through Maison Blanche. Elford and Dickie Attwood would dominate the race until a cracked bellhousing robbed them of victory three hours from the end. (GP Library)

Possibly Pedro Rodriguez's greatest race came in the 1970 Brands Hatch 1,000km. After a black flag incident, he drove for around 5½ hours in torrential rain to win by five laps.

Consistency paid off for Hans Herrmann and Richard Attwood at the 1970 Le Mans 24 Hours. Affected by prolonged rain, all the favourites dropped out and left the Salzburg 917K at the front. It was Porsche's first overall win at the Sarthe.

where many had difficulty just staying on the track. Trailing by five full laps came Vic Elford after an almost-solo demonstration of rapid wet weather driving, leading home the second Salzburg 917K of Attwood/Herrmann. After the disappointments of Sebring, it appeared Porsche were on a roll. With more effective Girling brakes, Rodriguez and team-mate Kinnunen headed three Ferraris at the Monza 1,000km. But the three other 917Ks had all hit problems at this event and there were signs Ferrari were turning the 512 into a front-line contender. But if there were any doubts left about the superiority of the 917K, they evaporated at Spa. Fitted with a new 4.9-litre version of the flat twelve, the two Gulf cars were in a class of their own for sheer speed. Siffert and Redman won and after Rodriguez/Kinnunen retired, Ickx and John Surtees finished on the same lap in their 512S. Vic Elford and Kurt Ahrens brought a 4.9-litre Salzburg 917K into third place.

Le Mans that year did not go John Wyer's way, but it did for Porsche. Three Gulf 917Ks were entered and all three retired. In a race greatly affected by heavy rain, only seven cars were running at the end, headed by the Salzburg 917K of Dickie Attwood and Hans Herrmann. Porsche had finally achieved the ambition – to win Le Mans – that had begun almost 20 years previously.

The two remaining championship events of 1970 both fell to the Wyer cars. Rodriguez and Kinnunen overcame a very healthy challenge from their team-mates Siffert and Redman at Watkins Glen, with both cars finishing on the same lap after 6 hours (and three laps ahead of the Andretti/Ignazio Giunti 512S). The Österreichring 1,000km nearly caused an upset when Jacky Ickx drove away from everyone in a new model of the 512. He retired and Siffert/Redman were leading easily until their engine

went off-song. The second-placed Alfa Romeo, driven by Henri Pescarolo began to close rapidly until, with just two laps to go, the Milanese engine blew. Porsche became constructors' champions for the second year running.

The reality of 1971 was that the 917 in all its forms proved its worth as one of the great racing cars of our time. Faced with the prospect of a strong challenge from the much-improved Ferrari 512M and the ever-improving Alfa Romeos, Porsche had to raise the 917's game to have a realistic chance of another championship. The internal competition did not get any easier either, the Porsche Salzburg team re-emerging as the strongly works-supported Martini Racing Team in 1971.

After a Gulf-Porsche victory led by Siffert and new co-driver Derek Bell at the Buenos Aires 1,000km in early January (this race being tragically marred by the death of Ignazio Giunti in the prototype Ferrari 312P), there was a shock in store for Porsche at Daytona. Ferrari sold a 512M to American Roger Penske and through outstanding preparation, his star driver, Mark Donohue, snatched pole position from all the 917s. But poor reliability would dog the big Ferrari. Pedro Rodriguez, with his new partner Jack Oliver, would win for Gulf-Porsche. At Sebring, it was the same race story. Blinding speed from the dark blue Penske Ferrari and then retirement. But this time it was Vic Elford who came through a gruelling 12 Hours to win for the new Martini team.

The Penske Ferrari would not be seen again until Le Mans, but at the first European round – at Brands Hatch – Alfa Romeo won from the improving 312P after the 917s ran into problems and Siffert/Bell could only finish third. Two 3-litre cars had beaten the 5-litre. But the next two courses were made for the big Porsche. First came Monza. Running full 5-litre cars and a new lower drag, finned short-tail, the two Gulf-Porsches flew away from their opposition. Rodriguez set a new outright course record of just over 154mph (248mph), which the Formula One cars only just beat by a fraction the following September.

If any course was made for the 917, then it had to be Spa-Francorchamps. The 'old, real Spa' as Vic Elford calls it. In practice Derek Bell shattered the lap record with a time of 3 minutes 16.0 seconds around the 8.76-mile (14.09km) track – an average speed of no less than 160.88mph (258.86kph).

Now Spa is not like Monza at all. It is not a series of straight straights linked by readily learned corners. For motor racing fans of a certain generation, Spa is the Mecca of motor racing. The course can be found near the E42 motorway near Malmedy in Eastern Belgium. Set in the richly forested and rolling hills of the Ardennes, it is somehow appropriate that a landscape that has for centuries been known as the battlefield of Europe should become the most respected battlefield in motor racing.

Dating from the 1920s, Spa vied with Reims for the title of being the fastest racing circuit in Europe. Made up of public roads, the course was notable for its significant elevation changes and very demanding high speed corners. Spa could not have been more different than the Nürburgring, located some 75 miles (120km) away in Germany. While both courses required instinctive skill and a fair dose of courage to drive quickly, Spa was fast, very fast.

The startline for the old course began on the hill down from La Source Hairpin, the only second-gear bend on the course. There followed what was possibly, the most famous corner in motor racing – Eau Rouge – a left-right-left 'S'

bend that dived and then rose sharply, ever willing to unsettle the nervous car or driver. The road went up the hill to the blind, left-turning crest that was Les Combes and then downhill at maximum speed towards the daunting Burneville curve. Speed through there was critical for a fast run along the Masta Straight. The brave drove this at over 150mph (240kph), unfazed by the corners of houses, telegraph poles and ditches that stand like tank traps waiting for the slightest mistake. In its time, the Masta Straight was one of the fastest places on Earth and the left-right kink halfway along tested the resolve of those who called themselves racing drivers. In 1971, the best said they could take the Masta kink flat out in a 917K – close to 230mph (370kph) – but others would admit to an inevitable pedal lift. The long, long climbing right-hand bend that marks the modern Stavelot Corner must have

The Brands Hatch 1,000km in 1971 was not a good showing for the Gulf-Porsches. Here, mechanic Peter Davies marshals Jo Siffert out of the crowded pits, while Pedro Rodriguez looks on. Behind the car, mechanic Gordon Wingrove (in Gulf anorak) looks worried while Jack Oliver is interviewed. Siffert and Derek Bell would finish a troubled third, while Rodriguez and Oliver retired. (LAT)

been short relief by comparison before the headlong thrash once more back up the valley, through Blanchimont and returning to La Source.

Today we can only look at the old Spa course in awe. It is narrow and bumpy and although the Masta is scarred by a thoughtlessly placed road junction, it is a place where you can – should – stop, breathe the crisp forest air and listen for the sound of 917s urgently echoing around the hills.

In that 1971 race, the two Gulf 917s battled wheel to wheel and when Rodriguez and Siffert had done their maximum time behind the wheels, it was left to Derek Bell and Jack Oliver to continue the high speed scrap. Siffert, convinced by now that the Wyer team were favouring his arch grand prix rival Rodriguez, frantically tried to signal Bell to overtake Oliver. But Bell held station and finished mere seconds behind. The Spa 1,000km in 1971 went into the record books as the fastest ever road race with an average speed of 154.77mph (249.02kph. Siffert's fastest lap averaged over 162mph (260kph).

For their final appearance as full works cars, the 917s came to Le Mans ready to win and break more speed records. The new long-tails had proven themselves far more stable than previous years and Oliver was the first to probe the maximum speed, calculated to be in the region of 246mph (396kph) on the Hunaudières Straight. The long-tails at Le Mans were around 20mph (32kph) faster than the two short-tails and the curvaceous 917/20 coupé also entered. But it was a short-tail – a Martini car – that won. Entered by the works as more of an experiment (like the 917/20) than with a serious expectation of winning, the Gijs van Lennep/Marko car was using a magnesium alloy chassis and cross-drilled ventilated disc brakes whose robustness for the 24 Hours was far from proven. Wyer was sure he was going to win in 1971, but it was not to be. The long-tails had the legs on the Penske Ferrari, for the only

Opposite: A man in a serious hurry! Pedro Rodriguez absolutely on the limit in the Gulf-Porsche 917K at Spa in 1970. He set a new outright lap record that averaged over 160mph. (GP Library)

Helmut Marko (here) and Gijs van Lennep were the surprised winners of the 1971 Le Mans 24 Hours in this Martini 917K. The car had an experimental magnesium alloy chassis and used perforated disc brakes for the first time in a long endurance race. (LAT)

time, but all the leading cars ran into trouble during the race. While the Ferrari (one of nine 512s entered) failed early, so did the 917 long-tails. The sole surviving Gulf 917 – a short-tail – driven by 1970 winner Attwood and Herbert Müller came home second after its own night to remember.

Porsche had won Le Mans once more with the 917, but it was to be the last time. With sports car racing changing to a 3-litre engine formula for 1972, development of the 917 coupés came to a halt after Le Mans. There were two more championship races, one of which produced another inspirational drive from Pedro Rodriguez at the Österreichring. Sadly, two weeks later the great Mexican driver was dead. There was little enthusiasm for the last race at Watkins Glen and it was an Alfa that took the last championship victory of 1971.

By this time, Porsche had decided to turn their backs on European racing and were helping Jo Siffert run an open-bodied 917/10 in the Canadian American Challenge. Siffert scored some notable finishes in the relatively under-powered car, but he too would tragically lose his life later that year in a Formula One race. It robbed Porsche of another great driving talent.

The Can-Am effort had its own momentum however. Much to John Wyer's later dismay, Ferdinand Piëch had agreed a secret deal at Le Mans with Roger Penske. It would be the American, not Wyer, who would run a Can-Am team

Jo Siffert used this 5-litre, normally aspirated 917/10 in the 1971 Can-Am races. Despite his tragic death before the final round, he finished in fourth place.

George Follmer stood in for the injured Mark Donohue soon after the start of the 1972 Can-Am series and ended by winning the championship.

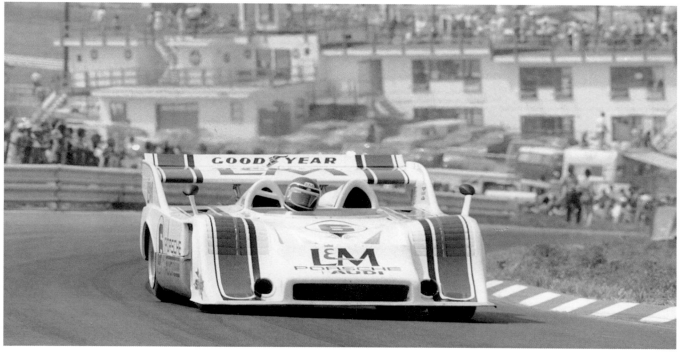

for 1972 and 1973 based around a new turbocharged version of the 917's 12-cylinder engine. Roger Penske was one who practised the business of running a racing team with astonishing attention to detail and in Mark Donohue, had a driver who gave 110 per cent whether engineering or racing the car.

After a fraught period of development, which went right up to the eve of the first race at Mosport Park in Canada, the Porsche turbo yielded the kind of technical superiority of which every race engineer dreams. Even before the green flag had been waved to start the first race, the new turbo-car threatened to blitz the Chevrolet-powered McLarens that had dominated Can-Am for so many years. Donohue's own technical contribution to the development of what was a very complex power plant was critical to the new car.

At Canada's Mosport Park, Donohue took pole, but in the race a pressure valve stuck on the new engine losing him three laps. He rejoined in ninth place and proceeded to drive around everyone in the 200-mile (320km) race except the two leaders, Hulme and Revson, in their McLarens. When they retired, Donohue collected a surprise win.

The campaign was not going to go like clockwork, however. In testing for the next race, Donohue crashed and broke his knee. After the whole development had centred around him, the team suddenly had to find a replacement driver. In George Follmer, Penske found a proven stand-in. But Follmer would go through a baptism of fire. He had no experience of the light-switch throttle characteristics of the turbo engine and no knowledge of Road Atlanta – the location of the next round of the Can-Am. But he won and after an off-pace engine and shot tyres spoiled the race at the following Watkins Glen event, he won again at Mid-Ohio. At Elkhart Lake, he won by a full lap from grand prix

The European Interserie was not as high profile as the Can-Am, but provided another arena for the turbocharged 917s. Willi Kauhsen did his fair share of the turbo engine's development and raced this Bosch-supported works car to second place in the championship.

star François Cevert in a McLaren. For the Minnesota round at Donnybrook, Donohue was back. As Follmer was now heading the championship, Penske built up another 917/10 for his lead driver. The race did not go to plan and Cevert won after Donohue picked up a puncture and Follmer ran out of fuel. By this time the McLarens were completely out-classed – even with their huge 8.34-litre V8 Chevrolets. Donohue made no mistake at the following Edmonton round, while Follmer was slowed to third place by a puncture. The Porsche Panzers (as the 917s were now nicknamed by the motorsport press) continued the roll at Laguna Seca. In practice, McLaren had tried an incredible 800bhp 9.26-litre Chevrolet – surely the largest capacity

racing engine seen in post-war international motorsport. But it was all in vain as it was Follmer's turn to win from Donohue and so take the championship. The final round at Riverside seemed routine for Donohue until he had a tyre problem and Follmer cruised home again.

The Porsche turbos had literally blown away the opposition but strangely, the total dominance was taken badly by almost everyone else. Strangely, because until Porsche entered with a full effort, McLaren had dominated the series to the point of boredom for five years. In Europe the story was largely the same in the lower profile Interserie Championship, which over its short life would be won each year by a 917 variant. Jurgen Neuhaus won the seven-

Opposite: Mark Donohue steamrollered the 1973 Can-Am championship in this Penske-entered 917/30.

In 1973, the previous year's 917/10s were outclassed by the 917/30, but provided the likes of Hurley Haywood with a strong contender for the other podium placings. Haywood finished the 1973 championship third overall.

round series in a 4.5-litre 917K in 1970 and the following three years, ex Gulf-Porsche driver Leo Kinnunen dominated in first a 'customer' 917 spyder and then a 917/10.

With the 917/30, Porsche stepped up the Can-Am effort for 1973, fully expecting both McLaren and Shadow to participate with competitive, turbocharged Chevrolet engines. The Shadow in particular had run at the final event at Riverside and despite consuming its engine in practice could have so easily turned into a real threat.

The reality was that just before the start of the season, McLaren pulled the plug on their Can-Am campaign and the Shadow never raced again with the turbo engine. It proved the point that the Porsche turbo was indeed something very special and underlined the expertise behind the effort.

Donohue had the 917/30 to himself, but the first two rounds did not go according to plan. Despite the immense pace of the new car, Donohue lost the lead – and the race – at Mosport Park after a collision with a slower car. The unlikely Charlie Kemp won, driving one of the previous year's 917/10s. Then, at Road Atlanta Donohue won the first heat by several miles, but was soaked in fuel in the second after a fuel valve burst. This time it was George Follmer, Kemp's team-mate, who climbed to the top step. But that was the only look-in the opposition would get that season. After this, Donohue steam-rollered the Can-Am. Mid-Ohio, Elkhart Lake and Edmonton all fell to the blue and yellow Porsche and then at Laguna Seca he had a scavenge pump fail and pulled off in the first heat. He made no mistake in the second heat or in the final event at Riverside. After he had taken the final chequered flag, the new champion announced his retirement from motor racing. He would return some years later, but not in the big Porsche.

In two year's of Can-Am participation, the Porsches had achieved such a level of superiority that the organisers felt moved to ban the cars. Despite being offered all kinds of inducements and concessions by Porsche to allow them to race, a new ruling was introduced which restricted fuel consumption (in a formula that previously had prided itself in having the minimum of rules). Spiralling costs and the coincident OPEC oil embargo in 1973 contrived to cripple the Can-Am in a way that it never recovered. By halfway through 1975, it was just a happy memory.

Somehow Roger Penske found a way of running the 917/30 at Mid-Ohio in 1974, with Brian Redman driving. But Redman found the car a real handful on the wrong tyres in wet and greasy conditions and came home third. It was the 917/30's last race appearance.

The world's most powerful racing car made its curtain call at the Talladega Super-Speedway in Alabama in 1975. Roger Penske asked Mark Donohue to take time out of the Penske Formula One programme to have a run at the world's closed course speed record. The effort had begun at Daytona in February 1975, but after a number of the very expensive engines had comprehensively blown, Porsche were asked to help give the engine enough reliability to run flat out for more than two minutes. It was a quite different use than that for a road racing engine. Intercoolers were added to help cool the red hot engine during its long run at full power. Donohue came back to Talladega and, with time and damp conditions working against him, he finally recorded an average speed of 221.120mph (355.782kph), beating the previous time by some 5mph (8kph). Tragically, just ten days later Donohue was killed while practising for the Austrian Grand Prix.

As for the 917/30, the world was just too small. It was a car that defeated its opposition simply by being in the paddock. And as Mark Donohue would have grinned, it was the perfect race car – a car with an unfair advantage.

Engineering

The heart of the new 917 was, like any Porsche, its engine. The Type 912 was a 180-degree, V12 with a central power take-off. Mezger's engineers had predicted 525bhp for the new engine and 540bhp was found easily on the initial bench runs. By the end of 1969, they had a reliable 580bhp. The twin spark, double overhead camshaft per bank design was restricted to two valves per cylinder by the air cooling. It was effectively two six-cylinder engines back to back. For this reason it was possible to separate the front and back exhaust packs and the 1969 cars had the front three exhausts from either bank exiting (very noisily) just behind the cockpit.

By re-using the pistons and barrels from the 3-litre 908 engine, the engine capacity came out at 4.5 litres. In late 1968, that was considered enough to win races, but the cylinder spacing was such that a full 5-litre capacity was still possible later. The central drive take-off overcame the problem of siting the driven gears at a point on the crankshaft where vibration was at a minimum. As a result the driven shafts and their bearings could be lighter. A spur gear at the crankshaft centre drove an upper accessory shaft, which in turn drove the gear drives to the four camshafts, the distributors and the fuel injection pump. The lubrication system was a further evolution of the system used on the earlier eight-cylinder engines. The central drive take-off virtually ensured the oil feed had to be through the ends of the crankshaft, but because this feed

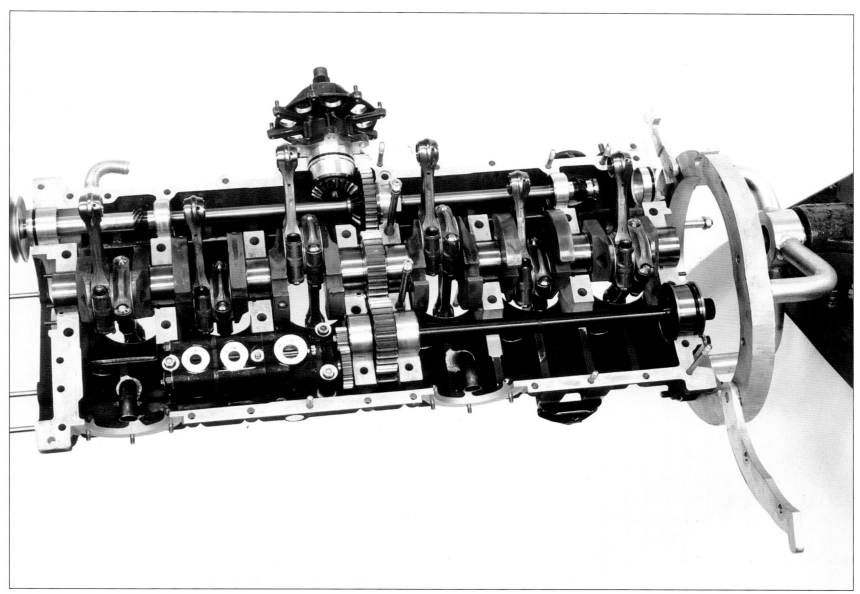

was unaffected by the rotating centrifugal forces, a much lower oil pressure could be used. Clever design of the cam lobe oil supply (so that oil was only squirted at the lobes just before the valve was lifted) meant oil circulation in the cylinder heads was kept to a minimum. Indeed, only 20 per cent of the engine cooling was performed by the lubricating oil. No fewer than six scavenge pumps resulted in an engine with very efficient lubrication and low oil splashing losses. The engine used all Mezger's experience of high technology materials and no less than 30 per cent was magnesium alloy, with extensive use of titanium alloy and aluminium. Even the cooling fan and its ducting did not

escape the weight-saving effort. Very thin section glass fibre replicated the strength/weight ratio of magnesium (this had been first tried on the 753 Formula One engine).

Another shaft, below the crankshaft, drove the transmission. This output drive layout meant the diameter of the clutch was very restricted and the 917 would use a triple-plate unit of little more than 180mm diameter. The gearbox in the 917 was always a point of contention with the drivers. The 1969 five-speed unit had a very close gate and wrong shifting became the greatest fear. Finding third instead of fifth at 150mph (240kph) was not something to joke about. For most of the 917's life as a sports car in

The insides of the type 912 12-cylinder engine. Drive from the crankshaft was taken through the central gears to two shafts above and below. The top shaft drives the cooling fan assembly and other ancillaries, while the lower shaft transmits drive to the clutch and gearbox (and also to the crankcase oil pump).

1970 and 1971, the teams preferred to run the more predictable four-speeder.

The aluminium space-frame chassis and suspension arrangement drew from the huge fund of knowledge gained with the earlier cars. The traditional Porsche 2,300mm wheelbase was well-proven and the first long-tail coupé body profile evolved directly from the 908 version (complete with suspension-controlled moving rear flaps). Although slightly wider, the 917 was actually shorter than the 908 long-tail. This reflected further extensive wind tunnel testing by Peter Falk and Helmut Flegl in the search for a reduced drag coefficient (if still not facing the problem of positive lift at high-speed).

The time available for 917 development through the 1969 sports car season was severely limited. The 1969 long-tail coupé was a very unstable machine, being nearly impossible to drive at high speed. With all the development effort going into the 908 that year, the problems with the 917 were given only minimal attention. There were changes to the suspension and tweaking with trim tabs, but the big problem remained unsolved. The brakes were given significantly improved cooling as these were found to be spongey due, it was thought, to overheating.

A special open-bodied spyder was built from one of the original 25 homologation cars and this used a body derived from the 909 hill-climb cars and the 1969 'flounder' 908/02. In North America, this spyder was extensively hacked around in the search for downforce and the combination of this experience and the alliance with the John Wyer engineers (who had helped solve the high-speed stability problems with the original Ford GT40s) resulted in a re-profiled short-tail in October 1969.

From this point the 917 was a winning machine. Improved during 1970 by edging the engine capacity up to first 4.9 litres and then a full 5 litres, power rose to a strong 630bhp. Another more refined long-tail surfaced for Le Mans but the car was still insufficiently confidence-building that the Gulf team (and the winning Attwood/Herrmann Salzburg car) elected not to use them in the race.

Over the winter of 1970–71, considerable effort went into refining the high speed aerodynamics. A parallel development effort was also run by the French SERA consultancy

Opposite: Car production at the Porsche factory almost came to a standstill while the 25 917s were built during March and April 1969.

The most elegant long-tail of them all, the 1971 917 Langheck in Martini colours driven by Elford and Larrousse.

Possibly the most powerful racing engine of the 20th century – the 5.4-litre twin turbocharged flat-twelve at high boost was capable of more than 1,500bhp.

in an attempt to evolve a shape that would have the stability of the short-tail, with the low drag of the long-tail. The car that resulted – the 917/20 – only partially met the objective, while Porsche's own development was a spectacular success. The 1971 917 long-tail remains one of the fastest, race-reliable cars ever to run at Le Mans.

John Wyer had described the upturned 1970 short-tail as 'having the aerodynamics of a grand piano' and during the season had evolved a small rear aerofoil to help reduce the

drag. During this time, Falk's team spent time analysing this arrangement and working on a lower-drag tail. The result of their efforts was a lower rear body with two vertical fins and a claimed 15 per cent less drag than the 1970 tail.

Jo Siffert went back to the Can-Am in 1971 with a new chassis developed specifically for the unlimited formula. What was not generally known at the time was that Porsche had considered running an astonishing 16-cylinder engine in the car. Mezger describes the sixteen as a simple devel-

opment of the twelve, with an extra cylinder at each corner, to give an engine that could be configured between 6 and 7.2 litres. On the dyno the 7.2-litre unit was said to produce no less than 850bhp, but the problem was its length. Fitted into a test 917PA, the change in weight distribution completely upset the handling. This effectively prevented any chance of Siffert using the engine in 1971 and he happily (and lucratively) ran with a sprint-tuned twelve producing around 650–680bhp. Any potential the sixteen might have shown was totally eclipsed by another experiment that was running during 1971. Porsche had begun to study turbocharging, first on a test six-cylinder engine and then on the twelve.

What captured the Porsche engineers' imaginations were the enormous flash power figures that the turbo engine was recording on the test dynos. But getting from a quantum-leap top end power figure to having a race-flexible engine proved to be a huge undertaking. It took the combination of Mezger, development engineer Valentin Schäffer, Helmut Flegl and the catalytic effect of American engineer/driver Mark Donohue to get to a workable – tractable – solution. The trick proved to be in the fuel delivery as the turbos were found to choke the mixture at low rpm. Schäffer spent many hours recording the engine characteristics with and without the turbos. This data was painstakingly analysed by the engineers at Bosch, and a new fuel pump – called the 'happy' pump – was delivered with a re-mapped fuel metering cam.

The resultant twin-turbocharged engine addressed the problems of throttle lag (although by today's standards this was still fairly extreme) and over-pressure. The early season 5-litre engine in 1972 had around 900bhp on race boost, with another 100bhp available when necessary.

For 1973, the capacity was enlarged to 5.4 litres, giving a race power of at least 1100bhp and significantly improved mid-range torque. This new engine was fitted into the 917/30, a completely revised chassis. The earlier cornering twitchiness of the 917/10 was addressed with a 200mm wheelbase extension and new, more powerful four-piston brakes were used. Two /30s were built, both with magnesium alloy chassis (the only magnesium chassis 917/10 was crashed by Donohue in 1972 and, it is believed, never raced). The new car looked much larger because of its coupé-style long-tail body and snow shovel nose, but it was still some way short of the original long-tail coupés (around 200mm shorter).

In anticipation of the 200-mile (320kph) Can-Am races, the 917/30 ran with a 400-litre fuel capacity. When tanked up, in project manager Helmut Flegl's own words, 'it was like a gas station!'

SPECIFICATION
1973 917/30KL

Engine: Mid-mounted type 912 air-cooled flat 12-cylinder with central power take-off from eight-plain bearing crankshaft. Layshafts to clutch and ancillary drives and gear-driven twin overhead camshafts per bank. Gear-driven horizontal cooling fan. Dry sump lubrication with seven oil pumps (one pressure and six scavenge) magnesium alloy crankcase and aluminium alloy cylinder heads, alloy barrels with nickel-silicon bores. Titanium inlet valves. Single-piece titanium connecting rods with forged aluminium alloy pistons. Twin plug Bosch ignition system with Bosch 12-plunger mechanical fuel injection. Twin Eberspächer turbochargers with driver-controlled over-pressure wastegates.

Capacity: 5,374cc

Bore/Stroke: 90mm/70.4mm

Maximum power: 1,100bhp at 8,000rpm

Maximum torque: 1,098Nm at 6,400rpm

Compression ratio: 6.5:1

Transmission: Quad plate Borg & Beck clutch with four-speed fully synchronised gearbox.

Chassis/body: Multi-tubular aluminium space-frame two-seat spyder chassis with mid-engine location. Lightweight glass fibre body with full-width rear aerofoil. 400 litres total fuel capacity in two side-mounted rubber bag tanks

Suspension and steering: Double wishbone with outboard rising rate titanium coil springs over Bilstein gas shock absorbers all round. 25 per cent anti-dive geometry at front. Driver adjustable rear anti-roll bar. Rack and pinion steering.

Brakes: Drilled and ventilated steel discs with aluminium hubs, four-piston alloy calipers.

Wheels and tyres: 12in front, 19in rear x 15in diameter magnesium alloy centre lock wheels with air extraction cones. Goodyear racing tyres.

Weight: 845kg (33 per cent front; 67 per cent rear)

Length: 4,562mm

Height: 730mm

Wheelbase: 2,500mm

Track (f/r): 1,670mm/1,564mm

Performance: Acceleration: 0 to 60mph (96.5kph): 2.1 seconds (Source: P. Frère)

Maximum speed: 231mph (372kph)

HEAVY METAL —
8
935

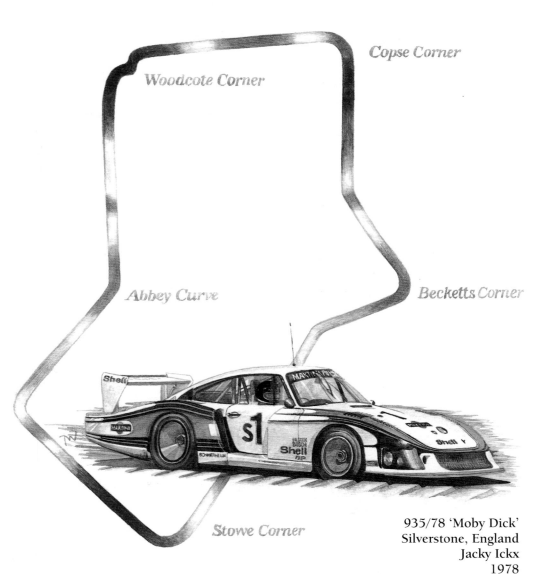

Copse Corner

Woodcote Corner

Abbey Curve

Becketts Corner

Stowe Corner

935/78 'Moby Dick'
Silverstone, England
Jacky Ickx
1978

A S THE 917 ERA CAME TO a conclusion, so the competition development of the 911 began. The material resources available after the departure of Ferdinand Piëch were far less than had been before, but the engineering talent that new Porsche head, Dr Ernst Fuhrmann, had at his disposal was almost priceless. Fuhrmann initiated a programme of development that would thrust the 911 to the forefront of the company's racing activities. Throughout the late 1960s and early '70s, the 911 had become a useful campaigner in the production GT class. Almost without anyone noticing, 911s had become the backbone of the Le Mans 24 Hours, providing a reliable, if not ultimately very rapid, platform for many private entrants.

The Carrera RS was the first sign that Porsche were not about to rest on their 917 laurels. But it was not easy for engineers who had been working at the very edge of racing car technology to suddenly turn their enthusiasm to a production-based car. Norbert Singer, who had been recruited by Porsche in April 1970, recalls the sudden change.

'It was a big change because these production cars were going to be used for, well, a little more than club sport. It was a rally car – a very good rally car in those days – and on race circuits it was quite good. But with a factory effort, it should be much more and so we started getting basic things in, like getting the torsion bars out and putting in coil springs and changing the suspension points for a better set-up. It was lots of other things. I remember we wanted to get the roll-centre higher at the rear.'

The work on the car that would become the RSR started in 1972, while the Can-Am programme was still running. The RSR was allowed an engine capacity of 2,808cc (being derived from the limited edition 2.7-litre RS) and, by using lightweight panels and components, weighed only 925kg. The 315bhp factory originals even dipped below 900kg in the search for minimum weight. Most importantly, the use of a rear spoiler (the classic 'ducktail') and a deep front air dam marked the first efforts to tame the 911's flighty high-speed aerodynamics.

'In those days lots of people said it was impossible to change the 911 in this way, that the car wasn't made for this type of modification. But we did the work and there it was.' Singer chuckles heartily at the memory. 'We raced the first two cars at Daytona [in 1973] and Peter Gregg [with Hurley Haywood] won overall. And then in May, Herbert Müller won the Targa Florio with the car!'

Straight away the car was winning world championship races and that year it also won the first European GT Championship. The 2.8-litre engine was soon enlarged to 3 litres and all the time the car's suspension and aerodynamics were being improved. The 'duck-tail' rear spoiler gave way to a new spoiler which quickly earned the name 'whale-tail' because of its shape when viewed from above, and its upturned rear edge. The road-going Carrera RS models were made in sufficient quantities to allow the race versions – the RSRs – to race in the FIA's Group 3 production GT class. Many of the later 3-litre cars were further improved to race in the Group 4 category. In this form, the 330bhp RSR would emerge as an extremely proficient customer racing car during 1974, and with their customers happy, the Weissach engineers turned to a new challenge.

'It became clear that the regulations were going to change,' says Singer. 'The 3-litre [prototype] formula was going to stop and everybody was talking about a production car formula. But the new regulations were a little late. And in '74 they made plans to apply them in '75. This was the reason we made a production race car as we thought. We had some guidelines early – how much clearance you had to have and that you had to maintain your production shape somehow. The baseline was clear and we had a car on the drawing board, so we started in the workshop. It was in '74 preparing for the '75 season. This was the Turbo-Carrera and we tried a lot of different ideas. But then they suddenly postponed the new regulations from '75 to '76!'

With all the knowledge from the Can-Am development resting unused at Weissach, it was inevitable that a boosted 911 would find its way into competition. The turbo arrangement used for the 1974 Turbo-Carrera was almost the same as the hardware for one bank of the 917/30's 12-cylinder. The resulting 490bhp 2.14-litre car (which, when factored by the regulation 1.4 was considered to equate to a 3-litre unblown engine) ran with distinction in the prototype class during 1974 against the mighty V12 Matra prototypes. The message that many took on board about 1974, especially after the 911 prototype finished second overall at Le Mans, was that Porsche had cracked the very

tough challenge of obtaining reliability with all that extra power.

Running the Turbo-Carrera in the prototype class allowed the engineers to considerably lighten the basic 911's chassis. Almost all the detachable steel body panels of the production car were replaced with lightweight glass fibre. The fuel tank was moved within the wheelbase (behind the passenger seat) to make it less sensitive to fuel weight changes and this allowed the front end of the car to be completely redesigned. At the rear, an aluminium sub-frame replaced the two longitudinal steel box sections and the rear cross-member. A full roll-over cage increased bodyshell stiffness and allowed the production dashboard (which helps with body rigidity) to be virtually eliminated. Again, for weight reasons, the torsion bars were replaced by progressive rate titanium coil springs. This in turn allowed lighter tubular front lower wishbones and at the rear, semi-trailing arms from aluminium. The Turbo-Carrera came out at around 825kg and with a torque curve that resembled the outline of the Eiffel Tower, the driver was assured of an exciting ride.

The 2.14-litre engine was extensively modified from the previous unblown racing engines and became known as the ATL (*Auspuff-Turbolader*, or exhaust turbocharger) and would feature greatly in Porsche's racing strategy for years to come. By the end of 1974, this engine was instantly recognisable not only for its single KKK turbocharger, but also because of the large air-to-air intercooler and horizontal

The RSR Turbo-Carrera claimed a surprising second place at the 1974 Le Mans 24 Hours. The car was run as a prototype and allowed the Weissach engineers to explore every aspect in the development of the 911 as a racing car.

cooling fan. The heavy turbo equipment – slung out to the rear of the rear-mounted engine – added to an already raw limitation in the Turbo-Carrera, namely the weight distribution. There was but 30 per cent of the car's weight on the front axle line. But the limitation was based more on the location of the rear engine and gearbox, rather than the actual weight of the chassis. Singer recalls that the weight saving options considered for the Turbo-Carrera went out to extremes.

'We wanted to get the weight down to that of the prototype cars, which as I remember were about 650kg. Our car was about 800kg or something. Then we had the idea like the American stock cars of those days, to get the steel bodyshell in an acid bath to make the metal thinner and to tape the pieces where we needed the strength. The thickness can come down from 0.8mm to 0.5 or 0.3mm. But it was too expensive as there was no bath to put the complete shell into. So we tried to get any possible weight out of the car and it came down to 700-something – and then you had the funny weight distributions.' Was it difficult to drive?

'Yes, for sure at the beginning! At the front we were running without any anti-roll bars and at the rear we had

17-inch wide tyres. But at least it worked.'

This was not a racing car in which you could pour on the power through a corner (although a locked rear axle did help). With the still-significant throttle delay, the Turbo-Carrera was only for the most instinctive of drivers. These characteristics make Herbert Müller's and Gijs van Lennep's second place at the 1974 Le Mans all the more impressive.

The development of the 911 took on new importance when, finally, the new regulations for the 1976 World Championship of Makes were announced. In Europe, sports car racing was regulated by the CSI (*Commission Sportive Internationale*) a committee of the FIA. The CSI defined three sports categories, namely Group 3, Group 4 and Group 5. Group 3 was for stock production grand tourers and at least 1,000 units had to have been built in one year. Group 4 allowed for limited production models where just 400 units had to be produced in two years while the new Group 5 was a silhouette formula for heavily modified GTs. Both Groups 4 and 5 were limited by a sliding scale which tied engine capacity to vehicle weight.

It was in the interpretation of the regulations for the new silhouette formula where Porsche would stretch the rule-

The first 935 was easily recognisable as being derived from the road-going 911 Turbo, although the bodyshell was lightened with glass fibre panels and clear plastic for the side windows. This is Jochen Mass at Vallelunga.

makers patience and at the same time develop a GT racing family that proudly took over the technical lead established by the much-missed 917s.

With the announcement of the 911 Turbo production car in late 1974, the basis for a comprehensive GT racing campaign was established. In Group 4, the 934 became the subtly modified offering to the company's racing customers. With the well-thumbed rule book in one hand and their slide rules in the other, project leader Norbert Singer and his fellow engineers went to work on the car that would emerge as the Group 5 935.

The coming years would produce a racing car as advanced and innovative as any Porsche had devised. 'I tried my best!' Singer grins today. 'We tried – everything.' Such was the perception of Porsche's preparations for the new GT categories, that few other manufacturers showed much interest in competing. This rather defeated the original aim of the championship which had been devised to attract the big manufacturers back into racing.

Race record

Only BMW, armed with their attractive 3.5-litre CSL 'Batmobiles', faced Porsche at the first 1976 World Championship of Makes race in Mugello, Italy. Driven by Jacky Ickx and Jochen Mass, the 935 won first time out and also the second race at Vallelunga. But this second victory was not without controversy and Porsche were forced subsequently to replace the air-to-air intercooler with a more compact water-cooled version. This upset the tune of the engine and both the following two events – the Nürburgring 1,000km and the Österriechring 1,000km – went to Munich. A further defeat came at the hands of the John Fitzpatrick/Tom Walkinshaw BMW at Silverstone when the clutch failed on Ickx right at the start of the race. But at Le Mans, the single Martini 935 gave everyone a glimpse of what was to come. Rolf Stommelen and Manfred Schurti were handicapped over the Group 6 cars on fuel tankage (120 litres compared with 160 litres) and the greater fuel consumption of their 2.85-litre motor. But despite being shunted heavily in the rear, problems with the lights and a long stop to change the turbo, the car finished fourth overall.

Porsche found themselves behind in the championship after the early season dramas and the position seemed to worsen when BMW had rolled out their own turbocharged missile at Silverstone. The Munich car proved to be very

Rolf Stommelen and Manfred Schurti demonstrated the potential of the 935 at Le Mans in 1976 when, after various delays, the car still finished fourth overall. (LAT)

The 935/77 extended the interpretation of the regulations still further, for example by clothing the whole of the production car's tail in a new aerodynamically efficient glass fibre casing. Stommelen and Schurti were unable to finish at Le Mans 1977 when the 630bhp twin-turbo engine had a head gasket fail. (LAT)

fast until it failed, but there was no doubting its potential. For the final two rounds of the championship, Porsche took along their test 935 to double their prospects of a result. It proved to be worthwhile because at Watkins Glen, although the BMW's faltered again, so did Ickx/Mass in the leading 935. Le Mans stars Stommelen and Schurti brought the second Martini 935 home first. Ickx/Mass made no mistake however at the final round in Dijon (although not until after Peterson had led comfortably and then retired in the blown BMW). There was relief indeed at Porsche as the championship for which they had worked so hard was finally won. Norbert Singer remembers the efforts of BMW to hold off Porsche's charge. 'They tried everything in '76. We had some bad races at the Nürburgring and at Zeltweg and we didn't finish. They were leading in the points and at the end we had a chance still to win the championship. We had to win in Watkins Glen and in Dijon. We were lucky to do that.'

Unfortunately, BMW decided to withdraw from Group 5 at the end of 1976, but Porsche decided to press on with the development of the 935. Over the winter, a small series of customer cars were built and it was these that would provide the principal class competition to the even more powerful factory 935/77. The 935s would win every round of the Championship of Makes in 1977, but the 935/77 developed a habit for head gasket failure. It was this that

Opposite: Porsche went to Watkins Glen knowing they had to beat BMW to win the championship. By this time the car had lost its original front wings and had acquired a full sports car tail.

The 'Baby' was an astonishing development driven by Porsche head Dr Ernst Fuhrmann's desire to show the company's technical excellence in the national motorsport arena. The 1.4-litre turbo engine produced around 370bhp.

Over the winter of 1976–77, a batch of customer 935s was produced. These became much sought after drives by professional and amateur teams. This is the Georg Loos 935 in a German national championship event, with Tim Schenken driving.

led to retirement of the single works car at Le Mans that year. What was most noticeable however, was the competitiveness of the best of the customer 935s. The Kremer cars were showing signs of extensive aerodynamic and engine development (begun the previous year), while the Georg Loos 'production' 935 ran as high as third before frustrating retirement in the 22nd hour. Customer 935s would win no less than four world championship events in 1977 to the factory's three.

It was the predictability of a 935 win in the 1977 World Championship of Makes that led to another remarkable 935 development. Norbert Singer takes up the story. 'Our Porsches were also racing in the German

national championship. There were two classes – up to 2 litres and over 2 litres. The Porsches were racing in the over 2 litre class because we had the larger engine. All the others, the Fords and BMWs, were racing in the small division and this was real racing. In the big class, it was just Porsches racing. They were all saying that we were a big company in the big class with no opponents, that the real racing happened in the small class.' When it was announced that the German national championship round at the Norisring in early July would be televised, but only for the smaller class, Dr Fuhrmann responded accordingly. Porsche would build a car that complied with the up to 2-litre class regulations. 'This was the origin of

the 'Baby'. It was just to show the others just where Porsche was.'

The 'Baby' was an astonishing development which came to the starting line barely eight weeks from its conception. The 1.4-litre turbo car was simply too new to score at the Norisring, but it won the next round at Hockenheim. 'The Norisring was just a little too early,' says Singer. 'It didn't really work, so we came back at Hockenheim. We just wanted to show we could do it. That's all.' After this the 'Baby' was retired, Dr Fuhrmann believing his company had shown the extent of his company's superiority and had thrown down the challenge to all-comers to take Porsche on in the top class.

During the winter of 1977–78, Porsche built a second 935 series based on the 935/77. At the same time, the stunning 935/78 was taking shape at Weissach. This ultra-sleek machine became known as *Moby Dick* for its lithe

profile and it was entered in just four races in the coming season.

The first time out at Silverstone, the car won by a massive seven laps. It retired at Vallelunga and the Norisring while at Le Mans it finished eighth after a catalogue of problems. In the hands of the highly experienced Stommelen/Schurti team, the outright speed of the 3.2-litre car stunned spectators, being timed at 227mph (365kph) on the Hunaudières Straight – fully 5mph (8kph) better than the winning Renault-Alpines and 17mph (27kph) faster than the 2.14-litre 936/78.

The 935/78 was a wonder car in the spirit of the 917/30. It was not raced again and the Silverstone event stands as the only marker as to its true potential. It was a complete turn-around on the result – or lack of one – that the 935/77 had achieved a year earlier.

The Silverstone 6 Hours in May had become a favourite

Once the train of events that created the concept of a heavily modified 911 Turbo was started back in 1974, the Moby Dick *almost became an inevitability. This virtual prototype racer went to the very edges of the regulations and graphically demonstrated how technology was overtaking motor racing in the 1970s*

event for sports car teams during the 1970s as its fast sweeps and high overall lap speeds made a demanding dress rehearsal for the following month's 24 Hours. The Northamptonshire circuit has acquired a charisma largely based on being one of the locations for the British Grand Prix. A former wartime bomber airfield, the old concrete runways and perimeter track formed a ready-made motor racing circuit in the late 1940s, once the aircraft had departed. More notable for its ability to thrill drivers with its opportunity for sheer speed, rather than excite the watching spectators, the first British Grand Prix was first held there in 1950. The circuit has been a popular option for this event ever since.

Rising concerns over safety in the 1980s inevitably resulted in changes to the fast layout that had prevailed from the late 1950s. By 1995, the original course had been disfigured virtually beyond all recognition, rendering the track suitable for grand prix cars and little else. Changes since then have introduced some relaxation in the zeal to take the fun out of driving there.

What the 935/78's drivers Ickx and Mass would have found at Silverstone in 1978 was a circuit that required a fair helping of courage. Despite a new chicane at Woodcote, the circuit was a flat-out blast around the outline of the old perimeter track. After the start came Copse, the first of many demanding high-speed curves. The run up a slight incline was followed by the left-right-left sweeps of the Maggotts, Becketts and Chapel. These curves were probably the most important bends on the track as it was vital to carry as much momentum as possible on to the main Hangar Straight. A heart-in-the-mouth entry into the right-hand Stowe Corner was followed by another short straight to Club Corner and up the slight slope to the left-hand sweep that was Abbey. This was followed by a straight run past the old control tower (roughly where the access bridge is today) into the flow-breaking right-left-right chicane at Woodcote and the start and finish line. The chicane had been introduced at Woodcote for the 1975 British Grand Prix and forced the cars to slow before they charged across the finish line. The chicane was inevitable and although it upset the driver's momentum around the 130mph (209kph) average track, a winning car would still need to have near-perfect stability and a driver with enough nerve to ignore the hard earth banks that lined this demanding course.

The sight of *Moby Dick* roaring around Silverstone, leaving long pouts of flame as its drivers lifted for the corners, left spectators with a profound statement about Porsche's technical supremacy in Group 5. The competition had little response to such a car, but at the season's end, and with little other manufacturer interest in the class, Porsche announced its withdrawal from racing.

However, 1979 was one of those year's which the Porsche engineers would have probably preferred to forget in terms of racing. While the Essex 936 effort ended in tears and the chosen new path of Indianapolis-style racing in North America was being nurtured, it was left to the company's now prolific 935 customer base to take up the Group 5 and International Motor Sports Association (IMSA) flags.

The Essex 936s were out before nightfall at Le Mans and the other possible candidate for overall victory – the Harley Cluxton-run Mirage-Fords – wilted soon after. It was left to the phalanx of 14 935s to produce a result, as the remaining Group 6 Cosworth runners were unable to maintain the Porsche pace. That it rained most of the Sunday made the race even more miserable. In the end, the best car did win – the heavily modified Kremer 935 K3 driven by the Whittington brothers and Klaus Ludwig, giving the 935 a notable triple. Earlier in the year both Daytona and Sebring had fallen to the big cars, starting a winning habit for the 935s in these American classics.

The 924 Carrera GTs took centre stage in the factory's attentions during 1980 and this time the non-Porsche Group 6 opposition blitzed the silhouette cars at Le Mans. However, in IMSA, the 935 had become the weapon of choice for the top competitors in the GTX category and some remarkable cars came to the line from the strongest

Moby Dick in the Silverstone pit-lane in 1978. Nowhere was the dominance of this car so marked than at the British circuit, where it won the 1,000km event by a full seven laps.

With both Essex-supported 936 entries retiring, the 1979 Le Mans was left to the Group 5 Kremer 935K3 of Klaus Ludwig, Don and Bill Whittington to overcome the IMSA-specification 935 of Dick Barbour, actor Paul Newman, and Rolf Stommelen. (LAT)

With both Essex-supported 936 entries retiring, the 1979 Le Mans was left to the Group 5 Kremer 935K3 of Klaus Ludwig, Don and Bill Whittington to overcome the IMSA-specification 935 of Dick Barbour, actor Paul Newman, and Rolf Stommelen. (LAT)

The 935K3 was a very familiar sight to drivers and spectators during sports car racing in the late 1970s and early '80s. The big Porsche became the ungainly choice of racing customers who wanted a strong, powerful racing car for endurance events. This is the Cooper, Bourgoignie and Wood car at the 1981 24 Hours. (LAT)

teams. Most of the front runners had their cars converted to the latest Kremer K3 specification, with upgrade kits provided by the factory. The 935 had become one of the best and most profitable racing cars in the company's history.

A snapshot of the car's dominance in American racing is witnessed by the entry and result for the 1981 Daytona 24 Hours, both the first round of the World Championship of Makes and the big-budget Camel GT series.

The Camel GT Championship had developed quite differently to the so-intense but cash-starved European GT racing scene. The American series had become very successful and well-funded, not least because it was the province of wealthy private teams. It was quite the norm for team owners to drive their own cars and some of these became extremely rapid racers. To achieve qualifying speed and race pace, these owners would hire professional drivers, usually well-known sports car or Indycar aces in the afternoons of their careers. By 1981, the Camel GT had become a 15-event series that appeared right across North America. The only blot on an otherwise relaxed and profitable enterprise was that IMSA race administrator, John Bishop, was growing increasingly frustrated by the total Porsche dominance of his series, the Carrera RSRs having been highly successful well before the 935s began to appear in 1977. That aside, the series usually produced good, close and competitive racing. What was more

important for the professional drivers was that it paid well and received good publicity.

Consequently, there was no shortage of well-prepared 935s in the pitlane at Daytona in 1981. Fifteen 935s were

entered and of the top ten qualifiers, nine were the big Porsches, with a Ferrari 308 in seventh position. Fastest was the Andial entry for veteran Rolf Stommelen – the evergreen Porsche driver blasting around the 3.84-mile (6.18km) speedway with its twiddling infield section at an average speed of 134mph (216kph). Other leading IMSA entries that figured in the top ten included the Ted Field Interscope car and John Fitzpatrick, making his debut as team manager, as well as driving. Reinhold Joest, the 1980 winner, shared a 935 with Jochen Mass. Jürgen Barth drove with four-times Daytona winner Hurley Haywood in Bruce Leven's 935, while Derek Bell drove another owned by Bob Akin. But the winner that year was an immaculate 3.2-litre 935 prepared and driven by the genial Bob Garretson, with co-drivers Bobby Rahal and Brian Redman. Porsche had won the Daytona 24 Hours for the fifth consecutive time.

The 935 would continue to be a force in the IMSA series into 1984, despite an increasing challenge from pure prototype chassis such as the Lola and March (both powered by Chevrolet) and the new Bob Tullius-run Jaguar XJRs. One of the saddest moments for IMSA and Porsche came with the news that Rolf Stommelen had been killed at the Riverside 6 Hours in April 1983, after the rear aerofoil of his 935 became detached in a fast curve. While the 935 had experienced a remarkable run of longevity, it was

perhaps the moment for Porsche to consider a new car for this high profile series.

Engineering

'Electrifying! Quite electrifying! This car is much more brutal than anything similar that I have driven.' That is how Derek Bell described his first experience of the Martini 935/77 in *Cars & Car Conversions* magazine in 1978. The 935 was a sledgehammer of a racing machine with raw power aplenty and little of the handling refinement expected in a more conventional sports prototype. It was a Porsche which became no less ground-breaking than any that had preceded it.

While Helmut Flegl was assigned the breakneck 936 development over the winter of 1975–76, Norbert Singer took over the preparation of the 935. Although it is easy to think the specification of the 935 was lifted directly from the 1974 Turbo-Carrera prototype, the reality was that because of the Group 5 ruling which linked the car's weight to its engine capacity, the first cars were more closely related to the new production 911 Turbo.

The Turbo-Carrera had used the 2.14-litre ATL engine, which, when factored for its turbocharger was considered to be at the class capacity limit of 3-litres. The production 911 Turbo's actual engine capacity was 3-litres, but applying the same 1.4 equivalency factor to this engine would have meant being classed as a 4.2-litre machine. This would have required the car to have a minimum weight which, for Porsche, was unacceptably high. By choosing a capacity of 2,856cc for the 935, the car's dry weight had to comply with a more attractive minimum of 970kg. The Turbo-Carrera had been extensively lightened – down to around 750kg – but much of this lightening knowledge was simply not required initially. This did not stop the 935 receiving many weight-saving details. These included plastic panels for all the add-on structures to the basic steel bodyshell, plastic side and rear windows and a comprehensive aluminium alloy roll-over cage. This did allow lead ballast to be placed in the car's front box sections and at the front of the passenger footwell, so that the dry weight distribution was a respectable (for a 911 anyway!) 40 per cent front/60 per cent rear.

The 930/72 engine was fitted with a single KKK turbocharger (being renamed KKK after Eberspächer had sold its turbo division) with a large air-to-air intercooler located over the top of the engine. With Bosch mechanical fuel injection (the Group 4 934 used K-Jetronic) and twin spark ignition, this gave an explosive 590bhp with 1.4 bar boost. An adjustable trimmer in the cockpit allowed the driver to control the boost.

The single-turbo all air-cooled engine of the 1976 935. The 2.85-litre twin-spark engine gave an explosive 590bhp on 1.4 bar boost.

The air-to-air intercooler was a lighter solution than the water-cooled system used on the 934, but it was bulkier. This gave accommodation problems under the regulation-standard spoiler mounted on the engine cover, but provided a rigid platform for the permitted extra 'biplane' rear wing mounted on top. This arrangement plunged Porsche into controversy early in the 1976 season, when the modified engine cover's side silhouette was considered outside the rules. The situation might perhaps have been negotiated with the CSI, except that Norbert Singer had already crossed their path by completely revising the front wings, moving the headlights into the front air dam and evolving a profile that fell to the front in the same line as the bonnet. This was not what the authorities had meant when they had allowed the wing profile to be 'free'. It was there to permit manufacturers to accommodate wider tyres! The stand off resulted in Porsche having to change to the more compact water-to-air intercoolers to re-establish the production Turbo's engine cover profile, but the sloping nose was allowed to stay. The radiators for the water inter-coolers were located just ahead of the rear wheels and resulted in large openings to draw in cooling air. Remarkably, the intercoolers yielded a full 100°C reduction in the inlet air charge, while the new front wings improved the car's penetration and stability in side winds. Louvres over the front wheels helped further with brake cooling.

In most other areas, the steel bodyshell itself was recog-nisable as a production item. The 911 Turbo's cast rear swing arms formed the basis of a sufficiently stiff rear sus-pension, and like the revised front suspension, used rising rate titanium coil springs. There were front and rear anti-roll bars, with the rear one being adjustable by the driver.

The brakes were carried over from the 917, with aluminium four-piston calipers acting on 32mm thick drilled and ventilated discs. As with the earlier 917s, the brakes were not drilled for Le Mans, to reduce the opportu-nity for cracking. Like the big Can-Am cars, keeping the brakes cool was a major concern. Large ducts in the front air dam carried cooling air to shrouds which enveloped the trailing area of the discs. The same air extractor vanes that had been used on the 917/30 were adopted on the front wheels in time for Le Mans.

The winter of 1976–77 saw no let up in the develop-ment of the 935. The 1977 model took to the tracks with significant changes as Singer capitalised on three important changes to the Group 5 regulations that were actually aimed at improving the chance's of the 935's competition! BMW in particular had struggled to find enough power with their turbocharged 3.0 CSL and initially had lobbied for more freedom. When the 935 began to make a habit of

The 935's brakes were carried over from the 917 sports car, being four-piston alloy calipers working on 35mm thick cross-drilled ventilated discs. Cooling air was closely ducted on to the front of the disc. The rising-rate titanium coil spring can just be seen behind the upper wishbone assembly.

winning mid-season, the rule-makers began to look for ways to enliven the championship. To help those manufac-turers with front-engine cars that wished to run tur-bocharged engines, three key changes were made to the regulations. First, extra space was permitted (supposedly for the new turbo ductwork) in the engine compartment by allowing the firewall to be moved up to 200mm into the cabin. To find enough space downstream of the exhaust manifolding to site the turbo installation, they allowed the floor to be defined at the level of the door sills. This would also allow the larger diameter exhausts to be routed out to the sides of the car (a problem that particularly affected BMW). Another change was aimed at giving these manufac-turers flexibility to fit strengthened – for which read larger – transmissions and drivelines and allowed design freedom outside of the front and rear bulkheads, effectively the extremities of the cabin.

Norbert Singer used the first and last of these changes to completely revise the 935's layout during 1977 and took up the second for 1978. Being able now to change the structure of the car ahead of the front bulkhead, Singer revised the mounting points where the front suspension lower A-arms (lightweight tubular items) attached. This change reduced front wheel camber changes – which was undesirable with the wide slick tyres. Unsprung weight was also reduced with a magnesium alloy hub carrier and, using aluminium alloy for the strut itself, while the adjustable anti-roll bar was moved from the rear to the front. A brake servo was briefly tried on the 1977 car, but was found to increase pad wear unacceptably. New, lighter four-piston calipers were used, however.

The body of the 935/77 extended the elasticity that

Singer could find in the wording of the Group 5 regulations. Leaving, as required, the standard car's body structure (less the rear wings), he evolved a snow-shovel front nose and clothed the whole of the rear of the car in a new aerodynamic tail, complete with a new and very large aerofoil. The lightweight tail structure was simply grafted on to the existing body. Typical of the detail was that this structure even covered the rear window, eliminating the turbulence-inducing step at its front edge. The result was a car with fully 10 per cent less drag for the same downforce.

Meanwhile, Hans Mezger's engine section came up with a revised specification for the power plant of the new car. The 2.85-litre engine used two smaller turbos which

The cockpit of the 935/78 was utilitarian, but still recognisable (just!) as a 911. The cockpit ventilation would not have been acceptable on a production car!

improved the throttle response and with changes made to valve lift, resulted in 630bhp. The changes did not alter the massive near-600Nm maximum torque available once the turbos spooled up. The horizontal cooling fan was carried over from the ATL engine. This arrangement had been found to improve engine temperature, allowing a measurable increase in boost pressure and so increasing maximum power by up to 15bhp. The fan drive was achieved by means of a toothed belt from the end of the crankshaft to a shaft running over the top of the crankcase. A pair of bevel gears turned the drive to the fan's vertical axis.

With over 600bhp and a weight distribution heavily biased to the tail, the 935/77 was a real handful to drive. As Derek Bell commented, 'With so much power at the wheels, it is lethal to get out of line.' Bell noted that the 935/77 went to 100mph (160kph) in less than seven

seconds, but handling the car well required great care. The huge turbo lag meant the driver had to feed the throttle before turning in, which in turn led to armfuls of understeer. With all the weight over the rear wheels, the tail was not slow to make its presence known. He concluded, 'You can't just drive a turbo, you have to think ahead. Once you have the power on, you have to balance it against the car breaking away.'

The next stage in development was the 935-02, better known as the 'Baby'. Norbert Singer again led this meteoric eight-week development. The single car assembled is important to the story because it had to meet the up to 2-litre class weight limit of just 725kg. As such, the 'Baby' became a target for every weight-saving trick that could be applied in the bare two months available for the development. Without the 935/77's lead ballast, this meant some

An aluminium frame replaced the production car's chassis at the rear. With water cooling for the new four-valve cylinder heads, air cooling was needed only for the cylinders, with the fan being noticeably smaller than the earlier, all air-cooled, engines.

180kg had to be taken off the car. 'We changed a lot on this car,' Singer recalls, 'because everything was for minimum weight. As far as I remember the car had to weigh 730 kilos and we got it a lot below that. And then we had to put lead in again to get it back up to 730!'

Drawing on the Turbo-Carrera experience, and stretching the regulations once again, Singer replaced the steel structure fore and aft of the bulkheads with cross-braced aluminium tube sub-frames, effectively forming a complete space-frame with the alloy roll-over cage. Even the steel rear bulkhead was replaced with a glass fibre wall.

Hans Mezger's team responded to the task of producing a 1.4-litre engine with a new crankshaft and smaller bores. The single turbo engine used a much lighter air-to-air inter-cooler installation and eliminated much of the complexity of the larger-engined version. Because the torque levels were lower, the lighter, five-speed 915 transmission became a very desirable bonus for the 'Baby'. The result was a car which needed some 15kg of lead ballast to meet the class weight limit.

Several head gasket failures on the larger capacity Group 5 cars during 1977 had prompted a new cylinder head design for the following year. An experimental engine with four-valve cylinder heads had been first tried back in the 1960s and it was accepted that water cooling was the only way to keep such a design cool (because the lower valves were shrouded from a cooling airflow). So for the 1977

season, the 935 acquired water-cooling for the cylinder heads (the cylinder head design was not regulated by the rules) and a new, more compact four-valve combustion chamber. Because the heads remained separate from each other but linked by common camshaft casings, they were welded to the still air-cooled cylinder barrels – and so eliminating the head gasket problem. The Group 5 regulations did not permit a change to full water-cooling as this was not a feature of the production 911 Turbo.

The new design (which used the regulation crankcase from the new production 3.3-litre Turbo) was drawn as a family of five engines, having capacities from 1.4-litres through to 3.2-litres. This covered all possible applications, including, as Paul Frère has noted, even the speculative design for a 1.4-litre engine suitable for Formula One. The 'Baby' engine never made it off the drawing board, but the 2.65-litre (935/72) engine was eventually built for the Interscope Indycar project, while the 2.14-litre unit (935/73) would go into the 936/78. For the 935, the options were the 3.2-litre (935/71) or the 2.8-litre (935/70) engines. The 2.8-litre engine was good for 600bhp with 1.4 bar boost, while the 3.2-litre produced up to 750bhp. The improvement over the all air-cooled engines was not so much in outright power, but that the same power could be achieved with lower turbo boost and so less stress to the engine.

Aside from the water cooling, the other obvious identifying feature of the new engine was the now-vertical and noticeably smaller cooling fan. This was conventionally belt-driven and could in fact have been deleted altogether as testing had revealed that natural convection kept the fins cooled well enough.

To keep within the regulations requiring 15in wide rear wheels, Singer asked Dunlop to manufacture 19in diameter tyres, which resulted in a larger contact patch. This change raised the axle line and so the transmission internals were turned upside down in a new casing so that the output shaft aligned more closely to the high axle line. The use of 16in diameter front wheels eased the task of the already over-worked brakes and after significant further development, Porsche confidently ran with drilled discs at Le Mans.

The rolling chassis for the 935/78 went all the way in its interpretation of the regulations, particularly making use of the three changes aimed at attracting other manufacturers into the top class of Group 5. Effectively the 935 became a full space-frame racing car, on to which the elemental remnants of the production car's upper cabin were riveted. Singer had cut off the production undertray at the level of the door line and replaced it with a glass fibre floor.

'Unfortunately' [for everyone else!], he laughs, 'the regulation was written so broadly that we said, OK, let's cut the floor off completely and make the car 80mm lower!'

This lowered the roof height by some 75mm. In fact, the 935/78 looked startlingly more 'right' as a racing car than the earlier 935s. Singer used the permitted overhangs to the fullest extent and came up with a flowing aerodynamic body – accentuated by Martini's swirling colours – that oozed speed. However, the new shape of the car which became the *Moby Dick*, soon drew criticism from the CSI and Singer had to modify the fairings placed initially over the doors, that linked the front and rear wings.

Porsche decided to use the longer legs of the 3.2-litre engine at Le Mans, accepting the extra capacity would mean the car would have to weigh no less than 1,025kg – 55kg more than the minimum for the 2.85-litre car. It was a sound decision as *Moby Dick* was the fastest car at Le Mans that year.

The development of the 935 was not taken any further by Porsche after 1978. There was no factory effort in Group 5 (or IMSA) for 1979 and this left the way open for some of the strongest customer racing teams to pursue their own ideas. Perhaps the most influential was the Kremer brothers evolution of the theme, known as the K3. This was an extensively reworked car (the third version of Kremer 935 development that had begun in 1976) whose 'roll-over cage' now began at the front suspension pick-ups and ended at the rear suspension. It was, in effect, a full space-frame. The aerodynamics were revised, particularly in the area of the tail around the rear aerofoil and included side fences on the front and rear wings. The other major difference on the K3 was the use of air-to-air intercoolers. The inter-coolers were lighter than the water types and, located just ahead of the rear wheels, and were force-cooled by having air drawn through them by the engine cooling fan. The pre-heat to the cooling air of the Le Mans-specification 3-litre engine was managed by a faster running fan. For sprint racing the Kremer's special 3.2-litre six-cylinder, on 1.7 bar boost, was good for over 800bhp.

Kremer's lateral thinking with the 935 was taken further with the K4 and Porsche themselves produced upgrade kits which allowed other customers to replicate the K3 specification. In IMSA several teams developed even more radical variations on the original theme to race in the GTX class. In particular, the concept of the full space-frame 935 was taken to its limits by the cars run by John Fitzpatrick, Preston Henn and Bob Akin.

That a 935 won the Sebring 12 Hours as late as 1984 only demonstrates further how durable the car had become.

SPECIFICATION
1978 935/78 *Moby Dick*

Engine: 935/71 flat six-cylinder engine with air-cooled cylinders and separate circuits for each water-cooled cylinder head. Gear-driven twin overhead camshafts per bank operating two inlet and two exhaust valves, each hollow and sodium filled (exhaust from Nimonic alloy steel). Single KKK exhaust-driven turbocharger and air-to-air intercooler per cylinder bank. Bosch six-plunger mechanical fuel injection, capacitative discharge electronic ignition with single spark plug per cylinder. Aluminium crankcase and Nikasil-coated air-cooled aluminium cylinders. 210mm diameter cooling fan driven by V-belt from the front of the crankshaft running at 1.34 times engine speed.

Capacity: 3,211cc

Bore/Stroke: 95.7mm/74.4mm

Maximum power: 750bhp at 8,200rpm (at 1.5 bar boost)

Maximum torque: 755Nm at 5,400rpm

Compression ratio: 7.0:1

Transmission: Type 930/50 aluminium case four-speed gearbox, inverted relative to the 1977 unit. Separate oil cooler. 240mm diameter single-plate Fichtel & Sachs clutch with sintered metal lining. No differential. 917-type titanium driveshafts, each with two Hookes universal joints and a single Guibo rubber doughnut.

Chassis/body: Basis was a 911 Turbo steel central cabin riveted to full structural aluminium roll-over cage. Full-braced aluminium tubular front and rear sub-frames. Engine bulkhead replaced with glass fibre and undertray removed at sill height and replaced with flat glass fibre floor. Engine cover, rear wings, front bonnet, front wings and integrated front air dam from lightweight polyurethane sandwich or glass fibre material. Side and rear windows from clear polycarbonate. Approx. 65kg of lead ballast located at front of car and in passenger footwell. 114-litre rubber fuel cell in front compartment with external filler. Engine water radiators located in front of rear wheels. Intercooler water radiator at front of car with oil cooler mounted behind.

Suspension and steering: Rack and pinion steering with column manufactured from titanium tubing.

Brakes: Twin circuit braking system, with balance bar for front-rear adjustment. 332mm x 35mm thickness ventilated (by curved internal vanes) and cross-drilled steel discs floating on aluminium alloy hub carriers. Four-piston alloy calipers all round.

Wheels and tyres: 10.5in wide, 16in diameter front, and 15in wide 19in diameter magnesium alloy wheels. Dunlop tyres.

Weight: 1,025kg dry (38 per cent front; 62 per cent rear)

Length: 4,890mm

Width: 1,990mm

Height: 1,200mm

Wheelbase: 2,273mm

Track (f/r): 1,630mm/1,575mm

Performance: Acceleration: 0 to 62.5mph (100kph): N/A

Maximum speed: 223mph (358kph)

TURBOCHARGER — 936

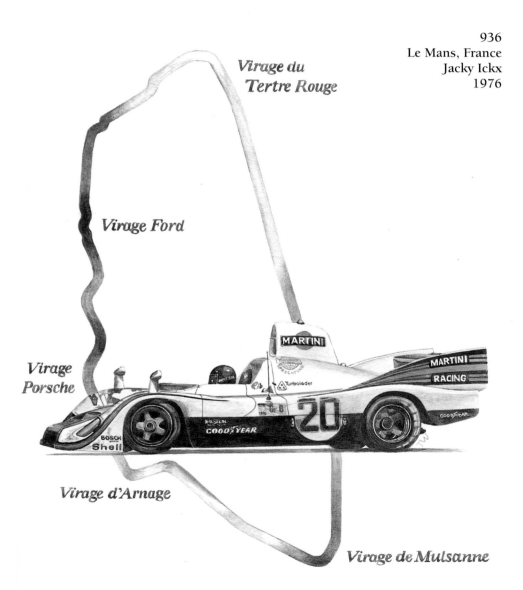

Virage du
Tertre Rouge

Virage Ford

Virage
Porsche

Virage d'Arnage

Virage de Mulsanne

936
Le Mans, France
Jacky Ickx
1976

ONE OF THE MOST INTERESTING questions regarding the history of motor racing in the late 20th century will concern the roller-coaster health of international sports car racing. When it has been good, it has been very, very good. But when it has been bad, it has been tedium exaggerated. From the mid-1960s, the rules have see-sawed backwards and forwards and just when it seemed a formula had been devised which produced large grids and close racing, everything shifted again.

At the heart of the matter in Europe has been the FIA (*Fédération Internationale de L'Automobile*) and their motor racing committee, FISA (*Fédération Internationale du Sport Automobile*) – previously known as the *Commission Sportive Internationale,* the CSI. Being based in France and wanting their national racing interests to flourish, it was perhaps typical of the racing world generally that self-interest should predominate in FISA. The first year of the revived World Sports Car Championship was 1968 and the change to the 3-litre prototype formula at that stage had been an attempt to facilitate French manufacturers progress towards overall victory. That had failed when first Porsche and then Ferrari had developed crushingly powerful 5-litre 'production' sports cars and the 3-litre machines (particularly those from Matra-Simca) were somewhat elbowed into the sidelines. The FIA was not impressed by the 917s and 512s and they dictated that these too would go from the end of 1971. The new formula would permit only 3-litre prototypes. The governing body could do no more than this to give the French racing car builders the head start they needed.

It did not quite go according to plan however. Ferrari perfected the 312P for 1972 and swept the board in the Manufacturers' Prototype Championship. Le Mans however, would be a different matter as the Ferrari was not able to offer a threat to Matra and the blue cars became the class of the 24 Hours for three seasons in a row. Ferrari devoted more and more attention to their Formula One effort in 1973 and new cars from Alfa Romeo and Gulf

Research Racing had disappointed. The Matra 670B was notable for the glorious shriek of its V12 and that year won five of the ten championship rounds, to Ferrari's two, with two other wins being captured by the Carrera RSR.

The following year, 1974, had proven little different in terms of overall results. The threat from the Gulf team again did not materialise and only a first round win by Alfa Romeo at Monza deprived Matra of a clean sweep in the ten round championship. Afterwards, the French team decided they had had enough.

As Matra-Simca bowed out of sports car racing, so Renault came in. While the former company had its technology base in the aerospace industry, the latter was a heavyweight automobile manufacturer. They saw an opportunity to go racing through the established Alpine team using a turbocharged version of their 2-litre V6 production engine. The Alpine-Renault prototypes completed a learning season in 1975, in the face of strong opposition from the flat 12-cylinder Alfa Romeo 33TT prototypes and various ageing 908s. But faced with a full-budget manufacturer effort, Alfa Romeo backed away from the series. Nevertheless, the cars were sold to Willi Kauhsen and by the end of the season, the Alfa effort was rewarded with the World Sports Car Championship.

Le Mans in 1975 demonstrated that a prototype was still the car with the best chance of winning the 24 Hours, when the Gulf-Mirage driven by Jacky Ickx and Derek Bell claimed the race. It seemed that 1976 would be little different. The Alpine-Renaults looked very strong for the new season and especially for Le Mans, despite the 'silhouette' formula GTs – including the new Porsche 935 – that were allowed in the new Group 5 class. Even a new fuel-conscious formula for prototypes did not deter this view, effectively demanding that cars such as the Cosworth-powered Gulf had to find 25 per cent better fuel consumption.

It was against this background that the subject of a new Group 6 contender was aired at Porsche. 'It was a very remarkable meeting,' recalls Norbert Singer, race engineer on the 935 project at the time. 'It was unthinkable how it was decided to make a new race car. There were a lot of people around the table – Dr Fuhrmann, Mr Bott (overall head of engineering), Mr Falk (development manager), Mr Hensler (engineering project leader), Mr Mezger (head of engine design), Mr Flegl (engineering project leader), Mr Jantke (racing team manager) and perhaps others. First, we were talking about the 935 project and suddenly Dr Fuhrmann asked "what do you think about the new sports car rules?" And nobody reacted. We were all thinking why is he asking this? But he continued. "You are always telling

me you have a lot of parts from the 917 in stock – uprights, A-arms and so on. And you have an engine. What do you think about making a sports car with the old parts. You could make a new space-frame and a new body." To that we said, with a new body we would have to go to the wind tunnel. He said, "no, no, you have the experience. You don't need any wind tunnel. We have the engine – from the 935 – it's a different displacement, but this isn't a problem." He went round the table asking everybody what they really thought about this. And everybody said well, no. We were racing the 935 and we were doing the world championship. Everybody said no, not really. And then he said, "I tell you, we are going to do it. And we'll meet in two weeks and you will tell me how we are going to do it!" The decision was made without any papers or anything. Just an order to do it.' Singer's engaging humour surfaces at this point. 'Dr Fuhrmann tried to keep that car really confidential. Top secret in Weissach. He didn't even tell Dr Porsche. Once when we had the mock-up made, there was a date with Dr Porsche to show him some production things in that workshop. Everything was covered, so he couldn't see anything. So they showed him what they wanted – I think it was a production fender or something – and when the meeting was over he went to the door. Then at the door he stopped and asked one of the guys, "Can I see it?" The guy asked what. And he said "the new car"'

The Jacky Ickx/Henri Pescarolo 936 retired early in the 1977 Le Mans 24 Hours with a broken connecting rod. Ickx was recalled to the sister car later in the race.

Singer rocks with laughter as he tells this story. 'So they went behind the curtain and showed him. He knew, of course.'

There were in fact many obstacles to such a car. The racing programme was already at full stretch developing the 934 customer cars and the new Group 5 935 for 1976, and as Fuhrmann had strongly hinted, this was to be no multi-million dollar development. On the positive side there were indeed shelves full of spare parts from both the 908 and 917 sports and Can-Am cars.

Fuhrmann wanted the programme on a tight budget – and there was not much time. He appointed Can-Am engineer and 928 development manager Helmut Flegl as project leader and almost from one day to the next, Porsche were building prototype racing cars again. The race department at that time was made up of perhaps five or six staff, plus three or four designers. This was at a time when the 935 was going through enormous change, it led to good-natured competition between the groups. Peter Falk, whose not inconsiderable task it was to manage Flegl (936) and Singer (935) recalls little conflict. 'Occasionally the workshop chief had some difficulties to organise the mechanics to do the different projects. Naturally there was

The first 936 was painted matt black to make it difficult to photograph when testing. This colour scheme was kept for the first race when, because of poor conditions, it was discovered nobody could take good pictures of the new Porsche racer!

internal competition, but it did not influence the quality of the whole work. We had run the development of the 908 and 917 like this.'

Race record

A little bit of secrecy always injects more mystery and enthusiasm into a project and Fuhrmann's desire to keep the 936 under wraps would keep Alpine-Renault completely unaware of Porsche's plans. The French team spent all the winter and the first part of 1976 thinking they would have little strong competition for that year's Le Mans. 'That car [the 936] was primarily designed for Le Mans,' recalls Helmut Flegl. 'So part of the tests had to be done at a high-speed test track and for this we used Paul Ricard. When we discussed matters of secrecy with Dr Fuhrmann, he wanted us to make sure that nobody would be able to take pictures of the car or get close. When we told him that we could not guarantee absolute secrecy, he got upset and said to paint it black. He wasn't really serious about it, but we did so.'

After shake-down runs at Weissach and at Paul Ricard, near Bandol in southern France, the 936 was revealed to the world at the April Nürburgring 300km. Still in its sinister black paint, but now with Martini stripes, the 936

lined up on the front row flanked by two surprised Alpine-Renaults. The race was caught in a typical Eifel storm and in torrential conditions, Patrick Depailler and Jean-Pierre Jabouille came together as they turned into the Nordkurve behind the pits. As they plunged into the catch fencing, Rolf Stommelen took his opportunity and slithered past into the lead. But the new 936 was slowed when the throttle cable stretched and the race was won by Reinhold Joest in his turbocharged 908. This was the last time the black paint was used on the 936 however, since the very low visibility appearance that had appealed in testing meant that in the 'Ring's downpour, the car was almost invisible! That was bad for media coverage. For the next race, the car was turned out in a new, predominantly white, colour scheme.

Porsche might well have raided the parts bin for the 936, but a strong driver team was going to be essential. There had not been a need to call up a top-line driver squad since the days of the 917, but with the likes of Depailler, Jean-Pierre Jaussaud and Patrick Tambay in the Alpine-Renault line-up, equally proficient skills were needed. For the single car that was campaigned in the remaining three races, just three drivers would be used, Rolf Stommelen had little to

prove at Porsche. The German driver had driven Porsches in endurance racing for more than ten years, during which there had been many highlights. Perhaps the example which most demonstrated his fearless speed was the 1969 pole-winning lap at Le Mans in the untamed, brand-new 917. By 1976, Stommelen was in his second season of Formula One, driving for Brabham-Alfa Romeo. He would subsequently also make his mark taming the new 935.

Belgian ace Jacky Ickx walked away from two poor (for him) seasons with the struggling Lotus F1 team to join Porsche. 'I contacted Jacky and offered him a drive with Porsche,' recalls then-competition manager Manfred Jantke. 'He had been a successful F1 driver in his early years and later showed great potential in sports cars and in long distance races in particular. That was why we wanted him.'

Ickx's efforts in the Wyer GT40s in the late 1960s had brought him universal respect not only for his outright speed, but also his ability to get a car to the finish of a long distance race. John Wyer had tried to retain him for the Gulf 917 effort back in 1970, but Ickx could not resist the lure of a Ferrari Formula One drive. Ferrari's 512S sports car was never the match of the 917, but what might have been with Ickx and the evolution 512M was demonstrated

The bodywork of the 936 recalled the lessons learned from the 917/30, particularly the benefit of having a large rear wing.

at the Österreichring in 1970 and later in Kyalami. Ickx drove the very agile 312P the following year and again gave the 917s a hard time. In this car and with Brian Redman, Ferrari strolled the 3-litre-only 1972 World Championship of Makes. The sports car wins had continued in 1973 in the face of Matra's onslaught, but the writing was on the wall. That year, the red cars had won only at Monza and the Nürburgring. At the season's end, Ferrari pulled the plug on sports car racing to focus on Formula One. Ickx subsequently found a welcome seat at John Horsman's Gulf Research Racing for the 1975 Le Mans 24 Hours, joining Englishman Derek Bell in a victory which would inspire a long term chemistry between the pair.

Peter Falk notes that Ickx had long enjoyed good contacts with Porsche before 1976. 'Jacky drove some laps in a 917 with Hans Herrmann at a test session on the old Südschleife [Nürburgring] during testing right after the [unforgettable!] 1969 Le Mans. After two years away from the big championships, we needed a new generation of drivers. Ickx had driven many manufacturers' cars, but not Porsche.' But Falk has no doubts as to why Ickx would find such remarkable success at Porsche in the coming years. 'It was many things – his reliability, his technical understanding, his detail work during testing and practice, his care for the cars, his smooth and steady driving style, his personal charisma, and his human relationship with the whole team.'

Jochen Mass was a rising star in Formula One. As teammate to 1975 World Champion Emerson Fittipaldi in the dominant Marlboro McLaren team, he was building a strong reputation as a charger. He had been awarded victory at that year's shortened Spanish Grand Prix, after Rolf Stommelen's car had crashed, killing four spectators. Mass drove for Porsche in 1976 as much as his McLaren commitments would allow and proved to be a rapid partner for Ickx.

Ickx and Mass came together for the first time at the Monza 4 Hours, where the 936 cruised to an easy victory. It marked the completion of the 936's initial development and at this point, Helmut Flegl moved across to the research department at Weissach. His role as engineering manager on the 936 was taken over by one of his staff, Wolfgang Berger. Berger had already made a name for himself as the driving force behind the early Carrera RS development and latterly the 934 customer racer.

The wins continued for the 936 at Dijon and Imola and another for Mass and Stommelen at Enna. Ickx raced the car alone at Canada's Mosport Park as did Mass at the Salzburgring.

A special effort was made for Le Mans, the course for which the car had been planned, with two cars modified for the longer distance. Surprisingly, Alpine-Renault entered only a single car, reflecting their lack of confidence to run for 24 hours. This duly retired during the night after electrical problems and then finally an overheating engine. For Porsche, the remainder of the run was barely troubled by a pair of non-turbo Gulf-Mirages or the Alain de Cadenet Lola. Ickx, partnered by Gijs van Lennep, drove the car that had first raced at Enna and won despite a long pit-stop to replace a broken exhaust manifold. It was Ickx's third Le Mans win and van Lennep's second. The sister car, the original prototype which had been used for the early season championship races, ran into various problems. It stopped at breakfast time on Sunday with a broken driveshaft.

In 1977 the 936 saw action only once – the Le Mans 24 Hours. The team did not race in the World Sports Car Championship and so was able to develop the car solely for the long Hunaudières Straight. It was a race that was filled with tension and drama.

This time there were four works Alpine-Renaults against two 936s. Renault had also taken out extra insurance by selling their engines to the Gulf-Mirage team. Porsche's extra card in the hand came from the Stommelen/Schurti 935/77 – the 650bhp car being the fastest on the straight, if not as nimble around the corners.

There is a breathtaking Dunlop film of Jürgen Barth driving the 936/77, which captures the essence of the old, non-chicaned, Le Mans. Barth says he dubbed on the soundtrack later in the comfort of his lounge, having run around the house beforehand so that his voice-over sounded more realistic!

The lap begins after the slow Ford chicane, with the cars accelerating hard past the old pits and curving gently right up the hill towards the Dunlop bridge. This section was completely unsullied by the chicanes of today. It meant the best cars were popping over the top of the hill at very high speed. Barth takes us down the hill, past the fairground on the left and through the Esses in one flowing and very fast sweep. The approach to Tertre Rouge is much as it is today. The corner on to the public road had yet to be re-profiled (a new intersection was built in 1978–79 between the Paris-Rennes autoroute and the Tours main road) and provided a very fast entry on to the 3.5-mile (5.6km) Hunaudières Straight. The Dunlop film shows the 210mph (338kph) 936/77 flying past 935s with a 30–40mph (48–64kph) speed differential – enough to demand the utmost concentration from every driver if disaster was to be avoided. And disaster was still not far away in the mid-1970s. By this time, the sand banks had gone and Le Mans was lined with double or triple layer Armco, but around

most of the high-speed sections, the dense woodlands extended to the edge of the track. There were few run-off areas. The 936/77 took the Mulsanne kink flat out, going light over the following crest and then hard on to the brakes to turn hard right at the Mulsanne cross-roads. The high-speed dash up to Indianapolis is flanked again by dense woodland at a point where the 936 runs up to 200mph (320kph) before braking for the second-gear (and left-hand) corner. There is a 400m squirt to the sharp right at Arnage, then another high-speed run leading into the new Porsche Curves (which were opened in 1972). The lap is completed after this with the twisting, speed-eroding turns of the Ford chicane.

This is a Le Mans without the skyscraper start-line complex, in the days when the pits were dark and damp booths with little protection from the weather. The paddock was a combination of grass and tarmac lanes and

the sandy topsoil could find its way into any engine that required maintenance in the open air. By the mid-1970s, the appalling accident that befell the 1955 event was but a distant memory, but racing car speeds were increasing rapidly. Niki Lauda's fiery Nürburgring accident in 1976 had brought track safety to the top of the list of racing concerns. Le Mans and its facilities had yet to find the new safety-conscious direction that professional racing drivers were beginning to demand. Perhaps it was this flirtation with high-speed danger that so appealed to drivers and spectators alike.

The result of the 1977 Le Mans was what Porsche wanted, but the race departed a long way from the planned strategy. The 935 flew off in pursuit of Jabouille's leading Renault, but the chase was impeded when the 935 lost all its oil. Then the 936 driven by Jürgen Barth and Hurley Haywood was delayed with a failed fuel pump and after

Le Mans, 1977. After a scorching drive through the night, headed by Jacky Ickx, the second 936 suffered a piston failure less than an hour from the end when Hurley Haywood was driving. The team's other driver, factory technician Jürgen Barth, took over and is seen here starting his final lap. He nursed the very sick car home to win. (LAT)

that the remaining 936 was put out completely by a broken connecting rod. At this point the first three cars were Renault, Renault and Renault. The fourth car had caught fire soon after the start. It was little more than three hours into the race.

The team switched Ickx to the remaining (Barth/Haywood) car and gave him orders to drive flat out. By midnight the car had climbed to fourth and when the second and third-placed Renaults ran into problems during the night, the Porsche found itself second. The leading Renault then expired in a cloud of smoke and the 936 was leading. All three Renaults eventually retired with the same piston failure. But with just 45 minutes before the end of the race, that was what happened to the surviving Porsche. Such was the size of the lead, the car was left in the pits until ten minutes from the end. The car had to complete just two laps to be classified – and win. Trailed by a long plume of oil smoke, Barth carefully nursed the crippled machine twice around the course to take a famous and very lucky victory. It was the 936's second successive, Porsche's fourth and Jacky Ickx's third consecutive (and fourth in total) win at the 24 Hours. The second-placed Gulf Mirage was more than 90 miles behind at the finish.

Ickx had more than justified the decision to bring him to Porsche. In later years Manfred Jantke would summarise the Belgian's skills, which went far beyond the cockpit and reveal why personal 'chemistry' is so essential to the successful racing team. 'His potential as a racing driver reached far beyond his speed and driving talent. Ickx was a person with management qualities. He permanently put a positive pressure on the team and he could force every circumstance during a race to his favour. He was an exceptional driver because of his intelligence, mental strength and charisma. He was the most impressive driver I worked with.'

Renault were heavily committed to a Formula One effort, but after three seasons developing their sports car, the French team could not rest until they had conquered Le Mans. The 24 Hours was the only sports car race they entered in 1978. They were represented by no less than four cars and each showed signs of significant development, with one using an enlarged 2.1-litre version of the twin turbo V6 engine.

Porsche responded in kind with three 936s and the infamous *Moby Dick* 935. Two of the 936s were using the new four-valve, water-cooled cylinder heads first tested on the 935, with the third car providing insurance with the well-proven two-valve all air-cooled engine. The 936/78s were again turned out in dazzling Martini colours and featured a very powerful driver team in what was expected to be a 24-hour sprint against the Renaults. Jacky Ickx and Henri Pescarolo headed the squad with Jürgen Barth and Bob Wollek in the second four-valve car. The two-valve 936/77 was driven by Hurley Haywood, Peter Gregg and Reinhold Joest. But despite this maximum effort, Renault's careful preparation and greater race speed won the day. For once it was Porsche that was in trouble – and right from the beginning. While the Barth/Wollek had to play chase with Jabouille in the 'hare' Alpine, the Ickx and Haywood 936s were in the pits almost immediately with fuel pressure problems.

By four hours it was an Alpine-Renault 1–2–4, with the Barth/Wollek 936 being the paté in the baguette. Behind them came the 935 and the recovering 936 of Haywood, Gregg and Joest. It was not over yet. But then as night fell the Ickx/Pescarolo car came in for a change of gearbox internals. Pescarolo had lost fifth gear – a fundamental disadvantage at Le Mans. While this car was in the pits, the two-valve car came in again, this time for a turbocharger change. Mirroring the previous year's change of strategy, Jacky Ickx switched cars and by Sunday morning, the Jarier/Bell Renault was out and the Ickx/Barth/Wollek car was just two laps behind Jabouille/Depailler. Jochen Mass had replaced Ickx in the second four-valve 936 and this was now making up ground after various problems. That run was finished just before midday on the Sunday when Mass went off the road and was unable to continue. But then the second-placed 936 lost fifth gear also and the

The drooping winglets on the 936/78 had their unlikely origins in a television repair shop in Zuffenhausen. Engineer Norbert Singer says the new wing provided a small advantage over the previous arrangement.

resulting three-quarter hour pit-stop saw them overwhelmed by the Alpine of Pironi/Jaussaud and the two-valve 936. When the leading Alpine stopped with a holed piston – a problem which Renault thought they had overcome after the previous year's failures – the race had yet another new leader.

The Pironi/Jaussaud Alpine led by a massive eight laps. It was too much for the Porsches to pull back. By the end, Barth and Wollek had reduced the gap to five laps, while the Haywood/Gregg/Joest two-valve car trailed in third. Alpine-Renault had achieved their ambition to win Le Mans and then, predictably, pulled the plug on their sports car effort. Porsche too, felt there was little to gain from racing against their own customers and announced soon after that they would be focusing their energies in other directions the following season. That other arena of turbocharged competition – Indianapolis – beckoned.

But it did not work out that way. Almost at the last moment, Porsche decided to compete again in 1979 with the 936 at Le Mans, with the Silverstone 6 Hours being used as the warm-up. It was very much a last-minute effort by Porsche and participation was prompted by lucrative sponsorship from Essex Petroleum. Competition manager Manfred Jantke explains the decision to race that year. 'After we had decided to do Indycar racing, our eight-year contract with Martini & Rossi had come to an end. Martini continued in sports car racing with Lancia instead. Essex boss David Thieme contacted me to sponsor another Le Mans entry in 1979 and as our Indycar effort was not yet ready, we agreed. This was in early April, as I remember. It was a kind of spontaneous decision, but there was still sufficient time for proper preparation.'

Drivers Jochen Mass and Brian Redman did not have a good weekend at the May Silverstone event. Initially, Mass simply flew away from the opposition, but then he picked up a slow puncture and as he crested the rise before Woodcote, the tyre bead came off the rim and he crashed heavily. It ended what appeared to be a gift of a race for Porsche. It was suspected the tyre had turned on the rim, causing the failure.

Two 936s were readied for the following month's 24 Hours. One was the Silverstone car and the other was the car Mass had crashed at Le Mans the previous year. With revised engines, the two Essex-liveried cars dominated practice. There were no Renaults and the race appeared to be in the bag for the last-minute entries from Zuffenhausen.

Brian Redman partnered Jacky Ickx in the lead car, bringing together again the pairing who had won the World Championship of Makes for Ferrari in 1972. But their race together was to be short and full of drama. First a wheel

came loose and later Brian had one of those memorable moments when a recurrence of the tyre problem seen at Silverstone returned. The resulting blow-out wrecked most of the left side rear suspension and bodywork. It took him 38 minutes to nurse the car back to the pits and then nearly an hour while the car was repaired. Ickx rejoined in 31st place and after a typically stirring drive, the car made its way up to seventh place during a cold, wet night. The charge was finally stopped for good by a broken fuel injection drive belt on Sunday morning. The other 936 of Wollek/Haywood had inherited the lead when its sister machine faltered, but was slowed soon after by fuel injection problems. They recovered to third during the night but probably because of the prolonged irregular fuel mixture earlier, the engine finally expired just four hours from the finish.

By Porsche standards, it was a poor showing, but technical head Peter Falk is more philosophical. 'You can lose Le Mans with the best prepared cars and a good crew. You can win Le Mans with virtually untested cars and a stressed crew (as we were with the 956 in 1982). Le Mans has its own laws! A faulty injection pump, a burned piston, a flat tyre, a weak belt: it can happen in each race.'

There was no factory representation in Group 6 at Le Mans in 1980, while the team experimented with the 924 Carrera GT. However, Reinhold Joest was loaned a 936/77 body to put on his old 908 and a 2.14-litre air-cooled twin turbo engine. Joest shared the heavily-modified car with

The entry for the 1979 Le Mans race was not decided until April and was initiated by a sponsorship offer from Essex Petroleum. The 917/30-style wheel centres had been run on the previous year's cars.

Jacky Ickx. The race went to plan until Saturday evening, when the Belgian was forced to change an injection pump drive belt out on the course after they had worked up into the lead. The car fell back to sixth, but overnight the pair recovered the lead again and there they stayed until midday on Sunday. At that point, fifth gear disappeared (as had happened in 1978) and the resulting stop let Jean Rondeau and Jean-Pierre Jaussaud through to win in their Rondeau.

The final year of the old Group 4, 5 and 6 formulas was 1981, before the 800kg, fuel consumption-based Group C formula was applied to sports car racing. The new formula did not dictate an engine capacity limit, but limited power by defining the maximum permitted amount of fuel that could be used per race.

This transition year brought out the best of both worlds at Le Mans. There was no engine capacity limit and fuel consumption was still unrestricted. With the Porsche Indy programme shelved after a last-minute rule change by the Indianapolis organisers, the 2.65-litre engine that had been developed for oval racing presented itself as being ideal for the new Group C. And where better than Le Mans to try it out? The two 936s were wheeled out of the Zuffenhausen museum(!) and new engines were fitted. The cars were given another new paint scheme – this time for the Jules clothing business. Derek Bell partnered Jacky Ickx to one of Porsche's most workmanlike victories in the 24 Hours. The winning car spent a minimum amount of time in the pits and finished more than four laps ahead of the second placed car – a Rondeau. It was not quite so easy for the second veteran 936. Driven by Jochen Mass, Hurley Haywood and Vern Schuppan, the car suffered a string of problems which began immediately after the start with a broken spark plug. Clutch trouble and fuel injection problems increased the frustration, but at least they finished – 13th. For Ickx and Bell however, it was a fine victory and would mark the beginning of a winning relationship. The Belgian ace could now claim a remarkable five Le Mans victories.

Having been created as something of an afterthought, the 936 became one of Porsche's most successful racing cars.

Engineering

The 936 was one of the best value racing cars Porsche have ever produced. It re-used experience and chassis components from the 917/908 programme and the engine from the prototype 911 Turbo-Carrera.

In 1974, when the Turbo-Carrera competed against the Matras and Alfa Romeos in the prototype class, the maximum capacity limit for a normally breathing engine

was 3-litres. For turbocharged engines, an equivalency factor of 1.4 had to be applied and this is the origin of the rather odd capacity of 2,142cc that Porsche used for their racing engine. The 911-based single turbocharger flat six-cylinder engine (the 911/78) developed 520bhp at 8,000rpm – better than the original Turbo-Carrera's 480–500bhp – with a 1.5 bar boost. This first turbo six showed that enough had already been learned about how to achieve both power and reliability to take second place at Le Mans in 1974. The engine represented a blend of experience from the original racing six used in the Carrera 6 and the turbo twelves of the 917 era. Nikasil coated alloy barrels and a magnesium crankcase were used. Instead of the very highly tuned 10.6:1 compression ratio of the Carrera 6, a less stressed 6.0:1 ratio was used with larger inlet and exhaust ports. The exhaust valves were made from the very hard Nimonic steel alloy as proven on the 917, while the inlet valves were sodium-filled. Twin plug ignition was used with mechanical six-plunger fuel injection. Carrera 6 titanium connecting rods ran on a standard 911 Turbo crankshaft, while the cooling fan was mounted horizontally, rather than the vertical position used on the production car.

The five-speed gearbox and transaxle came from the 917 sports cars (and was used on the unblown customer Can-

The factory team ran two world championship sports car campaigns in 1976. Here, at Le Mans team manager Manfred Jantke lines up with his cars and drivers, from left: 935, Manfred Schurti, Rolf Stommelen, Jochen Mass, Jacky Ickx and 936.

variation on the shafts was accommodated by the same large rubber 'doughnut' couplings as used on the 917/30.

'The chassis of the 936 was designed around the smaller engine [compared to the 917/30],' says project leader Helmut Flegl, 'so the tubular frame was new. Components like hubs, steering, etc. were genuine or modified 917 parts.' As with previous Porsche sports cars, the driver sat on the right side of the cockpit for better weight distribution on courses that generally turned right. Fuel tankage was 160-litres and this was disposed behind the driver and in the right-hand sill structure alongside the cockpit. For the first time in a Porsche racing car, the engine formed a structural member in the chassis, improving torsional rigidity. Paul Frère records that this change alone improved the chassis rigidity no less than 28 per cent.

The body was both familiar and unfamiliar to those used to Porsche's earlier sports prototypes. There was the recognisable long-tail section of the 917/30, the nose also recalling the 917/30, but with the area ahead of each front wheel built up to take two pairs of headlights.

The front and rear uprights and hub carriers also came from the 917, as well as the braking system and many of the suspension and steering components. Helmut Flegl tried again with aluminium alloy wishbones – these had given mixed results during the 917 Can-Am programme. To assist the stability of the car under acceleration and braking, the geometry included anti-dive at the front and both anti-dive and anti-squat at the rear. The 1971 917 sports car brakes were carried over and drilled discs were

Am cars). This was connected to the engine by an aluminium spacer that was no less than 235mm long – this length being necessary to get the desired 2,400mm wheelbase. Porsche were beginning to use electron beam welding more and more for highly stressed parts and this method was used for the drive shaft assemblies. Length

Lurking in the dark interior of the black-painted 936 hides Porsche's new secret weapon – the turbocharger. The 936 would take the first turbocharged victory at Le Mans.

used everywhere, except for Le Mans. The front wheels from the 917 sports car were used, with 10.5in wide Goodyears, but since Porsche did not have the right rim sizes for the preferred 14in wide rear tyres, 16in diameter BBS wheels were fitted at the rear. The complete car weighed in at just 20kg over the Group 6 minimum limit of 700kg.

Wind tunnel development by Norbert Singer and endurance testing at the Paul Ricard circuit in southern France further developed the tail and nose sections. This resulted in a full-width horizontal splitter around the front edge of the nose and a 50mm high spoiler along the rear edge of the tail, under the large aerofoil. This high-drag set-up was great for the car's first race at the Nürburgring, but by Le Mans, Singer had further refined the airflow to a lower drag configuration and improve the engine cooling (a concern in the early tests). This latter was solved by adopting a huge Formula One-style airbox behind the roll-over bar. This also fed cool air to both the air-to-air inter-coolers and the turbocharger inlet. Porsche had also been allowed to raise the height of the rear aerofoil by 200mm, in line with that being used by the Alpine-Renaults.

By this time a second car had been built, and had been the car used in the other Manufacturers Championship races by that point in the season. To gain as much advantage as possible on the long straight, the driver position on this second car had been reclined further, allowing both the front rim of the cockpit and the roll-over bar to be lowered (although this latter was now completely hidden by the large moulding integrating the airbox into the rear bodywork and cockpit sides). The 1976 Le Mans race also marked the first time a pits-to-car radio system was used by Porsche. The newer car won the race and recorded an overall fuel consumption of 41.8 litres/100km (6.7 miles to the imperial gallon). This compares well with the winning 1971 917 sports car figure of 47 litres/100km (6.1mpg).

For the 1977 Le Mans race, the 936/77 reflected considerable attention to low drag aerodynamics. By shortening the suspension arms, the track was reduced by 40mm at the front and 30mm at the rear. Much work went into refining the narrower bodywork and the result was a new shape airbox (with more integration of the roll-over bar cover into the cockpit sides), a new nose and a longer long-tail. Testing in both the wind tunnel and at Paul Ricard further honed the aerodynamic details. The large rear tail fins were retained but the chord of both the main plane and flap of the rear aerofoil was reduced by around 17 per cent (although a 10mm spoiler was still needed on the rear edge of the tail section to ensure the aerofoil had the necessary 'bite'). The shorter of two nose sections was chosen after some interesting lessons were learned on controlling the downforce over the front wheels. It was found that by opening or closing the gap under the wings ahead

The 1977 car was substantially developed from that of the previous year. It was narrower for lower aerodynamic drag and there was a new airbox for improved engine air supply and compartment cooling.

A 936/78 in final preparation at Weissach, with a spare water-cooled twin-turbo engine just behind. The 936 re-used many parts left over from the 917 programme, including the front and rear suspension uprights.

540bhp at 8,000rpm at 1.5 bar boost. Learning from the transmission failure on the second 1976 car, the long shaft between the engine and the clutch was increased in diameter from 20mm to 22mm.

Chassis changes concentrated on getting the best from the new Dunlop tyres and moving to thicker, 32mm ventilated (but still un-drilled) discs at the rear. The 1977 cars were some 20kg heavier than the 1976 versions, but the result was a car that was around 15mph faster on the Hunaudières Straight. To conserve the engines of the two cars in the race, a boost of 1.3 bar was used. This still could not prevent a piston melting on the winning car just 45 minutes from the end of the race. Ickx, Barth and Haywood had driven the 936 absolutely to its limits for some 20 hours, during which the Belgian had destroyed the Le Mans lap record with a time that was only three seconds off his qualifying best with a full boost engine!

The 936 went for a hat trick of wins in 1978 and once more the car underwent significant development. The 936/78 used as its basis the new four-valve engine which had been developed primarily for the *Moby Dick* 935. Originally a 3.2-litre engine, the 'Baby' 935 short-stroke (60mm) crankshaft was fitted and with the existing bore size (87mm) gave the regulation 2,142cc. The crankshaft main bearings were slimmed to reduce friction in the smaller capacity engine, while the air-cooled Nikasil barrels were electron-beam welded to the completely new cylinder heads. These were now water-cooled and contained four-valves per cylinder and a single sparking plug. The valves were smaller and more widely spaced than on the 935 engine but were driven by the same twin overhead camshaft arrangement, themselves driven by gears from the crankshaft. The water cooling allowed a tightening of the compression ratio to 7.0:1 and the result was an engine (the 935/73) that delivered 580bhp at 8,500rpm at a race boost of 1.4 bar and 625bhp with a 1.7 bar qualifying boost.

The radiators for the water-cooling system were located just ahead of the rear wheels and supplied with air drawn in by NACA-style inlet ducts along the sides of the body (with outlets on the top surface of the tail). The radiator location extended the wheelbase by 30mm.

The other obvious external difference on the new car was the rear aerofoil, which had grown long drooping winglets. There is an interesting story behind this wing, which began in a television repair shop in Zuffenhausen. 'I worked on this with Mr Flegl,' explains Norbert Singer. 'There was an amazing experimental 'plane that had been built by a guy in Zuffenhausen. It was amazing! Officially, it was a shop for TV and I don't know, electronic things. He pushed

of front wheels, and changing the number of open louvres in the tops of the wings, the front downforce could be controlled significantly with little drag penalty.

The engine reflected the need for greater top speed. Hans Mezger's thinking for the air-cooled six had resulted in each bank having its own, smaller, turbo and air-to-air intercooler but with a single, common waste-gate. This resulted in faster engine pick-up and an engine output raised to

somebody in the company to tell the racing people that they should please come and see this completely new wing design. He said that what we did on the race car was completely wrong and we had to do this new wing. So I visited this guy. I entered a normal shop with TVs in it and so on. And I asked for this gentleman and they said go through a door. It was a small building and behind the shop there was a complete aeroplane! I had a long discussion with him and it made sense. He asked why didn't we try it on the race car, so we did some basic stuff – a little bit on the *Moby Dick*. These were quite long metal pieces and this was the time when we started the 936 again. We tried to make it like these aircraft things. But we saw it in that shop!' The drooping winglets provided a small advantage, but as with many other aspects of aviation aerodynamics, what works in an open air stream proves to be quite different in the very turbulent flow of a racing car rear wing.

The new wing allowed the tail to be lowered in height, but this kept the small but very effective 20mm high rear edge spoiler. Because the cooling effect from the large airbox was less essential, this was narrowed by 50mm. The nose section was extended by 100mm and both the horizontal splitter and the louvres in the tops of the front wings were also removed. Inevitably, the 936/78 was heavier than the earlier variants. The two four-valve cars entered (there was one new car and the heavily updated original prototype) also had the full complement of radio, basic spares and tool kit, which had allowed Ickx to make temporary repairs at the Indianapolis Corner and get back to the pits in 1976, and a new pneumatic jack system. The best weight of the two cars was 804kg.

For the 1981 event, the 2.65-litre Indycar engine was used to gauge its suitability for the following year's new Group C fuel consumption formula. This 935/76 six-cylinder four-valve engine had a 66mm stroke with a bore of 92.3mm to give a capacity of 2649cc. With the Indianapolis-regulation single turbo replaced by twin turbos and individual inter-coolers, the engine was good for 620bhp and allowed Ickx and Bell to drive to an effortless win that year. The only other change to the pair of veteran 936s was to fit the stronger 917/30 four-speed gearbox.

Only three model 936 cars were ever built. Chassis numbers 001 and 002 did loyal service until 1977. No 003 was built for the 1978 race, but all three continued to be used until 1981. These three racing cars had brought Porsche no less than three victories (one apiece) and two second places at Le Mans over a period of six years. Compared with the Piëch era, when new cars would appear virtually at every race, that was exceptional value by any measure.

SPECIFICATION
1977 936/77

Engine: Type 911/78 air-cooled flat six-cylinder with dual ignition. Two KKK turbochargers with twin inter-coolers and single waste-gate delivering maximum 1.5 bar boost. Horizontal nine-blade cooling fan driven by V-belt and two bevel gears from the crankshaft. Cast aluminium alloy crankcase with forged steel plain bearing crankshaft, forged titanium connecting rods. Nikasil coated aluminium alloy cylinder barrels. Chain-driven single overhead camshaft per bank, single sodium-cooled exhaust and inlet valves per cylinder. Bosch mechanical fuel injection.

Capacity: 2,142cc

Bore/Stroke: 83mm/66mm

Maximum power: 540bhp at 8,000rpm

Maximum torque: 491Nm at 6,000rpm

Compression ratio: 6.5:1

Transmission: Type 917 five-speed gearbox with synchronisation on all forward speeds. Borg & Beck triple-plate sintered metal clutch. Titanium alloy drive shafts with Hookes (UJ) and Guibo (for length variation) joints.

Chassis/body: Multi-tubular aluminium space-frame with three-piece glass fibre outer body with long-tail. Integrated engine air box behind driver with sculpted high cockpit sides. Two vertical tail fins and full-width rear aerofoil and adjustable flap. Engine forms a rigid assembly with chassis to increase chassis stiffness. Twin bag-type fuel tanks (one behind driver and one in left-side cockpit sill) giving 160-litre total capacity.

Suspension and steering: Front and rear: independent with upper and lower aluminium alloy wishbones with twin radius rods, 917 uprights. Variable rate coil springs over Bilstein aluminium gas pressure shock absorbers, adjustable anti-roll bars. 917 rack and pinion steering with steering wheel on right of car centreline.

Brakes: 917-derived dual circuit with drilled, 32mm thickness ventilated disc brakes all round and four piston (finned) alloy calipers. Adjustable front/rear brake balance from cockpit.

Wheels and tyres: Centre-lock five-spoke aluminium alloy wheels 10.5in x 15in diameter front, and 15in rim by 15in diameter rear, with radially finned wheel discs. Dunlop racing tyres

Weight: 730kg (42 per cent front/58 per cent rear)

Length: 4,700mm

Width: 1,920mm

Height: 1,270mm

Wheelbase: 2,400mm

Track (f/r): 1,530mm/1,480mm

Performance: Acceleration: 0 to 62.5mph (100kph): N/A

Maximum speed: 216.9mph (349kph) (Source: P. Frère)

RIGHT FIRST TIME — 956/962

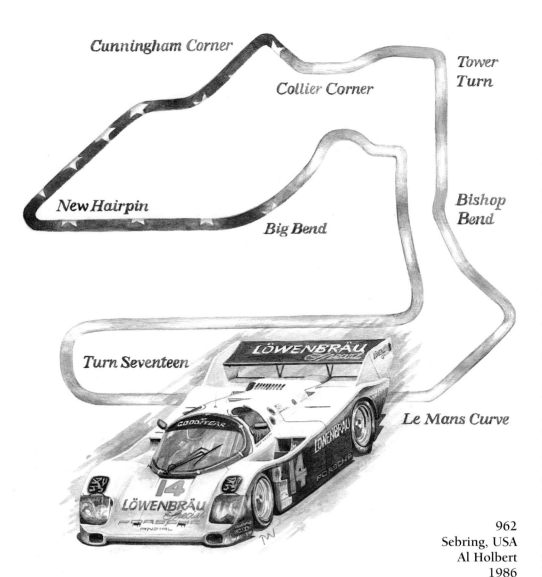

Cunningham Corner

Collier Corner

Tower Turn

New Hairpin

Big Bend

Bishop Bend

Turn Seventeen

Le Mans Curve

962
Sebring, USA
Al Holbert
1986

PORSCHE HAD WON LE MANS six times before 1982. The 936 had contributed three of those wins and the 917 two. But the records of these two great racing cars would pale when set against the car Porsche built for the new Group C endurance racing formula. Between 1982 and 1994 – an astonishing period of 12 years – cars from the 956/962 family would win the famous 24 Hours no less than seven times.

The influence of the 956 and the later 962 models on international motor racing was as fundamental as the 917 had been. But unlike the 917, it was not so much the ground-breaking technology which impressed (and that *was* very impressive) as the car's emergence as the backbone of international sports car racing through the 1980s. While other manufacturers such as Lancia, Jaguar and Sauber-Mercedes, built prototypes, won races and withdrew, Porsche built their own prototypes and then sold replicas to private customers. The result was full sports car grids and some very exciting races. While these sometimes were more like one-make challenges, for the first time the more-organised racing customers had a real opportunity to beat the factory racers. Everybody, it appeared, wanted to drive a 962 and most who did prospered.

It was a rule change and a new head at Porsche that opened the door in 1981 for a new racing sports car from Weissach. In January, Peter Schutz became head of Porsche AG. Schutz was a marketing man and fully appreciated the value of racing. Accepting that the ageing 936 would no longer be enough to overcome a dedicated assault on Le Mans from another manufacturer, he approved the construction of a new car to meet the 1982 regulations for the World Endurance Championship for Makes.

These new regulations were designed to give endurance racing a fresh start after several years of sporadic and unsatisfactory popularity with the big manufacturers. What caught the eye about the new rules was that there was no limit on engine capacity. But unlike the old Can-Am free-for-all, the amount of fuel the cars could use per race was limited. For a 1,000km race only 600 litres of fuel were permitted, while for a 24-hour race, the allowance rose to 2,600 litres. Maximum fuel tankage in each car (including the pipework, etc) could be no more than 100 litres and no more than five refuelling stops were allowed in any one 1,000km race. This effectively mandated that the car's fuel consumption had to be better than 4.7 miles to the imperial gallon and – by the accepted technology of 1981 – formed an effective limitation on engine size. Forced feed

Derek Bell brakes hard for the Mulsanne Corner in the 1982 race-winning 956 he shared with Jacky Ickx. (LAT)

fuel rigs as introduced to sports car racing by Roger Penske for the 1971 Ferrari 512M were outlawed in favour of gravity-only rigs that could deliver no more than 50 litres per minute. It threw an extra wild card into the racing because pit-stops would now take at least two minutes for a full refuel.

Group C defined a higher minimum weight than the previous Group 6. Within the 800kg dry limit for a car (without fuel or driver), a height restriction of between 1.1 and 1.2m steered designers towards a coupé body shape. The car had to be less than 4.80m long and no more than 2m wide. The requirement that the overhangs at the front and rear of the car had to be less than 20 per cent and 15 per cent respectively of the wheelbase would fundamentally influence the design of the new Porsche, as would the acceptance of aerodynamic ground effects.

This startling innovation, inspired by Colin Chapman, had revolutionised Formula One car design in the three seasons prior to 1981. The Lotus 78 had stunned the grand prix world during 1978 with its ability to enter corners at seemingly impossible speeds, while running very little drag-inducing wing. The secret was ground effect.

Chapman's fertile brain had reasoned that a partial vacuum could be generated beneath a car if air was drawn in at the front, accelerated through a narrow channel and then expanded again towards the rear. The accelerated air in the narrow channel resulted in a negative pressure – suction – at that point and forced the car down on to the track. The idea had been refined and developed by the Lotus engineers who drew further inspiration from the radiator installation of the wartime de Havilland Mosquito aircraft. They found that by placing the radiators in the narrow channels – there would be one either side of the cockpit – they heated the expanding air and so increased the effectiveness of the vacuum.

Letting air pass under a car was a complete anathema to racing car designers, who up to that point in time had gone to great lengths to *prevent* air passing under their machines. In this case, innovation in the face of convention was indeed the mark of brilliant engineering.

Mario Andretti had cruised to the World Championship and the following year, most of the Cosworth-powered *'garage-ists'* produced their own ground-effect cars. Enzo Ferrari's lack of competitiveness over the coming years (before the dawn of the turbo era) resulted from a dogged persistence with his flat-12 engine – a layout that prevented his cars from fully benefiting from ground effect.

The new Group C rules limited the degree of ground effect that the new sports cars could generate. The plastic skirts which closed off the gap between the ground and the sides of an F1 car were not permitted and a flat reference plate of 1m by 0.8m had to be fitted to the underbody within the wheelbase. Coming after the rule-stretching 917s and 935s, the challenge set by the new Group C must have been irresistible to the engineers at Porsche.

Race record

The 956 set many new standards at Porsche, not the least being the commercial association with Rothmans. Tobacco sponsorship of motor racing was already well established by the early 1980s, particularly in F1, but it was novel in sports car racing. Porsche's new public relations director, Manfred Jantke, brought the company into the sport to begin an association that would take them all the way to Formula One. Rothmans would support Porsche from the beginning of the 956 racing programme in 1982 to the end of the factory-entered programme in 1988.

Peter Falk became the new motorsport head. Falk, the quiet-spoken development engineer who had loved to drive the cars himself until a serious accident in 1969 at Hockenheim in a development 908 had prompted a more hands-off role, was a natural for the position. It was Falk who had initiated the gruelling destruction test (known today as the more politically correct 'bump' test) at Weissach which every new Porsche, including the racing cars, had to endure. Falk's ability to bridge the communications gap between the drivers and the famously untalkative engineers would mark him out as one of racing's great team managers. It is Falk who remembers with most pride that the 956 was quick from the moment test driver Jürgen Barth took it on the first exploratory laps around Weissach. 'The 956 was really ready to race after a few days testing. Unlike the 917, we had a lot of experience with the 936 and the 935, especially in aerodynamics. And we did not have a big boss (referring to Ferdinand Piëch) any longer who wanted only low drag cars!'

Resplendent in Rothmans's eye-catching white and blue colour scheme, the new 956 made its race debut at the Silverstone 6 Hours in May 1982. The British event was chosen as a curtain-raiser for Le Mans and to gauge the depth of the challenge from other manufacturers – notably the Lancia-Martini team. Being a transition year to the new regulations, cars of the old Group 6 formula were permitted. Managed by the highly respected Cesare Fiorio, Lancia gambled that for one year only a Group 6 car could beat the new Group C machines in the run for the drivers' championship. Their 1.4-litre 420bhp turbocharged LC1 open *barchetta* was unrestricted by fuel consumption and at 700kg was lighter and more nimble than the Group C cars.

The Italian plan looked good at Silverstone, when the brand new Porsches were totally handicapped by the new fuel regulations. Lancia took a surprise win. While no-one doubted the incredible speed of the Milanese cars, a big question mark hung over their durability.

That concern was ably demonstrated at Le Mans where both Lancias failed (as did the majority of the other Group C runners). For Porsche though, everything came good at the race. Painstaking testing beforehand paid off with a crushing 1–2–3 victory for the new 956s, perhaps the factory's most convincing win of all in the 24 Hours. Jacky Ickx and Derek Bell took a back-to-back victory (Ickx's sixth and Bell's third).

Porsche had only planned to run at Le Mans that year, but the temptation to race again was too much, especially when faced with the Lancia challenge. Jochen Mass proved the 956's sprinting abilities at the Norisring later in June, but three strong wins against the Italian cars came at Spa, Mount Fuji in Japan and Brands Hatch, England.

A typically autumnal Brands Hatch provided an opportunity for John Fitzpatrick and Derek Warwick to beat the factory cars in 1983 in their 962.

Around Brands, the full ground-effect (with side skirts) Lancia driven by Riccardo Patrese and Teo Fabi proved to be faster overall, but the race was stopped at nine laps after shunts damaged the track's Armco barrier. At the restart, the Lancia flew off into the distance in drying conditions as Porsche once again worried about fuel consumption. With 35 laps remaining, Jacky Ickx was over a minute behind the Lancia when the decision was made to go for it. Ickx hurled the 956 around the track like a man possessed, but by the chequered flag was still two seconds behind. However, when the aggregate of the two races was taken into account, Ickx and Bell were given the victory – much to the dismay of Ricardo Patrese, who had to concede the drivers' title to Jacky Ickx. The Italian gamble had failed and the LC1 was consigned to history.

Outside of Le Mans, Peter Falk reveals that it was unusual for Bell to partner Ickx. 'Ickx and Bell only drove together in Le Mans. This was because Derek was, like Jacky, an absolutely reliable driver who never crashed a car at Porsche. For that, Jacky put up that Derek was a little bit slower in lap-times. But this was not so important at Le Mans. For 1,000km races the combination Ickx/Mass was the number one.'

With nine customer cars being built for the start of the 1983 season, the 956 formed the bulk of the Group C grid that year. Lancia were back with a brand new car that looked to have real potential. The Dallara-designed LC2 coupé met the full Group C regulations and was powered by a Ferrari 2.6-litre twin-turbo V8. But the new V8 proved to be the Achilles heel of the car and while very fast, once again proved to have no durability.

Every race of that year's World Endurance Championship fell to the 956, with Lancia only winning at Imola in a race which only counted for the less-prestigious European Endurance Championship (and in which the factory 956s were not entered). The surprise of 1983 was that sometimes it was the customer 956s that won ahead of the factory cars. At Monza, Reinhold Joest's brand new car, driven by Wollek and Boutsen, outran Ickx and Mass while at Brands Hatch there was again a thrilling twist.

John Fitzpatrick, driving with Derek Warwick, closed off the engine cooling vent slots in the 956's underbody. This significantly improved the suction in the underbody channels and gave the customer car the edge over the factory cars. Race engineer Norbert Singer is philosophical about this defeat. 'We had an air-cooled engine and we were worried about over-heating. We had a closed floor with some slots to let the air out. But this destroyed the ground effects. It cost nearly a second [a lap]. Of course, we said to our customers keep them open or you will risk

an engine. At Brands Hatch it was raining and cold. And he [Fitzpatrick] said OK, I will risk an engine. He was successful and won the race. It was clever.'

Porsche strolled to the championship in 1983, with Jacky Ickx again becoming drivers' champion from Derek Bell. The following year, Le Mans was rocked with controversy as Porsche withdrew after the governing body decided not to implement a previously announced fuel allowance reduction for each race of the World Endurance Championship. It presented Lancia with a golden opportunity to win the 24 Hours, but it was not to be. The Italian cars were quite unable to take advantage of the situation, their best car finishing eighth in an otherwise clean sweep of customer 956s to ninth place. Victory went to Joest's New Man-sponsored car, driven by Klaus Ludwig and Henri Pescarolo. That year, the 956 again won every race of the World Endurance Championship, barring a poorly supported season-closing Kyalami event. Beside Joest's win at Le Mans, the other customer that flew the Porsche flag with distinction was Richard Lloyd, who at Brands Hatch led home a race that the factory did not enter. The drivers'

Reinhold Joest achieved a second consecutive win at Le Mans in 1985. With the advantage of cockpit-adjustable fuel mixture, a suspected higher specification engine and beneficial slipstreaming periods early in the race with the Richard Lloyd 956, the yellow and black New Man car was able to pull away from the field. Partnered by Paolo Barilla and Louis Krages (alias John Winter) this was Klaus Ludwig's third Le Mans win.

Double Le Mans winner, in 1984 and 1985, Reinhold Joest would repeat the feat again in 1996 and 1997.

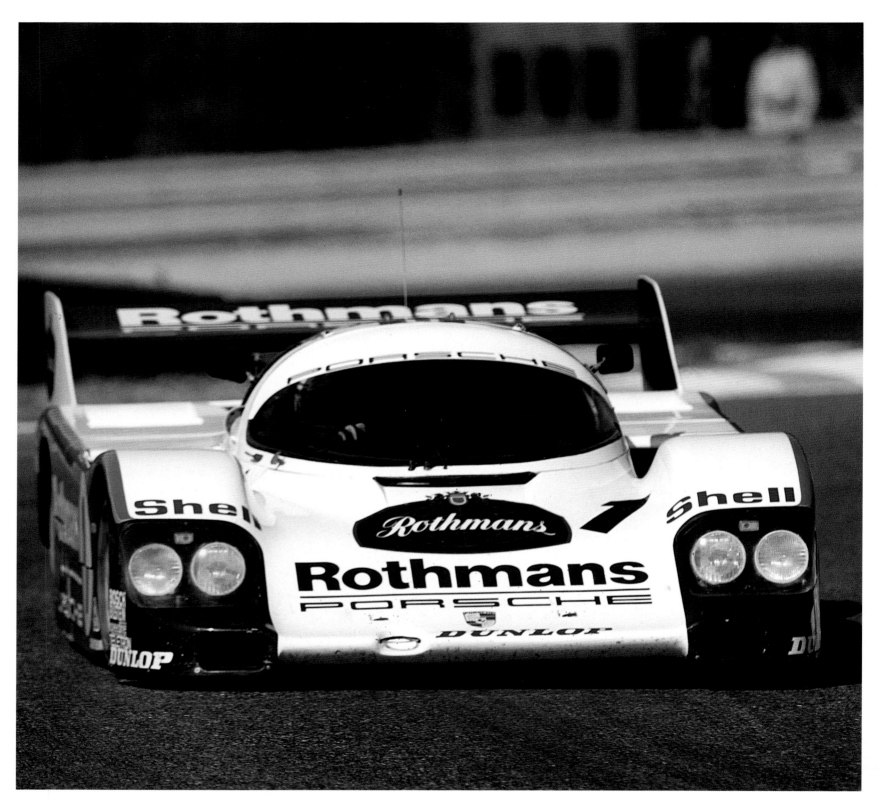

champion that year was the very promising Stefan Bellof, driving a Rothmans 956.

The following year, 1984, witnessed the arrival of the 962 in the American IMSA sports car championship. After a near-miss at the Daytona 24 Hours by the Andretti family, the new car progressively replaced the ageing 935s that had until then, been the only Porsche presence in the championship. The best of the 962s was the Löwenbräu-sponsored car driven by Al Holbert and Derek Bell, ahead of an array of competitive privately run cars in a field previously dominated by Holbert's own March-Porsche and the Bob Tullius Jaguar XJR-5s. The Holbert 962 took its first IMSA win at the delightful Mid-Ohio course in June and proceeded to pick up four more victories at Watkins Glen, Elkhart Lake, Pocono and Daytona. However, the new Porsche's late entry to the series gave it too much to do to catch the series-winning March-Chevrolet of Bill Whittington and Randy Lanier.

For 1985 and 1986, Al Holbert reigned supreme in what had become a semi-works machine. Holbert had taken over the Porsche motorsport activity in the USA and continuously searched for extra advantage with the 962, while attempting to keep pace with the somewhat variable regulations of the series. The main competition to the IMSA 962 clean sweep in 1986 was markedly inconsistent and came from a variety of machinery including the last of Tullius Jaguars (the 7.6-litre XJR-7), assorted March and Ford Mustang types. If any event came to underline how the 962 dominated in IMSA during the mid-1980s it was the classic Sebring 12 Hours. The 962 won this event four times in a row from 1985 to 1988, a remarkable feat of consistency at the bumpy, airfield course in central Florida.

Sebring is a sports car classic that it is easy to believe the Europeans value more highly than American race fans.

Opposite: The Rothmans-Porsches set the standard for Group C sports cars in the mid-1980s. This is Jochen Mass. (GP Library)

Al Holbert flat out on the Daytona banking in 1986 in the Löwenbräu IMSA 962. The turbo engine would become increasingly restricted in IMSA and Holbert, with engine builders Andial, tried various intercooler options in the pursuit of a reducing advantage.

The architect of Porsche's race team success with the 956 and 962 was long-time development engineer Peter Falk.

The Andretti family, Mario, (seen here talking to race engineer Norbert Singer), John and Michael, finished sixth at Le Mans in 1988 in the Shell-supported factory 962C.

Sebring is a survivor of not only the constantly changing climate of racing politics in the USA, but also of road racing culture in general. It is not a place that has the natural charisma of say, Watkins Glen or Elkhart Lake, but it has somehow maintained a firm grip on what the American sports car fan wants. There is an essential 'clubby' feel to Sebring that welcomes the spectator and racer alike. While other tracks have succumbed to the smoked glass, roll-up garage and chain link fence syndrome, Sebring still has grass in the paddock and a 'run what you brung' feel. The track used to be made up from the runways and perimeter track of the adjacent airfield, but by the 1960s it was largely permanent. It is tricky and fast to drive, despite the 3.7 miles (5.9km) having no elevation changes. Price Cobb's fastest lap in the third-placed 962 in 1988 was over 122mph (196kph). The 12 Hours is famous for breaking the very best. There is a saying that it is a 12-hour race that takes 24 hours out of the car. Most importantly, it is a track where even today, spectators can get close to the action. The 12 Hours in March is an almost religious happening for dedicated supporters.

The factory ran the more-competitive 962Cs for the 1985 European season, while the customer 956s waited to capitalise on any slip up in the Weissach campaign. The big upset of the year was Reinhold Joest's second consecutive win at Le Mans (a routine he would repeat in 1996 and 1997), using the same 956-117 chassis. His drivers, Bob Wollek, Paolo Barilla and 'John Winter' (Louis Krages), drove a perfectly executed and fuel-saving race to beat the Richard Lloyd Canon-sponsored 956 with the works 962 of Ickx/Bell trailing in third. There was a token victory for the 3-litre Lancia LC2-85 in the shortened Spa 1,000km, a race in which everyone lost the will to compete after Stefan Bellof fatally collided with Jacky Ickx as they raced into Eau Rouge.

Le Mans witnessed the second appearance of the Bob Tullius-entered Jaguar XJR-5s, which despite their strength in IMSA struggled in the 24 Hours. However, the American effort would trigger a works-supported Jaguar return to sports car racing in 1986.

The arrival of the Tom Walkinshaw-developed Jaguars that year would rekindle the spirit of competition that had become rather lacking. Jaguar's first season showed the cars to be very competitive, despite unreliability and occasional squabbles between their star drivers (including Warwick, Cheever, Schlesser, Lammers and Brundle). Their win at Silverstone almost certainly put the final nail in the coffin of the Lancia effort and the fast, but temperamental Italian cars were not raced again by the works. The British cars were not strong enough to take on Porsche at Le Mans and

Bell/Stuck drove to a comfortable win ahead of six other Porsches. It was during this race that Austrian Jo Gartner was killed driving the Kremer 962 in a high-speed night-time shunt on the Hunaudières. This was also the year in which Bell and Stuck used the automatic transmission PDK 962 in most races, but not at Le Mans. While Stuck is said to have liked it, Bell – who won the drivers' championship that year – was not a fan.

After taking a second straight win in the Daytona 24 Hours, Holberts's IMSA 962 looked set for another season of dominance in 1987. But as in Europe, the opposition was waking up. A win by the Electramotive-run Lola-Nissan at Miami set the scene for a variety of other winners during the year although these were mainly driving 962s. In 1988, Daytona was won by a Jaguar and after two 962 victories at Miami and a third straight victory at Sebring, the new Electramotive Nissan ZXT prototypes blew everything else away. From this point on, the 962 barely had a look in and would only score the occasional IMSA win.

The TWR Jaguars had defeated Porsche in the World Sports Prototype Championship in 1987, but at the Le Mans showdown Porsche emerged the victors yet again. Derek Bell, Hans Stuck and Al Holbert strolled to a 20-lap victory after the three-car Jaguar team faltered. The Porsche team drivers had no less than ten Le Mans victories behind them before this addition. It was Bell's fifth and Holbert's third win.

At the end of June, Porsche announced they were with-drawing their factory team of 962s, perhaps accepting there was little more to be wrung from the 962C, while the Jaguar was reaching its peak. What was needed was a new car, but other priorities would prevent that.

In 1988, the picture was indeed different. It barely seems relevant to say that this was the 956/962's seventh world championship season, but despite the dominance of the Jaguars, the 962 was still a force to be reckoned with. Because the factory's racing customers were represented in strength, the Porsches had become the cornerstone of the formula, ensuring full grids and close mid-field racing. Jaguar's main competition in the World Sports Prototype Championship now came from the much-improved Sauber-Mercedes. Peter Sauber's C9 cars enjoyed the full works support of Mercedes-Benz. The silver car's 5-litre V8 provided a 700bhp match for the Jaguar's 750bhp, with weight right down on the 850kg limit (the Jaguar was never able to lose an approximate 50kg excess).

At Le Mans, it was hoped that proven endurance would win the day for the factory 962s. The most obvious differ-ence from the 1987 cars was that the familiar blues and whites of Rothmans had been replaced by the reds and yellows of Shell, and a white car with Dunlop insignia. The odds were not good for Zuffenhausen with three works 962Cs against five Jaguars, but the supporting cast included no less than nine other 962Cs. The expected threat from the Sauber-Mercedes team evaporated after practice when one of their cars suffered an inexplicable high-speed crash, and Peter Sauber withdrew from the race.

The second head to head between Jaguar and Porsche produced a nail-biting duel between the two great sports car manufacturers, which only went the Jaguar's way by a mere lap after a day's very hard racing. The result, however, confirmed that the 962C had finally met its match.

Even though Porsche did not compete with works cars subsequently, the racing customers continued to take part in what had become a very healthy Group C formula. Sauber and Jaguar became the front runners in 1989 but there was the occasional upset. Typical was Reinhold Joest's win in the 300 miles (483km) sprint race at Dijon, by virtue of its Goodyear tyres, that worked better than the Jaguar's Dunlops or the Sauber's Michelins. This was to be the only championship respite for the Porsches however. Like every other championship race during the year, Sauber won Le Mans against the might of Jaguar and the Aston Martins. No less than 17 962Cs were entered that year,

Porsche were just beaten by the TWR-Jaguar XJR9-LM at the 1988 Le Mans. Finishing on the same lap after 24 hours racing, the Porsche was delayed during the night when Ludwig ran out of fuel and had to coax the 962 back to the pits on the starter motor.

Is it a road-going GT or a 962 racer? In 1994, the Dauer-962 gave everybody a preview of where GT racing was headed. Danny Sullivan prepares to go out while team chief Roland Kussmaul (on far side of the car, with a headset) supervises.

demonstrating how important was Porsche's contribution to sports car racing in general.

The following year was the last for Group C and the first for the newly chicaned Hunaudières Straight at Le Mans. The Saubers were now called Mercedes-Benz and the carbon fibre C11 took prototype sports car design into another league. The TWR-Jaguar XJR-11s won majestically at Silverstone, but the Silver Arrows repeated their Le Mans domination. The problem was that neither of these manufacturers was developing customer cars and as a result most others who wanted to race still ran 962s. It should have sounded warning bells for those involved in the organisation, but no-one was listening.

The Group C rules changed for 1991 to restrict engine capacity in the top class to 3.5 litres with no fuel allocation and a weight limit of 750kg. That signalled the entry of what became known as F1 sports cars, triggering spiralling costs for anyone going sports car racing at the top level. The result was grid sizes that reduced almost by the race. Typical of the new breed of car was the Peugeot 905. This was a full carbon fibre, high technology racer that made even the new Ford HB 3.5-litre V8-powered Jaguar XJR14s look dated, let alone the ten-year-old 962s. Jaguar however, won the Sportscar World Championship of Teams in 1991, while the surprise at Le Mans was that Mazda took the honours with its shrieking rotary, three laps ahead of a trio

of V12-engined XJR-12s. The most notable aspect of the 14-car 962C entry was that in the desperate efforts to keep the cars competitive, no less than eleven failed to make the finish.

In 1992, the advice from Porsche's new competitions manager, Max Welti, to the remaining customer 962 teams in endurance racing was to forget Le Mans. In the event, five teams put up a token Porsche presence. It was the same in 1993 as Peugeot raced against themselves and proved that their cars were reliable enough to win Le Mans a second time.

In IMSA too, the cost spiral had transformed the format of the starting grids. Since 1988, the rules had changed against the dominant Porsches and the races had been contested by the Valparaiso, Indiana-based TWR-Jaguars and the emergent Electramotive Nissan ZXTs. The 3.0-litre turbocharged Nissans mainly stayed away from Europe, but blitzed everything in North America, leaving only the odd race to a lucky 962 or Jaguar. It was a similar picture in 1990, this time the Japanese-powered grip being tightened by the Dan Gurney-run Eagle-Toyotas. That the 962 was still an enduring mid-field force in North America was shown by the last triumphant hurrah at Elkhart Lake in 1993.

Porsche returned to Le Mans in 1994 with a GT car based on the old 962. They had run a 911 Turbo GT in the GT class in 1993 with mixed results against purpose-built racing GTs such as the Jaguar XJ220. But with a minimum weight of just 1,000kg, the 911 Turbo was simply too heavy, especially as new contenders were rumoured to be coming from McLaren and Bugatti. To meet the competition, either Porsche would have to follow suit and build a very special limited edition car that would be light enough and powerful enough to be competitive in racing. But for Porsche to build the equivalent of the XJ220 or a McLaren was out of the question at this time. The company itself was struggling to survive a fierce recession in the production car business so they turned to those specialist builders who had converted the 962 into the road car of our dreams. Schuppan's carbon fibre 962 was a strong favourite but the company floundered, so they used a similar machine produced by Jochen Dauer.

Despite protests and cries for its exclusion as its purebred racing car origin went far beyond the original thinking for the production-based GT formula, the Dauers came to Le Mans in 1994. Norbert Singer was convinced his cars would not be able to match the pace of the rapid Group C Toyotas and he was nearly right, although the Toyotas had to refuel every 40 minutes to Porsche's one hour, the Japanese cars suffered from fragile transmissions.

The first Toyota dropped out during the night and despite Eddie Irvine giving a dazzling display of driving on the Sunday morning while leading, the car was robbed of the win when the gear linkage fell apart with less than an hour to go. That let the previously out-paced Dauer 962 driven by Yannick Dalmas, Mauro Baldi and Hurley Haywood into a lead they held to the end. The win was unexpected, but could not have come at a better time for Porsche. This season was a turning point for the company generally and the Le Mans victory was the icing on the cake.

Such was the clamour from other competitors, the Dauer-962 was not allowed to race again. But the point had been made. After seven wins at Le Mans and countless other victories in the FIA and IMSA championships, the 956/962 had proven itself a truly remarkable racing car.

Engineering

The engine for the new Group C challenger was the same 2.65-litre six-cylinder that had won Le Mans in 1981. This engine, with water-cooled four-valve cylinder heads and air-cooled Nikasil barrels, had been developed alongside the 2.1 and 3.2-litre engines during 1978. The plan for the 2.65-litre had been to run a Porsche-powered car at Indianapolis. Despite much testing during the early part of 1979, protective rule changes by the new Championship Auto Racing Team owners less than a month before the Indy 500 compromised the Porsche engine's power and the team withdrew.

The work on the Indy engine was not wasted however, because Hans Mezger considered the 2.65-litre capacity ideal for the new Group C. The engine was modified to run on petrol (the fuel/air ratio of methanol is much lower than that for pump fuel) and this included the addition of a vertical cooling blower – an item not needed on the methanol engine because of the cooling properties of the fuel itself. The big single turbo mandated for Indianapolis cars was replaced with two smaller turbos and air-to-water intercoolers, while the compression ratio was eased from 9.0:1 to 7.0:1. The big advantage over the 2.1-litre engine that had won Le Mans in 1978 was that for the same power everything was less stressed and ran cooler. The power was a strong 620bhp on sprint race boost. As 1982 progressed the compression ratio was eased up to 7.5:1, which offered the option of improved fuel consumption or around 620bhp at lower boost.

The five-speed gearbox was unusual for a racing car in that it had synchromesh. This replaced the old 917/30 four-speeder that had been used in the 936 the year before. A locked differential was the preferred set-up initially, but later, a Salisbury differential became somewhat of a secret weapon for the twistier circuits. The use of a limited slip differential was not fully accepted and the team even had some parts designed so that the locking factor could be adjusted from outside the casing. This variable slip differential was never actually tested.

At Le Mans in 1981 the winning Ickx/Bell 936 was timed at no less than 236mph (380kph) along the Hunaudières Straight, which was getting close to 917 long-tail territory. The calculations for the long-tail 956 suggested the new car would be good for 231mph (372kph). It was, and it was not too long before 956s were considerably exceeding that figure. In 1988 Hans-Joachim Stuck was recorded at a maximum speed of just under 247mph (397kph), putting him on a par with the best of the 917s.

The regulations governing the windscreen height determined a coupé body (for lowest drag) and for the first time Porsche chose a monocoque construction for the chassis. 'There was a lot of discussion about this in-house,' says Norbert Singer. 'Some people wanted another space-frame, but we wanted a monocoque for safety.' The sturdy fabrication was manufactured from aluminium sheet and aluminium sandwich panels which were glued and riveted together. 'We did a lot of tests during the summer [of 1981] and the beginning of winter and we built one monocoque just to practice how to do it. It was quite good. We measured the stiffness and all those kind of things and then we started on the race monocoque, which became the test car – 001.' The final monocoque consisted of the front footwell, which carried the braking system components, and a substantial bathtub cockpit, which tapered behind the seats to form the fuel cell cavity. (There were no side tanks.) A small sub-frame in front of the footwell projected forward to carry the nose body section and the cooling ducts for the front brakes. The engine firewall formed the rear of the structure and a separate alloy sub-frame was bolted to this that carried the mid-mounted engine, gearbox and rear suspension. A very substantial aluminium alloy roll-over cage helped with overall stiffness.

As with all the most recent Porsche racers, the driver sat on the right side of the car. The turbos and their wastegates were located right out on each side of the car – resulting in the two small exhaust outlets just in front of the rear wheels.

The body shape was the result of intensive development in the wind tunnel during late 1981 and appeared to pick up where the 917 long-tails had left off. There was of course, much more to it than that.

The body shape was less 'swoopy' than the old 5-litre cars, but the family resemblance was unmistakable. Air entered the underbody channels at the nose – where the oil cooler entry used to be on the 917 – and divided either side of the cockpit floor to form first the narrow venturi 'throat'. Each channel then opened out towards the rear of the car. The flat six-cylinder engine, which would have been a real disadvantage on a narrow F1 car (because the heads would extend into the underbody air channels), proved not to be such an issue on a 2m wide sports car. Even so, the entire engine and transmission assembly was pivoted off the rear of the monocoque with a 2-degree included angle to the horizontal, to improve the underbody airflow. The other potential problem was the prohibition of the moving side skirts in Group C, but Singer's experiments proved otherwise.

'At the beginning we just took Formula One practice and really, it was a drama! It didn't work at all. So we realised that there must be something different between an F1 car and our cars. Later it turned out that the F1 car is very narrow with these big side pods where you have a lot of opportunities which are not possible on a two-seat sports car. So we started to look for different shapes. We started with a model and we thought it would work, but it didn't. So we cut it and put new pieces in and I remember we were a complete week in the wind tunnel. We had to stop testing because the model was falling apart. No piece was original!'

After many experiments, Singer says they found an arrangement where the air drawn in at the sides of the car actually seemed to improve the suction under the car at speed. So the lack of skirts did not turn out to be a problem.

The water and oil radiators were mid-mounted and drew air in through large ducts in the top of the body alongside the cockpit. The exhausts for the radiator were sited in the top of the body, just ahead of the rear wheels. The engine cooling air exhausted through slots cut in the underbody

Right from the beginning there was a long-tail and a short-tail. The long-tail used every millimetre of the 4.80m maximum length and with a width just 5mm off 2m, the 956 came out as a big car. The wheelbase, at 2,650mm, was considerably longer even than the 917/30 (2,500mm) or the 936 (2,400mm), but since the regulations governed the amount of front and back overhang, the large central dimension was deemed necessary. It was certainly a long way from the traditional 2,300mm wheelbase. 'We knew a longer wheelbase could help us,' Singer says. 'We had no fear of the long wheelbase. When you keep the polar moment of inertia close to the centre of gravity, then you have the same moment and you have a very reactive car. And it gets even more reactive when the wheelbase gets longer. The problem is that when you have a long wheelbase you get more weight into the car and maybe less stiffness. If you take care of these two points, a long wheelbase is fine.'

The front suspension was by double wishbones and outboard rising rate titanium springs over Bilstein gas shock absorbers. The rear however, broke new ground. The importance of having as clear underbody airflow as possible meant it was worth paying a slight weight penalty to get the springs above the rising underfloor channels. As a result,

the rising rate springs were operated by triangulated pushrods. The bases of both spring units were located together above the gearbox on a tubular sub-frame that also carried the rear suspension and the powertrain.

One of the most remarkable developments raced on the 962 was the automatic shifting PDK transmission. PDK stands for *Porsche Doppel Kupplung,* or double clutch, and was first used at the end of 1984. While a clutch pedal was required to move off, changes on the move were made by a

The 1988 factory 962Cs faced the Jaguar challenge with a 3-litre water-cooled engine and the latest Bosch 1.7 engine management system with electronic waste-gate control. This latter feature was reputed to yield an extra 50bhp.

In what would prove to be a Nissan year in IMSA, 1989 opened with a narrow victory for Derek Bell, Bob Wollek and John Andretti in this IMSA 962 at the Daytona 24 Hours. Note the huge intercooler scoop on the rear deck.

sequential (front/back) lever, operating micro-switches in a manner similar to the old Sportomatic transmission on the 911. PDK was a much more advanced shift however, using an electro-hydraulic mechanism to change ratios on the two output shafts. Peter Falk explains: 'There were two clutches. If you were changing from third to fourth for instance, the first clutch was connected with third gear, while the second one with fourth gear. The gears were hydraulically preselected just when the driver pressed the corresponding buttons, which from 1986, were mounted on the steering wheel.'

While offering the opportunity to pre-select ratios (for instance going into a corner), there were problems with what was a complex and heavy system; it added 25kg. 'The improvement was a gear change without traction interruption and therefore a gain of some tenth of a second during each upshift.' Among the drivers however, PDK received a mixed reception. It won some races, but it lost others. 'The device was very complicated and cost us some nerves and victories in long distance races.' Falk says. 'But it was used successfully in the German Supercup sprint races.'

The 956B was the 1984 customer model and this offered the Motronic engine management system which had given the factory a continuous performance (if not always winning) edge over its customers the previous year. On the factory cars, Motronic allowed the engine's compression ratio to be raised and by the end of 1983, 8.5:1 was

typical, giving a race power of around 650bhp.

The other aspect of the 956's development that began in 1984, was experimentation with increases in engine capacity. Since Group C was a fuel consumption formula and the 935 four-valve engine had been designed back in 1977–78 with various applications in mind, the actual conversion was itself quite straightforward. The popular capacities became 3.0 and 3.2 litres, although 2.85 litres was also used. The increases were achieved either by lengthening the stroke, to 70.4mm for 2,857cc, and by using the crankshaft from the 1976 930/76 engine. The capacity could then be further stretched to 2,994cc using 95mm diameter barrels (and revised pistons) from the 3-litre RSR's 911/75 engine. Mix and match had never been easier and the factory's faster customers (notably Fitzpatrick and Joest) soon became very proficient at finding the right capacity for the fuel allocation available. However this was not so easy as from 1985 the fuel allowance was reduced by 15 per cent (to 510 litres) for 1,000km races – which perhaps demonstrated how good the Motronic engine management had become by this time. In 1986, the factory cars used the 3-litre 935/82 with air-cooled cylinders and in 1987 moved to the full water-cooled 935/83 3-litre.

After years of domination by the 935s, IMSA had not wanted Porsche's new 956 to continue the routine in 1982, so the rules were changed in the expectation that this would bar the entry. But Weissach's reaction was to build the 962, incorporating the mandated change that the driver's feet had to be behind the line of the front axle. This was achieved by extending the front wheels forward by 120mm, resulting in a remarkable 2,770mm wheelbase. This change called for various aerodynamic modifications to rediscover the car's high-speed balance and overall, the weight crept up to around 870kg.

The IMSA regulations were based on a scale of car weight and engine capacity – in stark and confrontational difference to Group C. The full four-valve, water-cooled 956 engine was ineligible in IMSA and a simpler two-valve, all air-cooled single turbo unit (the 962/70) was required to meet the equivalency regulations of the American GTP formula. IMSA 962s raced with around 680bhp from the 2.85-litre engine built by Andial in California, or 720bhp with a 3.2-litre unit (962/71). The extra thirst was accommodated by a 120-litre fuel tank. The IMSA engine regulations developed considerably through the 1980s and eventually four-valve water-cooled turbos were allowed, except that the engines had to breath through inlet air restrictors. The further development of the 962 for IMSA (particularly optimisation of the intercooler installation) was given a body blow by the death of Al Holbert in 1988.

'The very first IMSA 962 was a mixture between a Le Mans long-tail version with a little more downforce for the shorter races,' reflects engineer Norbert Singer. 'The regulations were a little bit odd because the wing had to be over the tail section. So we made the long-tail and used a bigger wing. But then the regulations changed again and customers could run more or less a short-tail. Later, we always tried to improve the car to improve the downforce and we made the tunnels wider. We were limited by the flat six's width and having the wheel outside. The tunnel size in that area was only about 120mm or whatever. So if you can make it wider by 30, 40 or 50mm there was quite an improvement in downforce. When I rang Dunlop and said I wanted a smaller tyre, they didn't believe me. But they said we could use a 19-inch rim tyre (on a narrow 14-inch wide wheel) and we would get nearly the same contact patch. We were able to get the moulds out we had used on the *Moby Dick!*'

Meanwhile in the FIA championship, the same footwell rules were announced for the 1985 season, with a two-year stay of execution for the old 956s. Porsche simply converted the IMSA car for Group C use, calling it 962C.

There were some interesting private developments by the more serious customers. The Richard Lloyd-entered 956 pursued development of the chassis, adopting a full aluminium honeycomb construction in the search for extra torsional stiffness (and also improved crash safety). The Lloyd development triggered a series of honeycomb chassis 956 and later 962 chassis built for privateers by John Thompson in England and Fabcar and Holbert in the USA. These included tubs for Kremer, Brun and Joest among others. Lloyd would continue to follow his own (produc-

Faced with a real shortage of entries in the new 3.5-litre sports car formula from 1991, the 962 was allowed a reprieve at Le Mans in the following years, running to the 1990 Group C regulations (albeit with a weight penalty). This is the suitably painted Obermaier 962 in the 1993 event.

SPECIFICATION

1982 956

Engine: Type 935/76 (late season) flat six-cylinder engine with water-cooled four-valve cylinder heads and air-cooled (Nikasil-coated) alloy cylinder barrels. Vertical cooling fan located at front of engine. Cast magnesium alloy crankcase with eight plain main bearings. Steel crankshaft with titanium alloy connecting rods, forged alloy pistons. Two gear-driven overhead camshafts per bank. Two KKK K26 turbochargers with twin air-to-water intercoolers. Bosch Motronic 1.2 engine management with single spark plug per cylinder.

Capacity: 2 650cc

Bore/Stroke: 92.3mm/66.0mm

Maximum power: 620bhp at 8,000rpm (at 1.2 bar boost)

Maximum torque: 608Nm at 5,400rpm

Compression ratio: 7.2:1

Transmission: Type 956 magnesium case gearbox and aluminium clutch bellhousing. Five forward speeds with synchromesh and reverse. Single-plate Sachs clutch. Locked differential.

Chassis/body: Aluminium monocoque tub with additional aluminium tube roll-over cage and rear steel sub-frames to carry semi-stressed engine/gearbox/rear suspension. Honeycomb aluminium sandwich used for footbox area (safety feature) and bonded Kevlar sill (side) boxes. Seven-piece Kevlar body reinforced with carbon fibre. Laminated glass windscreen with heating, clear plastic side windows. Long and short-tail options (with matching nose and rear underbody pieces). Underbody with suction-inducing longitudinal channels each side of centre section. 99-litre rubber fuel cell located between the driver and engine bulkheads. Integrated compressed air jacking system.

Suspension and steering: Rack and pinion steering. Front suspension by unequal length wishbones and titanium rising rate coil springs over Bilstein alloy gas shock absorbers. Rear suspension by lower wishbone and parallel upper links with inboard rising rate titanium coil springs over Bilstein alloy gas shock absorbers, operated by fabricated rocker arms pivoted at upper links.

Brakes: Dual circuit braking system with all-round four-piston Porsche-designed alloy calipers on drilled, ventilated 325mm diameter steel discs.

Wheels and tyres: 12in wide front, 15in wide rear centre-lock magnesium alloy 16in diameter six-spoke Speedline wheels with Dunlop Denloc tyres (front: 16/600/280; Rear: 16/650/350).

Weight: 840kg (40 per cent front/60 per cent rear)

Length: 4,770mm

Width: 1,990mm

Height: 1,080mm

Wheelbase: 2,650mm

Track (f/r): 1,648mm/1,548mm

Performance: Acceleration: 0 to 62.5mph (100kph): N/A

Maximum speed: 217mph (349kph)

tive) course in the development of the 956/962 throughout the late 1980s. Kremer went one step further in 1989, by building an all-carbon fibre monocoque. However, the 962 CK6 and another carbon fibre chassis car built by Vern Schuppan did not meet their hopes and were little more than mid-field runners against the Saubers and Jaguars.

The entry of Jaguar into sports car racing in late 1985 considerably increased interest in what had virtually become a Porsche one-make formula. Jaguar contracted Tom Walkinshaw to lead the programme and with an engineering team led by Tony Southgate – an old adversary of Porsche – cars were developed for both Group C and IMSA championships. The ex-Shadow Can-Am and Formula One engineer opted for a full composite chassis construction. The 7-litre all-alloy 60 degree V12 engine used to win Le Mans in 1988 developed around 745bhp but weighed 240kg. (The 962 3.2-litre engine weighed some 45kg less.) That weight disadvantage was carried over to the overall weight of the car compared with the 962C.

In their search for extra power, the Porsche engineers used the full water-cooled engine (935/83). By this time, a factory 962C could offer 700bhp for practice and a reliable 650bhp for racing. The 1988 factory cars for Le Mans used electronic control of the waste-gate for the first time (an idea proven by Nissan in IMSA), with the new Motronic 1.7 engine management and this yielded an extra 50bhp.

One customer proposal might have gone further. Peter Falk says that Kremer built a mock-up 928 engine in a 962 chassis and asked for help with the engine management, clutch and gearbox. 'We declined because by then we had no budget for it. But this way would have been the right one.' Both Jaguar and Mercedes had shown that the rpm of a big displacement engine were much lower than that of the smaller Porsche engines. 'That means less friction power loss and so less fuel consumption. The higher torques at lower revs led to better handling in the corners and better acceleration out.'

The 962 would have one last blaze of glory in 1994, when Singer persuaded the Automobile Club de L'Ouest (ACO) to let the Dauer 962s run. However, with a flat bottom, the previously stable 962 became quite dangerous at speed. Urgent modifications were made to the body aerodynamics, the brakes and various changes to the suspension to run narrow, 14in rear tyres. This led to Porsche having to re-type approve the car in its new form, considerably upsetting the ACO and eventually the other competitors. But although the two cars entered at Le Mans were some 15 seconds a lap faster than the other GT cars, they were some way from the full venturi 962s of just a few years earlier, which were perhaps ten seconds a lap faster still.

SURPRISE, SURPRISE! – TWR-PORSCHE WSC-95

FROM THE FIRST YEAR OF ITS LIFE, the International Motor Sports Association (IMSA) has enjoyed a productive if combative relationship with Porsche. Founded in 1969 to develop a professional sports car series in North America which would encourage manufacturers into racing, series promoter John Bishop gained the close support of Rudolf Hoppen, motorsports co-ordinator for Volkswagen-Audi of North America, the then importers of Porsche cars. The 911 had been prevented from running in the rival Sports Car Club of America Trans-Am series and Porsche wanted a new stage on which to demonstrate their racing abilities. The problem was that from the very beginning, the Zuffenhausen company absolutely dominated the new championship. First came the Carrera RSR, which won three consecutive IMSA titles for Peter Gregg. Then along came the 935 – which won, and won, and won. The 935 would keep on winning in IMSA until Sebring 1984.

By the early 1980s, Bishop seemed desperate to seek an alternative to the Porsche domination of his series. There was an opportunity to link up with the FIA's ideas for Group C in 1982, but Bishop went his own way with a formula based on the car's weight and engine capacity. The previous Grand Touring Experimental (GTX) which had become the private property of the 935s, was replaced by Grand Touring Prototypes (GTP). The rules were (in theory) factored in favour of normally aspirated stock-block engines such as the Chevrolet V8 and Europeans such as BMW's M1 and Jaguar's V12.

There was an equivalency formula for turbocharged engines and using this, it was hoped (by IMSA) that the Porsche steamroller could be halted. Specifically, the all-conquering 935's twin-turbocharged, water-cooled four-valve engines were ruled out in an effort to gag the turbo's power.

Porsche built the 956 to compete in the new Group C and plans were proposed to run the car in IMSA events.

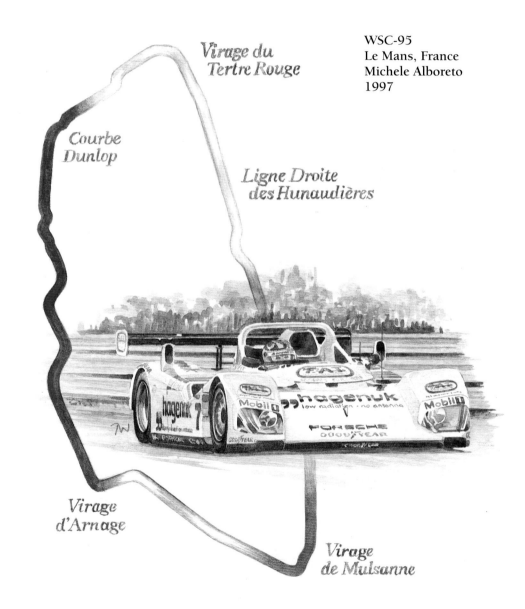

WSC-95
Le Mans, France
Michele Alboreto
1997

However, Bishop saw the 956 coming and banned the car before it could turn a wheel. He did this by identifying that the driver's feet on the 956 were ahead of the axle line of the front wheels. He declared that all IMSA machines must be so constructed that the driver's feet were behind the axle line. What he did not expect was that Porsche would then build a car to his new regulations, based on the 956. The 3-litre single turbo all air-cooled 962s – with the driver's feet behind the axle line – proceeded to dominate again until IMSA insisted on power-sapping air restrictors in the induction manifolding in 1988. That left the field clear for other makes who were finding it so difficult to beat Porsche – namely Jaguar and Nissan, but still left open the odd event where the 962's durability could win the day.

In 1994, IMSA went in a new direction by proposing World Sports Car (WSC) prototypes. Such was the desire to rid the emergent series of the Stuttgart cars, Bishop declared what amounted to an effective ban on the turbo – for which read Porsche turbo – engines. 'It was not really banned by the letter,' says Porsche race director Norbert Singer with a good-humoured chuckle, 'but by the numbers in the regulations. They did it with the restrictors and the weight. We got another 30 or 40kg and the restrictor was reduced a lot. So we realised they didn't want us. They did not want just to tell us to stay at home, because that wouldn't have been so polite, so they said have some extra weight and more restrictor and you are welcome!'

The only concession was made for the Daytona 24 Hours, at that time the blue ribband event of the IMSA

The TWR-Porsche WSC-95 was announced at the end of 1994 and on the first test at the Charlotte Motor Speedway was found to have various teething troubles.

championship. That year, Porsche ran the GT Turbo at Daytona and Sebring (where Röhrl, Stuck and Haywood won) and meanwhile turned their attentions to giving the Le Mans organisers, the Automobile Club de L'Ouest, what Singer describes as a 'preview' of the future of GT racing. The Dauer 962 stretched the understanding of the GT rules, but after some hard negotiating with the ACO's technical head Alain Bertaut, Porsche gained entries for the racer-turned GT-turned racer. The Dauer won, but everyone knew the car would never race again.

In August 1994, the ACO announced that cars built to the year-old WSC regulations would be eligible for the following year's Le Mans 24 Hours (calling the class Le Mans Prototypes or LMPs). Given that IMSA had already relaxed their strict turbo engine restrictions for their 24

Hours, Porsche began to think in terms of a racing programme based only around the three classic endurance events – Daytona, Sebring and Le Mans.

The ACO's announcement left little time to develop a brand new car for Daytona, in early February, the following year. But Porsche did want to race. Buoyed by an astonishing resurgence in their production car business, Zuffenhausen wanted to put on a show in North America and come back to Le Mans with a car that would challenge the best. Porsche wanted to run a GT to reflect the basis of their production car business, but as Singer explains the spyder has many advantages, especially for long distance racing. 'In principle, the people at Le Mans want both kinds of cars to be equal – even today. But everybody would like to do a prototype even when they are not faster

For the January Daytona test, a deep horizontal splitter had been added to the nose section, with tabs on each side of the nose. This is Mario Andretti. The car was some 2.3 seconds a lap slower than the best Ferrari 333SP, and the team was still accused of sandbagging the performance.

than a GT. It is an open car, so the driver is cooler, the tyres can be a little wider and a little softer and you can run three stints or two stints when the GT car can only do one or so. So on race performance there are small advantages and a little bit from the fuel consumption.'

It was at this point that Alwin Springer, Porsche's motorsport head in North America, suggested matters could get a jump-start with a link-up with the Tom Walkinshaw organisation in the USA. The TWR Jaguars had been a force in IMSA ever since they had arrived in 1988. The Ross Brawn-designed XJR14, powered by the 3.5-litre Ford HB V8 engine had consolidated Jaguar's leading position in endurance racing during 1991, winning the Sportscar World Championship, and had also won two races in the IMSA GTP championship (Davy Jones at Road Atlanta and Mid-Ohio) in 1992. While not having the durability of the long-legged 7.4-litre V12 XJR12s, the feature that all the drivers loved about the '14 was the handling fluidity of its carbon fibre chassis.

The calibre of the basic design had been further proven at Le Mans in 1992, because by this time Mazda had contracted the UK-based TWR organisation to produce a sports prototype to follow-up their victorious 1991 Le Mans campaign. The Mazda MXR01 was instantly recognisable as being from the XJR14 family, although in this guise the car used a 3.5-litre Judd V10 engine.

Given that there was no time to develop a new chassis, the option of using the XJR14's basic rolling chassis presented itself as being the only way to go and TWR were willing to help. To fit the flat-six Porsche engine as an unstressed member, in place of the previous V-engines and to completely revise the bodywork to that of an open spyder was no small task, but by January 1995, the first car – named WSC-95 – was running. However, building the car and racing it would provide two quite different challenges.

Race record

The all-white car ran for the first time at the Charlotte Motor Speedway in December 1994. The new Porsche ran over two days and it soon became clear that the aerodynamics were something of a disaster. 'When we tested the first time in Charlotte,' Norbert Singer recalls, 'I think it was Scott Goodyear who was running a little bit on the oval and a little bit on the small infield. I remember when he was passing the pits and he said, 'Can you see what I am doing? ' At first I couldn't see anything. When he came by next time he said again, 'Look, look!' and he was on the steering going from side to side and the car was still going straight ahead!' Singer rocks with laughter at the memory.

'We took it in the wind tunnel afterwards and found it had a lot of lift at the front!'

But despite the testing problems, Porsche were still ready to go to Daytona with an all-star driving team led by Mario Andretti, Bob Wollek and Goodyear in one car, with Hans-Joachim Stuck, Geoff Brabham and Thierry Boutsen in another. Plans were being made to compete at the Sebring 12 Hours that March.

The next test came at Daytona the following January and although the car was better, the best time was still some 2.3 seconds off the pace-setting Momo Ferrari 333SP and just slower than the other principal WSC competition, the Rob Dyson-run, Ford V8-powered Riley & Scott Mk 3.

The 333SP was in its second year as trend-setter in the new World Sportscar Championship. Powered by a 4-litre, five valves per cylinder V12, this new generation Ferrari sports racer was a stubby, utilitarian *barchetta* with an impeccable pedigree. Designed by Mauro Rioli, Giorgio Camachella and Gian-Paolo Dallara and guided during development by Tony Southgate, the 333SP (the 333 came from the cubic capacity of each cylinder) was a state-of-the-art aluminium/carbon fibre customer racer. Its 600bhp was delivered with true Ferrari panache. During 1994, the car had quickly become accepted as the class of the field and its superiority had been extended further for 1995. The 'melted jelly' bodywork benefited from Southgate's huge experience and if not perhaps the most elegant of the classic red cars, that V12 had the most glorious wail which even the contemporary McLaren-BMW V12 could not emulate. In having a chassis not designed and built in Maranello, the 333SP paralleled the WSC-95 in its 'convenience store' background. In Maranello as in Weissach, you will always be told the heart of the car is its engine. No-one would argue the heritage of a Ferrari V12 and similarly there were no doubts about the provenance of the twin-turbo flat-six in the back of the WSC-95.

Despite the apparent lack of the WSC-95's pace at the Daytona test, the prospects of an exciting contest in the World Sports Car class were good. Unfortunately, the other competitors did not see it that way. The problem was that many believed the TWR-Porsche team was sandbagging, that its drivers were holding back on the car's real performance. Just the suggestion of the TWR chassis combined with the well-proven 3-litre twin turbo Porsche engine was enough to bring on cries of 'foul' before the cars had clashed in anger.

A week later, the Scandia Ferrari team accused Porsche of not showing its potential speed at the Daytona tests. Given that the other competitors would have been well aware of the background between the Daytona organisers, IMSA, and Porsche, the clamour was taken to fever pitch. Another viewpoint to the controversy was coincidentally revealed by the same, 19 January 1995 issue of *Autosport* that recorded the Daytona test. It carried the announcement of the new McLaren-BMW GTR. Ron Dennis, with engineer Gordon Murray, had moved the GTR into the frame as a prime contender for the GT1 category in European racing – and Le Mans. Porsche were caught in the middle of a high-stakes game.

It can only be guessed at how many telephone calls were made to Mark Raffauf, the new IMSA chief, and from whom, in those last two weeks of January 1995.

Singer takes up the story. 'We had the test in Daytona and a week after they came up and said 'Ah, OK. We saw your lap times, but you were sandbagging.' So we sent them the data on the boost, we gave them the records of the engine and the car to compare with the other cars so that they could see we were not sandbagging. And then they decided one or two weeks later to increase the weight limit and the restrictor size.'

Increasing the car's weight by around 45kg and reducing power by some 80bhp effectively gagged the Porsche in a move which reeked of self-interest. It was just days before the Daytona 24 Hours and it became clear that the decision was not about to be changed for the Sebring 12 Hours either. So with their racer almost fuelled up and ready to go, Porsche pulled the plug on the whole WSC-95 activity – including Le Mans. The two cars were shipped back to Weissach and covers thrown over them.

For 1995, Porsche would have nothing more to do with IMSA, which itself floundered later. For information, the car that crossed the line first at Le Mans that year was a McLaren-BMW GTR – a commendable first-time-out win by a team that was alleged to be a full works effort. With Porsche out of Le Mans, McLaren had seized their opportunity with both hands.

Controversy has never been far from sports car racing and it dominated in 1995.

At this stage, the WSC-95 looked set for the same fate as the late 1970s Indycar project – a place in the museum in the section for interesting experiments that did not quite make it. Enter Reinhold Joest, veteran of 14 Le Mans drives and twice winner as a team owner with the same New Man-sponsored 956 in 1984 and 1985. Although in 1996, his team were running the works Opel Calibras in the International Touring Car Championship, Joest wanted to come back to Le Mans. He believed the WSC-95 – running in the Le Mans Prototype (LMP) class – was the car he should have. 'It was Mr Joest who suggested it.' Singer says. 'And we said why not? From the factory side we couldn't do it because of the GT car. He went to Dr Porsche and the board also said "why not?" But because of the GT development effort, the arrangement only included the loan of the two cars that were in Weissach, with little spares or development support.

While all the press attention at the April 1996 test weekend focused on the controversial 911 GT1 contenders, the Frankfurt-based Joest team put some low-key

By Le Mans 1996, the WSC-95 had received an aerodynamic make-over, particularly to the nose section. Significant wind tunnel work went into the airflow around the cockpit, with the result that the original transparency was replaced by more built-up cockpit sides and improved fairings to the roll-over bar.

mileage on the two open prototypes. Like the 1995 factory effort, Joest's team featured an all-star cast of drivers including Manuel Reuter (a Le Mans winner with Sauber Mercedes in 1989) American Davy Jones (who had driven the XJR14 and tested the WSC-95 in 1995) and rising Austrian driver Alexander Wurz. The second car was piloted by F1 refugees Michele Alboreto, Pier-Luigi Martini and Belgian Didier Theys – all experienced drivers who were very familiar with the new breed of flat-bottom sports cars and masters in the essential 24 Hours art of combining speed with mechanical sympathy.

Le Mans in 1996 was a quite different course to the classic non-chicaned *piste de vitesse* of earlier years, but the challenge was no less daunting. The ACO have always enjoyed a stimulating relationship with the sport's governing body, and while significant safety improvements had been made through the 1980s, great effort had been made to retain the essential character of the famous course. In particular the Hunaudières remained – quite easily – the fastest place in road racing. But it was that speed which gave so much concern to the drivers. It was not that the top drivers were afraid of the place – although it must have still been daunting in a flighty car – it was the absolute knowledge that if anything did go wrong, there was no run off.

The improvements to the course since the Porsche Curves by-passed the old, and very tricky, Maison Blanche section in 1972 included a re-profiled Tetre Rouge for 1979 and the slip road at the Mulsanne Corner in 1986 to miss the new roundabout. The FIA were growing increasingly concerned about speeds past the start-line and in 1987 insisted that a chicane be placed just after the previously very high speed (160mph+/255kph+) Dunlop Curve. However, there was no doubt that the FIA had become

In the race the white car ran strongly behind its team-mate until Pier-Luigi Martini beached it in a gravel trap. The car was later retired with a broken drive shaft. (LAT)

fixated with forcing the ACO to slow the cars on the Hunaudières. The highly risky heart-in-the-mouth top speed attempts like the 253mph (407kph) blast by Roger Dorchy in the WM-Peugeot in 1988 had the potential to bring motor racing in general some very bad press. Very few indeed have mastered the aerodynamics of the racing sports car at speeds greater than 200mph (320kph) and as the late 1990s showed, even the most famous names can get it wrong. The 'nanny' state kicked in for 1990 and two chicanes broke up the Hundaudières in nearly equal thirds, while large gravel traps at various places gave the drivers some insurance against technical failure or error. One wondered what the real benefit was however as that same year, Jonathan Palmer in a 962 was very lucky indeed to survive a 200mph impact with the barriers approaching the second new chicane.

Le Mans finally shrugged off its 1950s-image of rain-swept grittiness in 1991 when the magnificent new start-line complex opened. Gone were the old poorly-lit pit bunkers – reminiscent of the old days at Monza or Reims – and the sand in the paddock – to be replaced with smoked glass, roller doors and even hot showers behind the garages! There is little doubt that the ACO's re-investment

in their facility in the early 1990s was instrumental in the 24 Hours becoming a huge success in the latter part of the decade. With a further tightening of the Dunlop 'S' in 1997, the course maintained its international rating as simply one of the best in the world. This in itself is a remarkable feat for an 8.5-mile (13.68km) long course. Most importantly, a lap around Le Mans today, even when the *camions* are thundering along the N138, will get your pulse racing. The famous names like Tertre Rouge, Mulsanne and Arnage are carved deep in motor racing history and each has its own story to tell. Go into Le Mans city centre and you will find references to the 24 Hours everywhere – look for the bronzes set into the ground throughout the pedestrian areas. The race is part of the local culture and actively encouraged by the Département de la Sarthe.

It was to this much-improved Le Mans that Reinhold Joest returned in 1996. He had a head start, since there was only half the expected competition in the LMP class. Only the Scandia Ferrari 333SPs had their late entry accepted by the ACO, with the near-winners at Daytona, Momo boss Giampiero Moretti's 333SP, being refused.

The main threat to the WSC-95 at the 1996 race was the advanced GT1 racers from Toyota, Nissan and of course

Dark horse. At Le Mans in 1996, Alex Wurz brings the winning car through the Ford chicane at dusk. The WSC-95 benefited from a trouble-free run throughout the 24 hours to beat all the pre-race favourites. (LAT)

Porsche themselves. But after careful testing at Paul Ricard, Reinhold Joest came to Le Mans with an ace up his sleeve. With their regulation 80-litre fuel tanks, the WSC-95 could run 12 laps in between fuel stops – that was three laps better than the 'gas guzzling' Riley & Scott and one lap better than the rapid Scandia Ferrari or even the similarly-engined Courage-Porsche prototypes. Crucially, it was only a lap down on the expected interval for the 911 GT1s which were allowed 100-litre tanks. It would turn out to be a pivotal equaliser in the WSC-95's run against the more powerful but 200kg heavier, narrower-tyred GT1. Joest had achieved a similar advantage in 1985 and his plans for 1996 would work with equal success. Lucky number 7 would deliver again for Joest.

Despite a higher than expected oil consumption, the Joest mechanics only had to tend to the very rapidly driven Jones/Reuter/Wurz car's consumables – fuel, oil and pads. The pit-stops took no longer than the minimum time – essential for a winning Le Mans run in the 1990s – and this while all the other contenders hit troubles of greater or lesser magnitude. The two Ferraris fell out on the Saturday evening and the other GT1 contenders were left gasping by the pace of the Porsches. The 911 GT1s were simply out-run by the sports car, which led them for 23 of the 24 hours. The factory cars also lost crucial minutes in the pits during the night after minor offs. The Stuck/Wollek/Boutsen GT1 chased the black-painted WSC-95 through the night, often less than a lap apart. The

GT1 grabbed the lead at breakfast time, but the prototype came back and opened up a one and a half lap advantage by the end.

Joest's second WSC-95 began the race well, running with the other team car. As team manager Ralf Jüttner remembers, 'The performance was not bad at all. The car was lying second to number 7 when Martini went off and the problems started.' Martini beached in the gravel after missing his braking point for the first Hunaudières chicane, then the car developed engine management problems before finally stopping with a broken drive shaft. But the car that had been shunned by everyone had come back with a vengeance. Against all the odds, the black swan of the family had surprised everyone. Such was the sprint between the top GT1 and the winning WSC-95, the winner covered no less than ten laps more than the Dauer 962 in 1994 – the last completely dry 24 Hours. After the race, the white number 8 WSC-95 was retired to the Zuffenhausen museum, while Joest retained number 7.

When, the following year, the factory returned with an improved version of the GT1, Joest dusted down his one remaining car again. The factory GT1s were running new modifications which gave them a significant performance advantage over their customer GT1s, but the now white-painted WSC-95 – driven by Michele Alboreto, Stefan Johansson and Tom Kristensen – snatched pole position from the best factory GT1 driven by Boutsen, Stuck and Wollek.

In the race however, both factory GT1s showed what a year's development could achieve and they seized the advantage. Lucky number 7 trailed the two works cars through the night until Wollek in the leading GT1 hit the wall at the Porsche Curves. Joest's team manager, Ralf Jüttner, increased the pressure on the remaining GT1, driven by Dalmas, Collard and Kelleners, from early Sunday morning. The Joest team did not hold out much hope, but with more than eight hours to run, a lot could still happen before the chequered flag was unfurled. And it did. With just two hours to go, the surviving GT1 caught fire and was out. Joest was handed the race, albeit chased to the end by the consistent Gulf-McLaren GTR. Joest nonetheless had achieved a remarkable second back-to-back victory.

Joest took his Le Mans winner to the Donington round of the International Sports Racing Series (ISRS) in July 1997, in a head to head with the 333SPs. The Italian cars were much more suited to the sprint format of the ISRS, but once again the WSC-95 demonstrated the value of a well-developed chassis and engine package by winning.

By all accounts that should have been the finale for the WSC-95, but in 1998 the factory came back with a pair of

The cockpit of the WSC-95, just before the start of the 1997 24 Hours. The most notable aspect is the lack of dials – only a rev counter giving information and everything else being looked after by warning lights. The big rotary switches are fuel mixture and a selector for the LED display beneath. The driver shares the cockpit with various telemetry and radio black boxes.

brand new carbon fibre GT1s, and for insurance they took the Joest team under their wing and developed the two open prototypes as a full works effort, renaming them LMP1-98s.

The test weekend was not promising when the newly revised bodywork gave the car an instability that had not been present on the earlier model. However, by official practice the Alboreto/Johansson/Dalmas car lined up second fastest in the prototype class with a time around 1.5 seconds slower than the fastest Williams-built BMW spyder. The Pierre-Henri Raphanel, David Murry, James Weaver car was oddly some five seconds slower. How things had changed in the GT class for 1998 was shown by the speed of the pole-winning Mercedes CLK-LM. Bernd Schneider hurled the silver coupé around the course some 3.3 seconds faster than the BMW prototype. Unless some major problems sidelined the leading GT teams – in the form of Mercedes, Toyota and Porsche – then the proto-types looked to have little chance. The odds were made worse because the GT cars were getting at least one extra lap on the prototypes because of their larger fuel tanks.

Reinhold Joest did not come away from Le Mans in 1998 a happy man. There was not even the opportunity to play a waiting game with the fast GT runners. Firstly, lucky number 7 stopped on the Hunaudières on Saturday evening after climbing to sixth following a slow start. The second car shadowed its team-mate in the climb through the front runners and by midnight lay fifth. Then shortly after one o'clock, the car lost a rear wheel after a routine stop and dropped back to eighth. By dawn it was all over, the car retiring after a miserable night's racing. This time the Porsche GT1s did not falter. The headlines proclaimed 'Porsche wins Le Mans', but it was not a hat trick for the WSC-95.

This inauspicious appearance marked the finale in top-level competition for a car which had delivered far more than its creators ever dreamed. It had taken the competi-tion two long years to overcome and in the end it was another Porsche which did the job. Reinhold Joest remains the most successful private entrant in the history of Le Mans, with four overall victories – all with Porsches carrying the number 7.

Engineering

Although not a Porsche design, the WSC-95 chassis has impeccable design credentials. The parentage can be traced back to the proven Jaguar XJR14 that Tom Walkinshaw Racing, based in Oxfordshire, England, had developed for the 'F1-specification' Sportscar World Championship of Teams in 1990–91. These cars were built to take 3.5-litre normally aspirated V8 or V10 motors that theoretically

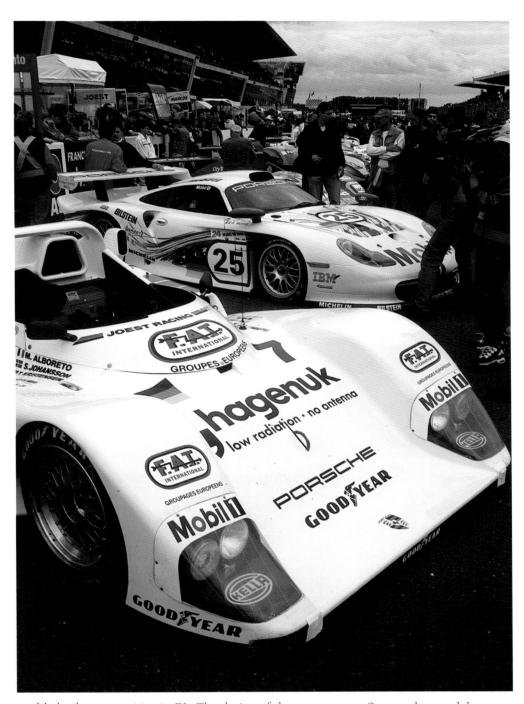

could also be competitive in F1. The design of the cars was orientated towards the shorter 480km sprint format races that the FIA were favouring from 1990. As a result, the original Ross Brawn XJR14 coupé was a very high specifica-tion machine, designed within the 750kg minimum weight with a full carbon fibre chassis. The most notable aspect of

One year later and the WSC-95 is still ahead of the latest version of the GT1 on the Le Mans grid. The GT1 had the speed in 1997, but not the ultimate durability.

The double Le Mans winner came to the Donington round of the International Sports Racing Series in July 1997 and won again. This is Pier-Luigi Martini. (Stephen Mummery)

Reborn as the Porsche LMP1-98, the car featured extensive changes to the original specification including the 500bhp version of the full water-cooled 3.2-litre flat-six. (LAT)

The new nose section included deep gullies and small winglets each side of the nose, in the search for more downforce.

this car was its extremely narrow monocoque which did not have the wide box section sills so typical of the conventional racing sports car. In the Jaguar's case, power was provided by a Ford HB V8 engine and in this form the car won three races, and in 1991, beat off Peugeot to the championship.

As an aside, Jaguar subsequently withdrew from the Sportscar World Championship and for 1992, TWR won the contract to build Mazda's new Judd V10-powered endurance racing machine. The modifications were supervised by Nigel Stroud and the result was the MXR01, a car which was clearly derived from the XJR14, but which was developed to run 24 hour races not short sprint events.

After racing in IMSA in 1992, the XJR14s did not race again and were stored at the TWR Inc facility run by Tony Dowe at Valparaiso, Indiana. But with the start of the new World Sports Car formula in North America, Dowe's organisation began to think about using the basis of the XJR14 for a new spyder. In the autumn of 1994, Porsche approached the team to see whether the two chassis could be converted to take the 962's proven water-cooled 3-litre

flat six twin turbo, five-speed gearbox and the 962's braking and hub units. The big difference was that the Porsche six was not capable of taking the rear suspension and chassis loads in the way that the Cosworth HB could. It meant that virtually the whole of the rear end of the car had to be redesigned. This work also involved blanking off the deep venturis in the floors to meet the flat bottom regulations then in force in endurance racing, slicing off the bubble-top coupé bodywork to turn the car into a spyder and incorporating the intercooler entry ducts. The weight of the car came out at around 880kg, somewhat heavier than the Jaguar and even the endurance-prepared Mazda (which weighed approximately 780kg). As a result, the springs – torsion bars at the front and coils at the rear – needed to be stiffened.

Aside from the obvious difference of changing to an open cockpit from a coupé, the WSC-95 bore a marked similarity to the Mazda, save for the deletion of the small front aerofoil and the huge biplane rear wing. On the WSC-95, the rear wing was replaced with a regulation narrow chord, two-element device.

Opposite: Worried looks in the Team Joest garage. Norbert Singer (left) and Reinhold Joest wait in vain for their spyder to appear. Both prototypes retired after being outclassed by the best GT1 runners.

All in all, the aerodynamic changes between the well-adjusted XJR14 and the WSC-95 proved to be critical. The changes made by Joest ahead of the entry at Le Mans in 1996 addressed the significant aerodynamic problems encountered earlier by Porsche at Charlotte and Daytona, and also included fitting a completely new fuel system. Norbert Singer helped Joest with some wind tunnel work on the car that produced quite extensive visual changes. 'It ended with a completely new floor, windscreen, wing and a new nose (including how it was mounted),' recalls Joest team manager Ralf Jüttner. The new front bodywork took on a classic snow shovel concave profile between the wheel arches and re-introduced the top wheel-arch vents as seen on the XJR14, but which had been deleted on the Mazda.

These were supplemented with vertical slots cut into the body behind the arches which, by Le Mans, were simple cut-aways to the lower body behind the wheels. The new nose helped clean up the airflow around the reprofiled cockpit bodywork which, with a revised back to the large airbox, helped feed less turbulent air to the rear aerofoil. The larger, double element rear wing was therefore altogether more effective than its predecessor. The other obvious additions to the WSC were two large scoops on the upper rear body and louvred grilles on the body sides in front of the rear wheels, to keep the rear brakes and turbos cool.

For the 1997 single car entry at Le Mans, Joest largely followed the old rule of 'if it ain't broke don't fix it'. There were detail changes however, to the aerodynamics (most notably the deletion of the top wheel arch vents), the suspension and the area around the engine.

The aerodynamics went through another iteration for the 1998 Le Mans race and in the process the cars became known as the LMP1-98. The most noticeable difference was the new nose section. This featured a single seater-style raised centre section with deeply carved gulleys each side and small, fenced trim tabs on the front edges of the wings. The profile of the body between the wheels no longer dipped down to the radiator entry, but followed a near tangential line between the wheels, with the main radiator openings being on the top of the body and recalling the arrangement used for the 962. At the rear the large airbox was deleted completely and a new double element wing was used.

The previous 3-litre six-cylinder engine was replaced by a 500bhp version of the twin-turbo 3.2-litre full water-cooled engine as used in the GT1-98. The five-speed gearbox was also replaced with a brand new sequential change six-speed unit. In this form however, the car proved to be under-developed for 24 hours racing.

Engine: Type 935/85 all-aluminium flat six-cylinder engine with full water cooling. Aluminium crankcase with aluminium barrels and cylinder heads. Dry sump lubrication. Two gear-driven overhead camshafts per bank with four-valves per cylinder. Two KKK K27 turbochargers with two charge air intercoolers and two 33.2mm diameter air restrictors in the inlet manifolding. Bosch Motronic 1.7 engine management.

Capacity: 2,994cc

Bore/Stroke: 95mm/74.4mm

Maximum power: 550bhp at 7,800rpm

Maximum torque: 510Nm at 5,000rpm

Transmission: Five-speed all-synchromesh gearbox with Automotive Products triple-plate clutch and Salisbury self-locking differential. Gearbox cooled by separate oil system with pump and oil to water cooler.

Chassis/body: Tom Walkinshaw Racing-designed, two-seat spyder carbon fibre monocoque. Carbon fibre/Kevlar bodywork with flat bottom aerodynamics. Automatic fire extinguisher system. 80-litre FT3 safety fuel tank with reserve. Mid-mounted water radiators and oil heat exchangers. Transmission-mounted full-width two element rear aerofoil. Integrated air jack system. Two Hella DE project module and two paraboloid Xenon gas discharge headlights for main and dipped beams.

Suspension and steering: Front: double wishbone with pushrod actuated torsion bars with four-stage Pfeifer telescopic gas pressure shock absorbers. Rear: Double wishbones with pullrod-actuated coil springs over four-stage Pfeifer gas pressure shock absorbers. Anti-roll bars front and rear.

Brakes: Axially ventilated Carbone Industrie 355mm carbon brake discs and disc pads front and rear. Brembo fixed six-piston alloy calipers front with fixed four-piston calipers rear.

Wheels and tyres: BBS wheels with centre-lock attachment: 13in wide front and 14.5in wide rear, 17in diameter rims. Goodyear 25/5 x 12.0-17 front, 28/5 x 14.5-17 rear racing tyres.

Weight: 880kg

Length: 4,650mm

Width: 2,000mm

Height: 1,050mm

Wheelbase: 2,785mm

Performance: Not available

GRAND DESIGN –
911 GT1

12

**GT1 Evo
Laguna Seca, USA
Allan McNish
1997**

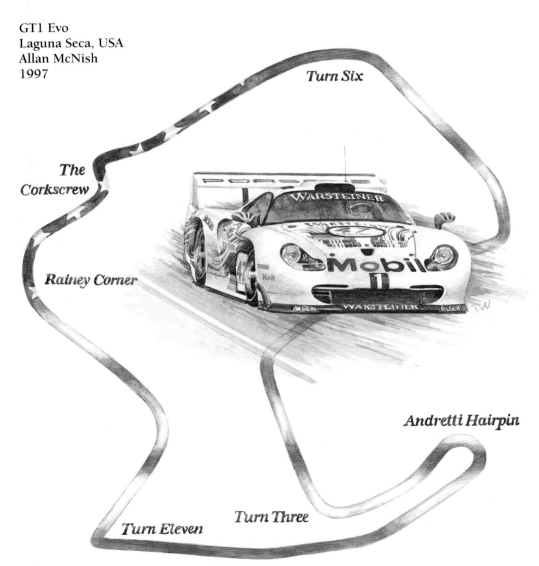

Turn Six

The
Corkscrew

Rainey Corner

Andretti Hairpin

Turn Three

Turn Eleven

THE 911 GT1 CAME TO LE MANS in 1996 as very much the upstart challenger to the then-undisputed king of the flourishing GT sports car class – the McLaren F1. It was a new beginning for Porsche's GT effort, which had produced mixed results over the previous three years.

In 1993, GT racing had emerged from the ashes of Group C in the form of the BPR International Endurance Series. BPR (the surname initials of the series' three creators: Porsche's Jürgen Barth, race organiser Patrick Peter and Venturi's Stefan Ratel) had picked up sports car racing with a strategy that was founded on production-based Grand Touring (GT) cars like the 911, not prototypes such as the 962. And wanting to support this new direction, Porsche produced a new car in 1993 – the 911 Turbo GT.

The development was approved by the Porsche Board at a time when the production car business was in a seemingly endless downward spiral. With extremely limited resources, only a single entry was sanctioned for that year's Le Mans. The result was a fairly conventional car and while drivers Hans Stuck and others showed all the necessary determination, the effort proved to be just too little and it retired early.

The following year, Porsche studied the regulations carefully, looking for a new opportunity. They found it in the Dauer 962 and in adapting this racer for the road, jump-started the development of GT racing.

Norbert Singer, the architect of the Dauer and later GT programmes, looks back sagely on the beginning of this most recent chapter in the history of the racing Porsche. 'We could see the GT regulations coming in 1993. We at Porsche produce GT cars and it was right Porsche should run in the GT series. First there were the slightly modified road cars and then what we could call advanced road cars – a little less than a 935 perhaps because they were nevertheless road cars. Everybody said they wanted no more *Moby Dicks*! So it had to be based on road cars. Our first attempt with an advanced road car was the GT Turbo. But in 1994

Gordon Murray came up with his McLaren and it was clear it was still a GT car. It was also clear it was a much better car than the GT Turbo. We already had a further development of this car in mind, but when we saw the McLaren we knew there was no way. And then the idea with the Dauer came and we said "OK, when they make a GT car, we can also make a GT car". And of course we already had one of these new GT cars (in the 962 racing car)!' Singer unleashes one of his booming laughs at this point, relishing the memory of tangling with two highly respected adversaries – the ACO's technical head Alain Bertaut and McLaren's Gordon Murray. 'OK, this was one step further maybe!'

The drivers came to terms with the somewhat slippery cornering characteristics of the Dauers and powered by the well-proven water-cooled 3-litre turbo, Le Mans was won. For Porsche it was a psychologically important victory, boosting spirits in a year that had also begun to see the company re-emerging in the production marketplace with the new 993-bodied 911.

The Le Mans authorities allowed the Dauers in 1994, but it was clear their future was limited. Using a full race prototype, converted only so as to make it road legal and then coming back with it as a GT car was stretching everybody's understanding of the rules. For 1995, Porsche would plan to go in a new direction, or so they thought.

The WSC-95 fiasco was a salutary learning experience. The car did not race in 1995 and would later prove what might have happened at Le Mans that year. McLaren would win the 24 Hours after a race that was notable for Porsche's absence and a great deal of rain. During 1995, thoughts in the Racing Department at Weissach turned to the now very healthy European-based BPR Global Endurance Challenge GT series.

There was little opposition to the fabulous-sounding, 6-litre BMW V12-powered McLarens. But Porsche felt that with detailed interpretation of the GT rules, a heavily modified 911 could give the Woking cars a run for their money.

Flushed with a much-improved balance sheet (a direct result of remarkable sales of the new production 993 model), Board approval was given to build a brand new GT challenger. Plans were made for a car that would take the battle to McLaren. However, Norbert Singer's first stop was the Le Mans rule book and after extensive scrutiny, he went to Alain Bertaut at the ACO, ready for some tough negotiating.

After the Dauer, Porsche perhaps could have expected an uncompromising reception, but Singer's view of his discussions with Bertaut were that they were hard, of course, but they were fun. It was quite different to the confrontational

discussions with IMSA in the days of the WSC-95. 'Yes, on the Le Mans side it was completely different,' recalls Singer. 'They have a regulation and they stick to that regulation. The freedom you have is in the interpretation. You cannot make a regulation 100 per cent otherwise you are in the Porsche Carrera Cup. Then you have to say that you don't touch the car at all. Only that way can it be 100 per cent. But when you want to have engineering spirit, you cannot do it.' A lovely choice of words perhaps, but it sums up Porsche's whole approach to racing. You need that little bit of ambiguity. 'That was what was really fun and I think Mr Bertaut also has fun with that. It was a discussion. It was pretty hard, but it was friendly and clear. We went through the regulations letter by letter, saying that we felt this or

Porsche returned to GT racing in 1993 with this 911 Turbo GT, an altogether conventional approach to the emerging GT regulations.

The Dauer formed the bridge between the old sports prototype cars and the new generation of high technology GT racers. Just to prove there was a road car, Porsche presented the real thing at Le Mans in 1994.

The 911 GT1 first ran in 1996 and responded to the competitiveness of the McLaren F1 GTR (following here).

The 911 GT1 was first announced in May 1996 to yells of approval from the company's friends and howls of protest from everyone else. It proved to be another perfect example of Norbert Singer at his cryptic best, exercising the regulations in a way that nobody else had dared.

Race record

The new 911 GT1 was ready for the traditional April test weekend at Le Mans. But before that it had been exhaustively shaken down at the Paul Ricard and Lurcy circuits in France and at Estoril in Portugal. Between the test weekend and the race itself Porsche performed a full 24-hour test on the new car. As was typical, nothing was being left to chance in the pursuit of the company's 14th overall victory. Team captain Hans-Joachim Stuck made Porsche's gameplan clear when he set a fastest time of the weekend with a lap of 3 minutes 50.995 seconds, an average of just under 132mph (212kph). But the problem for the 911 GT1s came not from other makes.

The team faced up the two Porsche-powered WSC-95 prototypes that had been loaned to Reinhold Joest. Joest had his own impressive record at Le Mans (including an excellent tactical victory over the factory 956s in 1985). His challenge in 1996 was billed as Porsche's Trojan Horse by *Autosport* and with an all-star driving team, the Reuter/Jones/Wurz car triumphed over Wollek/Stuck/Boutsen in their GT1 by a mere lap, with the second factory GT1, driven by Dalmas/Wendlinger/ Goodyear in third place. The factory GTs had lost the race after night-time problems with damaged bodywork had kept them in the pits for crucial minutes. The journalists could roll out their well-worn headline 'Porsche win Le Mans', but it was not quite the way the factory had wanted it to be.

'OK, in '96 we were second – the sports car was faster.' Singer shrugs. 'But we won overall, the sports car class and the GT class, so it was quite a big success.'

Perhaps the best performance of the GT1 in 1996 came at England's Brands Hatch circuit. Brands is a world away from the high-speed sweeps of Le Mans, but as the GT1 had shown earlier in the year at Spa-Francorchamps, it was indeed a very versatile racer. The GT1 proved to be completely at home on the undulating twists and turns of the Kent track. The authority of Stuck and Boutsen's victory had the opposition claiming that Porsche were once more sandbagging their real performance. And unlike the situation with the WSC-95, this time there was some justification. Porsche had due concern that their cars were not seen as too dominant, because the FIA was threatening to restrict the GT1's performance the following season.

The rules did change and Porsche were forced to use

that was our interpretation. And he would say no, the spirit is different. And we would agree if he said no.' If ever you wondered why Porsche seem so well prepared for Le Mans, it is because every detail of the campaign has been examined, but particularly the regulations.

smaller air restrictors on their turbos in 1997 that deprived them of some 50bhp at the beginning of the year. Combined with the deletion of ABS, the GT1 was now positively handicapped against the much-improved McLaren GTR and particularly against the brand new Mercedes CLK-GTR. In the FIA GT Championship the handicap was so marked that after two races, the restrictor change was lifted, but it was not until the cars appeared in second generation 'Evo' trim that visible progress was made, although it was barely enough to keep pace with the powerful Mercedes

Night stop for the Dalmas, Wendlinger and Goodyear GT1. Damaged bodywork during the night delayed the car, resulting in a third place.

With fluorescent advertising and piercing Xenon headlights, the new generation of sports cars make a spectacular sight when racing at night. This is the Wollek/Boutsen/Stuck GT1 'Evo'. (LAT)

and the championship fell easily to the three-pointed star.

The opportunity for Porsche to score with the GT1 came at Le Mans, since their rapid Stuttgart neighbours declined to enter. The new 'Evo' GT1 still had to contend with the very strong BMW-backed McLarens and once more the ever-competitive Joest-run WSC-95.

The progress in the GT1 from 1996 to the 'Evo' model was measurable. This factor would cause significant

acrimony among those racing customers who had bought 1996-specification GT1s, only to find them completely out-performed.

Rows aside, Thierry Boutsen hurled the new car around the 8.53 miles (13.65km) Le Mans course in 3min 43.363sec. That was nearly four seconds faster than Stuck's pole position time the previous year. The irritation was that somehow, the WSC-95 snatched pole position with a time

that was nearly two seconds faster. Perhaps Joest was using a special engine for qualifying?

It looked probable, because in the race the sports car could only play a back-up role to the two GT1s. The car driven by Wollek, Stuck and Boutsen edged into the lead after four hours racing and ran comfortably in that position through the night. However, at breakfast time poor Wollek suffered an inexplicable spin at the Porsche Curves and

planted his GT1 firmly in the wall. The car retired on the spot, and so once more this great personality was denied his first Le Mans win in no less than 29 attempts. That left the remaining factory GT1 of Dalmas, Kelleners and Collard out in front with the race seemingly sewn up. But with just two hours to go, Kelleners was forced to bale out on the Hunaudières when the car caught alight, an oil leak being the source of the fire. The car that slipped into the

Wollek, Stuck and Boutsen finished just a lap adrift of the winning WSC-95 at Le Mans in 1996.

lead was the Joest WSC-95 of Alboreto/Johansson/Kristensen. For the second year running the 911 GT1 had been beaten – by the very same car!

Singer once more adds a laconic comment to this agonising defeat. 'The GT was quicker than the sports car that year, but unfortunately it didn't finish.' He grins. 'And of course you have to finish first before you can do anything at Le Mans. Being fast in qualifying and in the first 18 hours isn't enough.'

In the remaining rounds of the FIA GT Championship, Porsche learned to understand the meaning of pain. The

class act was undoubtedly Mercedes, who despite consistent competition from the Schnitzer and GTC McLarens, became champions. In truth there was much politics involved because no-one wanted to pour any cold water over the return of Mercedes to sports car racing. The reality was that the CLK-GTR drove a coach and horses through the GT rule book (as, it must be said, Porsche had done in the past). GT racing was back to being a very big budget factory-only championship, which in truth, was the way the FIA wanted it.

The highlight of Porsche's 1997 season came at just the

right moment, the last race of the season. A third 911 GT1 'Evo' was entered at Laguna Seca for the team's test driver, Scotsman Allan McNish, partnered by Ralf Kelleners. McNish found something in the GT1 that day that the others hadn't and for the first hour kept everyone – including the Mercedes – behind. McNish was new to GT racing and he drove the race as if the car was a single seater. Whatever the attributes of the car, McNish – a former McLaren test driver and out in the racing wilderness at the time – grasped the opportunity with both hands. Perhaps his attacking drive was what had been missing all year, because for that single hour in California, the Porsche had the pace of the CLK on a dry track.

Laguna Seca is a fairly twisty, changing elevation course that has many similarities to Brands Hatch (where the previous year's GT1 had earlier excelled). Run on a non-profit basis, it enjoys the reputation as the West Coast's leading road racing course and is set in an area classed as parks and recreation land. Located between Monterey and Salinas in Southern California. It has become most well known in recent years for hosting the closing event of the Champ Car (formerly known as Indycar) series and is also a popular venue for the FIM World Motorcycle Championship.

Unlike most of the tracks where the sports car teams race, the course runs anti-clockwise. Laguna Seca's facilities are best described as basic, but the track itself is a delight. Set in sparsely wooded, sandy hills, Laguna is notable for few real straights (not even long, fast curves) but includes plenty of braking, accelerating and gear changing. The bleak areas of desert scrub that one has as a first impression is further strengthened by the uninviting Champ Car-inspired ribbons of whitewashed concrete walls that line the track. The drive is made interesting by some pronounced elevation changes – particularly through the S-bend known as the Corkscrew. The 2.38 miles (3.83km) length favours an agile car, but not one carrying an excess of weight.

Sadly, it all went wrong for Allan McNish at Laguna Seca in 1997 during the first pit stop. The mechanics were unable to get the wheel nuts off the GT1, after a misunderstanding about torque settings. It handed the race and the championship to Bernd Schneider in the CLK, who led home the GT1 of Yannick Dalmas and Bob Wollek, with McNish and Kelleners finishing third. The second overall place was a big confidence boost for the team after being out-classed all season. Up to that point, the private Roock Racing team had looked set to record the best performance in the championship by a GT1, with their 1996 specification customer car in Helsinki, Finland. Meanwhile, in McNish, the factory

had discovered a great new sports car talent.

Few would argue that Mercedes were set for another year of crushing superiority in 1998. The team had the luxury of 6-litre V12 cars for the FIA GT series, but for their comeback at Le Mans rolled out similar capacity V8-powered machines. The wild card for Le Mans 1998 however, would be Toyota and perhaps the new BMW spyders. The new Toyota looked startling and stretched the spirit of the regulations to their fullest extent. This was surely a flat-bottomed F1 car by another name. The BMW effort was lower key, but with their proven V12 engine at the heart of a very complete package, the potential was there for all to see.

Car 25 led the 1997 Le Mans 24 Hours until Sunday morning when Bob Wollek crashed in the first of the Porsche Curves. (LAT)

Allan McNish's run in the third 911 GT1 at Laguna Seca was the only time the GT1 'Evo' looked a match for Mercedes-Benz in the 1997 FIA GT Championship. (LAT)

Porsche wanted no more mistakes or mishaps in 1998. After two successive defeats for the GT car, the Weissach team came to the 24 Hours better prepared than ever before. There was real bounce in the team's step and a noticeable confidence among the drivers. The GT1s were all-new – the cars taking the CLK's direction of being a racing car first and a road car (the original intention of the GT class) second.

In the two opening rounds of the FIA GT Championship at Oschersleben and Silverstone, the GT1-98s had claimed pole position against the previous year's CLK-GTRs. But Le Mans practice not only demonstrated how much better the GT1-98 was from the previous year, but also the progress that had been made by the others. Jorg Müller recorded a time of 3min 38.407sec in qualifying, but his five-second improvement over the previous year was not enough to

capture the prestigious pole position. In the chill, dry conditions of the Thursday evening, it was Toyota and Mercedes who dominated, the fastest being Schneider's silver car on 3min 35.544sec. But speed in practice, does not necessarily give any pointers to the favourites for the race.

When the flag dropped, it was Martin Brundle who led after the first lap, his Toyota scorching off into the lead and trailed by the Porsches and Mercedes. The race quickly became a catastrophe for Mercedes-Benz and before two hours both their cars had retired. The GT1s were clearly out-pacing the prototypes and into Saturday evening, the Toyotas managed to keep just ahead of the two chasing 911 GT1s, who in turn were chased by the surprisingly quick Nissans. But then the Toyotas began to run into gearbox problems. The cars were quite obviously faster than the Porsches and it became a question of whether the hard-worked Japanese mechanics could replace the gear sets faster than they failed – they had perfected this practice down to just ten minutes! The chase went on through the night and by morning, after 18 hours of very hard racing, there were still only four seconds between the now-leading Porsche and the second-placed Toyota.

The 1998 Le Mans was a personal triumph for the Scottish driver Allan McNish. An element of his speed in the GT1 was down to having confidence in the team around him. He says it was worth as much as half a second a lap. 'If you see a driver with confidence, you can feel that air about him. You can see the air when he gets in the car. You can see how he attacks a fast corner.' And McNish certainly found that confidence during the night in 1998, driving double stints during the night to maintain the slender lead (at that time) over the chasing Toyota. Partnered with Laurent Aiello and Stefan Ortelli, it was remarkable to see the way these super-fit drivers sprang from their cars, still fresh as daisies after 50 minutes in the claustrophobic space-age cockpit.

In the crisp, clear sun of Sunday morning, the leading cars emerged from a gruelling night's racing oil-streaked and covered in layers of dirty, black carbon brake dust. They looked like prize fighters weary after a long and sustained fight. The new generation of GT1 machines were putting on a spectacular demonstration of modern high technology motor racing. All the top cars were touching 200mph (320kph) routinely before the first chicane, between the Mulsanne Hairpin and Indianapolis and on the run up to the Porsche Curves from Arnage. The night-time imagery had been surreal, with the new generation of variable focus, high-brightness headlamps marking out the flame-spitting faster cars from the yellow-tinted halogen

Tired but on a winning roll. The mechanics refuel the winning car of McNish, Aiello and Ortelli early on Sunday morning. At this stage the car was locked in a fierce duel with the remaining Toyota.

lights of the rest of the field. Many of the leading cars carried luminescent advertising and when greeted by a battery of flash cameras would explode out of the darkness in a blaze of colour. The sounds were no less electrifying, the deep rumble of the Porsche turbos mixing with the wail of the V12 Ferraris and the McLarens. It was Le Mans at its very best and a testimony that not everything about technology was bad for motor racing.

The battle continued at sprint pace through the morning. After 21 hours racing, at 11 o'clock, the gap was just 1.5 seconds. But the Toyota's transmission would be its downfall. Just 80 minutes from the end, and although it was proving to be consistently faster than the Porsche, the Japanese car rolled to a silent halt. Boutsen could not find any gear to get the car moving again and desolated, he had to leave the car. The scenes in the Japanese pits were no less distraught. Norbert Singer watched the stationary Toyota on one of the television screens in the Porsche pits and let slip a wry smile.

Over the years, Porsche have had their fair share of bad luck near the end of this most-punishing race. Think of Hans Herrmann losing by ten seconds to Jacky Ickx in 1969, or in '78 when the 936 lost fifth gear or in '88 when Ludwig missed his pit stop and had to get his car back to the pits on the starter motor. The 962 lost the race to Jaguar by a single lap. Singer has been going to Le Mans with Porsche since 1971 and he sheds no tears if he can benefit from his adversaries problems in the final stages.

'At Le Mans you need a car which is reliable, working well and you need good organisation.' Singer reflects. 'In 1998, everyone said we won it by good luck, but I think Toyota made a strategic mistake. Going to Le Mans saying they can change a gearbox in 10 or 12 minutes, I think, is wrong. Going to a 24-hour race, you have no time and they were thinking of changing two times. You have no 20 minutes normally. This was a real mistake on their side. Even today, people are saying that they can change a gearbox in seven minutes or five minutes. This is the wrong approach for Le Mans. You have it every year where the leading car has spent five minutes extra in the pits and that can lose the race.'

The 1998 victory was a very sweet one for Porsche. It was the company's 50th anniversary year as an automobile manufacturer. The icing on the cake was that the other team car had overcome the strong challenge from the reliable Nissans to finish second. It seemed like a resounding 1–2 victory but in fact it had been one of Porsche's most hard-earned wins.

The 1998 Le Mans triumph would be the last for the 911 GT1. It was clear from the very beginning of the 1998

season that Porsche would have no reply to the huge resources being played by their Stuttgart neighbour in the FIA GT Championship. The hard truth was that the GT1 was no match for the silver cars in the three or four-hour sprint races. The new CLK-LM had won first time out at Hockenheim and was on top for the rest of the season. Uwe Alzen's somewhat desperate move on Brabham's Panoz at Silverstone led to a 30-second stop-go penalty and this certainly deprived the GT1-98 of its only chance of an FIA GT victory that year. McNish had good runs at Suzuka and again at Laguna Seca, but each time the race ended in the gravel. Six third place finishes over the season summed it all up.

As has become the custom, the GT1s were retired to the factory's museum to join their illustrious forebears.

Engineering

The 1996 911 GT1 could be described as an advanced 911, in the same spirit as say the 961 racer that had run at Le Mans in 1986–87. The GT regulations in 1996 still required the car be derived from the production machine and had to pass a crash test. To overcome all the qualification issues, Porsche took a production shell and developed the car from that basis.

The first 911 GT1 used the bodyshell from a production 993 to avoid the need for additional type approval.

A very rigid roll-cage filled out the cabin area and extended forwards to stiffen the front suspension mountings and rearwards to support the engine, transmission and rear suspension. Carbon fibre was much in evidence, if not used for the main chassis section, and used for ducting and ancillary fittings around the car. A regulation 100-litre fuel tank was mounted amidships. The suspension used double wishbones and coil springs front and rear (with the rears operated by F1-style pushrods).

The 3.2-litre water-cooled six-cylinder engine, used twin KKK turbochargers, twin intercoolers, four valves per cylinder and the very latest TAG 3.8 engine management. The result was a reliable 600bhp at 7,200rpm, with a staggering 650Nm maximum torque at 5,500rpm. The engine was coupled to a brand new six-speed gated transmission which featured oil to water heat exchanging to keep it cool.

The GT1 ran on 11.5in wide front and 13in wide rear Michelin racing tyres, that were mounted on BBS 18in wheels. Integrated air jacks heaved the GT1 into the air as soon as the car dived to a halt in its specially marked pit box, making the wheel-changers' task less onerous in the early hours of Sunday morning. Anti-lock braking was by this time a well-proven means of shortening braking distances and, hinting at how tiring this powerful machine was to drive over 24 hours, the GT1 enjoyed power steering. The regulations permitted full carbon brake discs

and there were no less than eight piston calipers at the front and four piston calipers on the rear.

From the outside, the 911 GT1 was instantly recognisable as derived from the 911 – albeit a squashed example of one. Black plastic mouldings (in place of the rear three-quarter windows) and carefully sculpted cockpit windows were the features that most gave the car its 911 'look'. At the front, there was a huge opening for the engine water cooler and front brake cooling ducts, while a large scoop over the cockpit drew air down to the turbo inlets and kept the engine compartment cool. A scoop just forward of the rear wheel arches drew air to the rear brakes. Another feature of the GT1, which Le Mans spectators did not see until dusk fell, was the purple-tinged blaze of Litronic variable focus headlights. Across the rear deck, a single plane rear wing finished off the racer look. Of course, this factory Porsche was painted in white base colour, but the GT1 was given an abstract highlighting of red and blue to compliment the large logos of principal sponsor Mobil.

For 1997 and the GT1's second attempt at overall victory, Weissach came back to Le Mans with an evolution of their first model. Side by side, the 1997 'Evo' car appeared just that little bit less like a 911 and more like a closed sports racer. While the engine and transmission were outwardly unchanged, there were signs everywhere else that the car had been subjected to a very detailed engineering appraisal. The new bodykit of the GT1-97 still had a very stubby appearance, but many of the original machine's curves were more rounded, the nose and tail were longer, the wing deeper. The car had clearly spent much time in the Weissach wind tunnel. There was still the vestigial 911-style design of the cockpit glass and the front of the car still used the 993's undertray forward of the dash. But with the announcement of the new 996-bodied 911, the GT1 was now turned out with replicas of the production car's 'eggs-over-easy' headlamp assemblies, while the scoop over the cockpit roof was markedly larger. On a technical level, the front suspension was reworked and while ABS was now deleted, at 1,050kg, it was 50kg heavier than the original.

The third evolution of the GT1 was not really an evolution at all. It was a major redesign. 'We had to stay with some of the steel pieces,' says Norbert Singer, 'but we went to the maximum allowed by the regulations, so this one had a carbon chassis. We had to do the crash test, but it passed.'

The GT1-98 was a very serious effort to take the battle to the expected very competitive challenges from Mercedes and Toyota. With only vestigial resemblance to the 911 road cars, the GT1-98 was the most advanced racing car Porsche had built to date. The chassis was brand new,

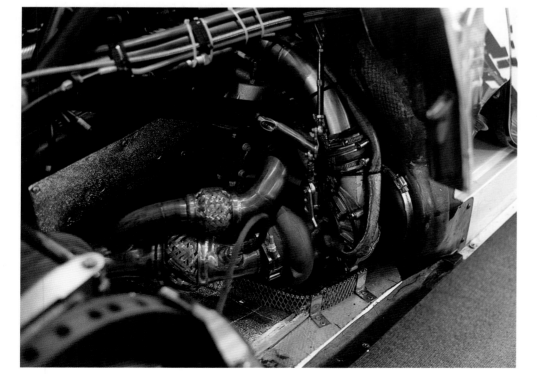

The turbocharger installation is squeezed into the sides of the engine compartment. Note also the very substantial chassis tubes.

being Porsche's first full carbon fibre monocoque. 'We had some help from CTS for this.' Singer says, 'this is the ex-Lola cars composites consultancy.' A total of six chassis were made in Huntingdon and transported to Weissach so that two race cars could be assembled. The most notable aspect of the car's basic design was its very long-legged, 2,785mm, wheelbase. But Weissach were on known territory as such long wheelbases had been proven with the 2,770mm 962. The new car was 207mm longer than the previous year's GT1. Porsche's love affair with speed on the Hunaudières Straight produced a car with a delicious coke-bottle profile and sculpted long tail, which as well as the full-width aerofoil, featured an up-turned duck-tail. The 100-litre fuel tank was housed again behind the driver and

ABS once more brought astonishing braking reserves to the 950kg car.

The proven 3.2-litre six was retained but a new six-speed sequential transmission gave the drivers a very fast gear change. This was combined with a triple-plate clutch that replaced the previous single-plate version.

The new car proved a delight to drive. Le Mans winner Allan McNish sums up the winning factors which, he reveals, were not all technical. 'It is more like a single seater; it's a little bit stiffer with the carbon chassis. It brakes a little bit better and I can throw the car into the corner and I've got confidence in it. You're more comfortable when you're driving near the limit.' McNish also refers to the confidence the Porsche team gave him. 'It's different. I'm lucky that I've

A very substantial cast bellhousing was linked to the rear chassis tubes and provided a location for the engine, gearbox and rear suspension.

driven for probably two of the best F1 teams in the modern era – being Benetton and McLaren – in a testing capacity. Porsche are very professional, but it's like a family the way they treat you. I thought it was PR speak, but it was not. They put their arm round you and make sure you're not subject to a lot of the difficulties racing drivers have – in the areas of working with the media and various other areas. They're very, very good and I appreciate that.'

The cockpit of the GT1-98 was notably snug compared with the earlier cars (even the compact 962) and when the helmeted driver was installed the appearance was more like a space capsule than a racing car. McNish notes that much thought went into the layout of the cockpit. 'It has to be like that because the ergonomics of the cockpit are thought out quite carefully. Take the light switches for example, they've got to be where you can easily access them, in the

dark and without thinking where they are. Because you can be coming up behind a GT2 and you're in a braking zone and you need to flash him or something. You need to know instinctively where they are. It was actually Bob (Wollek) who laid out the dashboard on this year's car. If I'd just jumped in the car and said we need this there and that there, we'd have probably missed something.'

McNish also gives us some idea of the difference between driving the GT1 and a regular production Porsche Turbo. 'We have a top speed at Le Mans of about 320kph [200mph] – and that's not really much more than a Turbo – but we get there very, very quickly. The difference is in the aerodynamic grip that we have on the car. For example, I looked at the speedo (there is a small digital speed read-out on the GT1) as I went through the Indianapolis corner, which was the worst thing I could have done – and it was

The factory effort for the 1998 Le Mans 24 Hours was very substantial. The cars were the most advanced technology racers ever to emerge from Weissach and in the words of McNish were a 'delight to drive'.

248kph [155mph]! And that was through a left-hand, 90-degree bend! I would have thought you would go through there at around 150kph [90mph] in a Turbo. The advantage is purely because of the aerodynamic grip we have on the GT1.'

But if Le Mans brought out the best in the GT1, the performances in the FIA GT Championship that year also demonstrated how limited a Le Mans-specific design can be everywhere else. The new Mercedes CLK-LM completely outclassed the GT1-98.

In its seasonal review, *Autosport* summed up the advantages the CLK-LM enjoyed over GT1-98 as being down to the crucial use by Mercedes of Bridgestone tyres rather than the Michelins used by Porsche. The superior, more driveable power of the normally aspirated Mercedes also played its part in making the CLK more adaptable to every kind of circuit rather than just the faster courses that suited the Porsche. Subsequently, Norbert Singer was able to describe the disadvantage that his turbo engine had against the powerful V12 Mercedes-Benz. 'The turbo was at a disadvantage because of its restrictors. With the big, normally aspirated engines, those with 6 or 8 litres, they have big torque from low revs and the power is cut by a restrictor. And at the top end the turbo is also cut by the restrictor, but also the boost is lower, so you have two limitations. You can talk about boost pressures and so on, but when you watch a car accelerating out of a corner, it is very hard for the driver to control the boost, because he is stepping on the throttle and the boost comes up and it is too much. So he lifts off and he loses everything. Then he goes again and maybe the second or third time he is on the straight and away he goes. With an aspirated engine he can feed it in very precisely. We saw it at Donington (the seventh round of the FIA championship). We lost everything out of those hairpins and we were sure we had the same torque as the Mercedes – but it was everything or nothing. I think by that stage the aspirated engine had the advantage.'

At the Porsche awards ceremony in December 1998, Porsche announced that it would not compete at Le Mans in 1999 in GT1. It was an acknowledgement that the 911 GT1-98 had reached the extent of its development potential and yet still was believed to be out-classed by the large capacity normally aspirated engines. After just a single season's racing, it was declared obsolete – such is the pace of contemporary motor racing development.

The following two years would be marked by Porsche priorities away from the race track. A new, normally aspirated V10-powered spyder was running by November 1999, but late that year the factory declared that Le Mans 2000 was not going to be the target for an attempt at win 17.

SPECIFICATION
911 GT1-98

Engine: Design: Flat six-cylinder, aluminium head and block, both water-cooled. Dry sump lubrication. Twin, gear-driven overhead camshafts per bank, operating four valves per cylinder. Two exhaust-driven KKK K27.2 turbochargers with individual air restrictors and charge air intercoolers. TAG 3.8 engine management. Multipoint sequential fuel injection with Lambda control.

Capacity: 3,200cc

Bore/Stroke: 74.4mm/95.5mm

Compression ratio: 8.5:1

Maximum power: 550bhp at 7,200rpm

Maximum torque: 630Nm at 5,000rpm

Fuel: Complies with Le Mans regulations (Super Plus 98 octane)

Transmission: Six-speed sequential gearbox with triple-plate sintered metal racing clutch. Gearbox lubricated with oil pump and oil-to-water heat exchanger. Variable lock differential.

Chassis/body: Carbon fibre monocoque with integral air jacks. Automatic fire extinguisher system. 100-litre FT3 safety fuel cell with integrated catchtank. Le Mans rapid fillers. Hella-Xenon gas discharge (Litronic) headlights.

Suspension: Double wishbones front and rear with pull-rod spring operation. Torsion bar front, coil spring rear. Bilstein four-level adjustable shock absorbers front and rear. Anti-roll bars front and rear. Power steering.

Brakes: 380 x 37mm carbon brake discs front and rear with Brembo eight-piston front, six-piston rear calipers. ABS.

Wheels and tyres: BBS 19in racing wheels with centre locking nuts. 11.5in front rim width, 13in rear. Tyres are Michelin, front: 27/67-19; rear 31/70-19.

Weight: 950kg

Length: 4,890mm

Width: 1,990mm

Wheelbase: 2,785mm

Performance: (Factory figures for the 1997 road car prototype.) This car was fitted with a 3.2-litre 544bhp water-cooled flat-six engine. The car weighed around 1,100kg. The 1998 racing cars would be better in both acceleration and top speed. Acceleration 0 to 62.5mph (100kph): 3.7 seconds

Maximum speed: 202mph (325kph) (but electronically limited to 192mph/309kph)

INDEX

Nordschleife

Südschleife

Virage de Muizon

Virage
de la Garenne

Virage de
la Hovette

Thillois

Virage du Gresil

L'Etoile

Virage
Sanson

Nouveau Monde

Turn
One

The Kink

Turn Four

Turn Three

Turn Two

Campofelice

Collesano

Cerda

Caltavuturo

Bergwerk

Karussell

Pflanzgarten

Aremberg

Döttinger Höhe

Flugplatz

Südkehre